a Place of
EXCELLENCE

A CHRONICLE OF

WEST VANCOUVER

1912-1987

a *Place of* EXCELLENCE

BRUCE RAMSEY

Published in
Commemoration of the 75th Anniversary
of the Incorporation of West Vancouver

by

THE CORPORATION OF THE DISTRICT OF
WEST VANCOUVER, B.C.

Published by The Corporation of the District of West Vancouver — I.T. Lester, Municipal Manager.

Cover Design by Dave Webber the Artist.

ISBN 0-88925-749-3

Printed in Canada
by D.W. Friesen & Sons Ltd.
5748 - 176th St.
Cloverdale, B.C.
V3S 4C8

To the Memory of the Author's parents, the Rev. Canon F.A. Ramsey, C.D., L.S.T., Rector of St. Stephen's and St. Francis-in-the-Wood, 1931-1941 and his wife, Gussie, and to all those who have lived in and loved West Vancouver.

Contents

Preface

A history of West Vancouver is a history of independent, courageous people who dared to be first, who dared to meet the challenges of a wilderness, who dared to leave their comfortable surrounds in "civilized" Britain and Europe and who dared to be leaders in a new land and in a new mountain and marine-oriented Municipality. This is the story of those people.

The story will be told of the first European sighting of this coast, of the friendly greetings by the indigenous people, of the Municipality's Founding Fathers, John Lawson, Charles Nelson, George Hay, and others. This book tells of community leaders such as Francis W. Caulfeild who laid out "a bit of old England" in the Caulfeild Estates, and of the contribution of Major General Victor W. Odlum, a Canadian war hero. It describes the development of the first shopping centre in Canada at Park Royal and the development by the Guinness family of England of the finest residential area in the country known as British Pacific Properties.

The story will be a blend of humorous anecdote, reminders of hardships and examples of community spirit, all of which have provided a foundation conducive to a way of life, a manner of living and inspiration for excellence which captains of industry and leaders of our society, Federal, Provincial, and Municipal, have been pleased to call their home.

West Vancouver's people aspire to greatness and excellence. We are indeed fortunate that the example of our forebearers in providing leadership is continuing in the aspirations, work and results of today's West Vancouver citizens.

Donald A.S. Lanskail,
Mayor
1987-

Introduction

This is a "homecoming book," written by one who is not a pioneer, not really an oldtimer and not even a resident of West Vancouver. In search of an identity befitting the situation, a happy phrase came to mind that puts the problem to rest, and so I proudly proclaim being an "expatriate West Vancouverite."

It was early in September, 1931 when I arrived in West Vancouver from Victoria to enter the halls of learning at Pauline Johnson School and I lived there until 1946.

What changes have taken place since those days of yore! Then it was a community made up largely of unpretentious homes, wooden sidewalks, and not many of those, of streets lined with ditches, vacant, bush-covered lots and tall trees, but there is one thing that has not changed and that is the driving spirit of the people toward attaining, in the words of Mayor Derrick Humphreys, "A Place of Excellence."

Perhaps I can be forgiven for introducing into this Chronicle a certain amount of trivia — little things that happened that by themselves have no real importance, but when put into the context of the book and its **raison d'etre**, they fit in to the mosaic of life at that particular time.

For me it has been like going back in time, and I have been ably assisted in that journey by a number of old friends, in particular, Rupert Harrison, former municipal clerk and now archivist, whose patience, by the way, was remarkable as he dug out old files and other research materials for me. To Nigel Snelgrove and his wife, Bea, Mrs. Dolly Cartwright, Miss Lucy Smith, Mrs. David Wilson, Mrs. Arthur P. Mackenzie, Norman R. Hacking, Hugh Addison, John Kirkwood, Mrs. Tony Eberts, and many, many others, I owe a debt of gratitude and I hope I have not let them down in this endeavor. And my special thanks to Len Norris for his permission to use three of his cartoons.

Another shoulder I relied on was provided by Mrs. Doreen Sullivan, of the reference department at the West Vancouver Memorial Library and I also acknowledge the invaluable assistance given by Jack Mounce, the librarian. To Bernie Holt and all the members of the West Vancouver Museum and Historical Society, I also extend my thanks.

The bibliographical references are contained in the text, so I have refrained from listing them here, but I have used initials to credit those who loaned photographs: West Vancouver Municipal Archives (WVMA); West Vancouver Memorial Library (WVML); Vancouver City Archives (VCA); Provincial Archives (PA); Nigel Snelgrove (NS); David Moon (DM); British Pacific Properties and Park Royal Shopping Centre (BPP); Capilano College (CC); North Shore Museum and Archives (NSMA); Ed. Prescesky (EP); Herbert Bibbs (HB); Mike Wakefield, **North Shore News** (MW); Pacific Press (PP), and West Vancouver Museum and Historical Society. (WVMHS).

To my wife, Betty, (she is not from West Vancouver but I had the good fortune to meet her at Kew Beach), my loving thanks, and to all in West Vancouver, thank-you for extending me the honor of writing this Chronicle.

Bruce Ramsey.

Sparwood, British Columbia.

11

Chapter One

THE SHIPWATCHERS

The world was in a very sorry state of affairs during the summer of 1941. On the war front, which had, since September 1939, been the dominant thought in the minds of men and women, there had been occasional glimpses of a silver lining to the dark clouds, but they were few and far between. The boys and girls from next door were now wearing the uniforms of the Canadian Army, the Royal Canadian Navy and the Royal Canadian Air Force or were members of the non-uniformed Merchant Navy. Many of them were serving overseas and some were now seasoned veterans of the Battle of Britain and the Battle of the Atlantic. But in mid-August at Ambleside Beach, which even after the passage of a dozen or more years since that name had been officially sanctioned, oldtimers continued to call East Beach, all the heavy cares of a nation at war were set aside to celebrate a great historic occasion. The **fiesta**, and no better word can describe the euphoria of that moment, was to mark the 150th anniversary of the landing here of the Spanish navigator **Piloto** Jose Maria Narvaez, a landfall which, incidentally, never took place, but nobody cared. It was time for a party and nobody gave a hoot about the facts. The bash they had in mind was to be **the** best and **the** gayest the municipality had **ever** experienced.

Marine Drive, especially around Ambleside Park, took on the appearances of a street scene from Bizet's opera **Carmen,** with bands of strolling guitar-plunking troubadors, ladies in brightly-colored dresses and men in sparkling matador outfits. Old Spain had never seen such get-ups! A bullfight was scheduled, and a New York manufacturer of wire fencing offered to supply, free of charge, not only the protective fence but a world-famous

13

matador in exchange for free advertising. Then a spoil-sport made his appearance. It was probably a lawyer. At a meeting of the West Vancouver Lions Club, sponsors of the event, he read a section of the Criminal Code of Canada which strictly forbade what was called "bull baiting." There the matter might have ended, but the club was bullish about having a bull fight, and so were members of the 31st Heavy Battery, Royal Canadian Artillery, who manned the guns beneath the Lions Gate Bridge, and they rose to the occasion by staging what the press called a "burlesque bull-fight." It was, indeed, a "burley-cue" show because at one point, the south pole of the bull became detached from the headquarters and performed its own little topless revue. The crowds loved it and they applauded as loudly and excitedly as if they were in the stadium in Madrid.

The supreme moment, however, had come a bit earlier in the afternoon with the arrival of the ship **Santa Saturnina**, an event which was marred only by the appearance of Military and Naval Police who, without a greal deal of enthusiasm, forbade the taking of photographs because of wartime security. It was an effort in futility on their part because photograph albums in the hands of "oldtimers" in West Vancouver are filled with graphic pictures which show in the background the Narrows North gun emplacements which were officially located "Somewhere in Vancouver" — not one of the best kept secrets of the Second World War by any means. After being carefully scrutinized by the censors, John Graham and Lew Gordon, news coverage of the event was stamped "Approved" and the world was informed of the "arrival of the **Santa Saturnina** under full sail and with its rails lined by a picturesquely dressed crew of Spaniards was an impressive sight." Narvaez would have been shocked. There were ladies aboard! "Brilliant sunshine made the disguised **Romance** , with its owner, Captain E.O. Green at the wheel, a ship of extreme beauty as with her sails full of wind she slid before the shore." A party of Indians in native dress, led by Chief Andy Paull met the newcomers to West Vancouver and, according to the press report were "acting their part as they heard fire arms for the first time, nervously beating their tom-toms, fingering their bows and arrows, they stared, gesticulated and jabbered. (Paull had been asked by the committee to have the Indians dressed as they might have been when Narvaez arrived. He replied they were probably nude. The idea, then, collapsed.) Then ashore came a landing party consisting of Thomas Greenall, Arthur Hill, Sam Payne and Lister Sinclair (**Note the Spanish names**) representing Narvaez and his officers. They made friendly gestures to the Indians, were thoroughly examined, felt all over, and finally accepted as humans, although white, were invited to sit down and smoke the pipe of peace."

"The next ceremony was the unveilling by Councillor Jack Richardson, Lions president, of the Narvaez Cairn containing a drinking fountain, which he presented to Reeve J. Edward Sears representing the municipality. Indian maidens in the party danced a native dance and Pro-Rec Girls responded with European dances, although no explanation was given as to where Narvaez had conjured up the white maidens."

Soon afterwards, the plaque disappeared and many thought irate blue-blooded historians had stolen it but this was never proved. Years later it was found by accident at the North Vancouver city dump and has now been re-instated.

To be truthful, Narvaez *did* see what is now West Vancouver but only from a distance, and while other Spaniards would see the heavily forested slopes of Hollyburn Ridge and Sentinel Hill at close range over the next year or so, it was the British officer, Captain George Vancouver, RN, in June, 1792 who entered a description of the land and its people on the printed page. Now, when the shadows fall from the Lions Gate Bridge to the "old" mouth of the Capilano River, our minds must turn to the village of Homulchesum which once stood there and to the very beginnings of a long-established tradition in West Vancouver, that being ship-watching. What the Indians saw that June day in 1792 was not one of the great sleek white **Empress** liners nor the huge container ships, heavily laden to the Plimsoll line, which now pass through the First Narrows, but an unpretentious long-boat from HMS **Discovery** powered by a sail and the muscle of men of the Royal Navy. This is how Captain Vancouver described the event:

"From Point Grey we proceeded first up the eastern branch of the sound **[Burrard Inlet]** where, about a league within its entrance, we passed to the northward of an island which nearly terminated its extent, forming a passage from ten to seven fathoms deep, not more than a cable's length in width **[the First Narrows and the "island" is present-day Stanley Park]**. This island lying exactly across the channel, appeared to form a similar passage

15

to the south of it, with a smaller island lying before it. **[False Creek. The other "island" has not been identified]**. From these islands, the channel, in width about half a mile, continued its direction about east. Here we were met by about fifty Indians, in their canoes, who conducted themselves with the greatest decorum and civility, presenting us with several fish cooked, and undressed, of the sort already mentioned as resembling smelts. These good people, finding we were inclined to make some return for their hospitality, shewed much understanding in preferring iron to copper.

"For the sake of the company of our new friends, we stood on under an easy sail, which encouraged them to attend us some little distance up the arm **[Vancouver's inner harbour]**. The major part of the canoes twice paddled forward, assembled before us, and each time a conference was held. Our visit and appearance were most likely the object of their consultation, as our motions on these occasions seemed to engage the whole of their attention. The subject matter, which remained a profound secret to us, did not appear of an unfriendly nature to us, as they soon returned, and, if possible, expressed additional cordiality and respect. This sort of conduct always created a degree of suspicion, and should ever be regarded with a watchful eye. In our short intercourse with the people of this country, we have generally found these consultations take place, whether their numbers were great or small; and though I have ever considered it prudent to be cautiously attentive on such occasions, they ought by no means to be considered as indicating at all times a positive intention of concerting hostile measures; having witnessed many of these conferences, without our experiencing afterwards any alteration in their friendly dispostion. This was now the case with our numerous attendants, who gradually dispersed as we advanced from the station where we first met them, and three or four canoes only accompanied us up a navigation which, in some places, does not exceed an hundred and fifty yards in width.

"We landed for the night about half a league from the head of the inlet **[Port Moody]**, and about three leagues from its entrance. Our Indian visitors remained with us until by signs we gave them to understand we were going to rest, and after receiving some acceptable articles, they retired, and by means of the same language promised an abundant supply of fish the next day; our seine having been tried in their presence with very little success. A great desire was manifested by these people to imitate our actions, especially in the firing of a musket, which one of them performed, though with much fear and trembling. They minutely attended to all our transactions, and examined the color of our skins with infinite curiosity. In other respects they differed little from the generality of the natives we had seen: they possessed no European commodities, or trinkets, excepting some rude ornaments apparently made from sheet copper; this circumstance, and the general tenor of their behavior, gave us reason to conclude that we were the first people from a civilized country they had yet seen. Nor did it appear that they were nearly connected, or had much intercourse with other Indians, who traded with the European or American adventurers..... at four in the morning of Thursday the 14th, we retraced our passage.... As we passed the situation from whence the Indians had first visited us the preceding day, which is a small border of low marshy land on the northern shore, intersected by several creeks of fresh water, we were in expectation of their company, but were disappointed, owing to our travelling so soon in the morning. Most of their canoes were hauled up into the creeks, and two or three only of the natives were seen straggling about on the beach. None of their habitations could be discovered, whence we concluded that their village was within the forest. Two canoes came off as we passed the island, but our boats being under sail, with a fresh favorable wind breeze, I was not inclined to halt, and they almost immediately returned.

"The shores of this channel, which, after Sir Harry Burrard of the navy, I have distinguished by the name Burrard's Channel.... On the northern side the rugged snowy barrier, whose base we had now nearly approached, rose very abruptly, and was only protected from the wash of the sea by a very narrow border of low land. By seven o'clock we had reached the N.W. point of the channel, which forms also the south point of the main branch of the sound: this also, after another particular friend, [who cannot be identified] I called Point Atkinson ..."

Vancouver now began the exploration of Howe Sound, and on his return he was surprised to see two Spanish ships, the **Sutil** and **Mexicana**, anchored off Point Grey. The natives of Homulchesum at the mouth of the Capilano River had also seen these ships which were commanded by Don Dionisio Alcala Galiano and Don Cayeto Valdez, and there is a charming story

17

told by Tom MacInnes in his little book **Chinook Days** about the meeting between the Indian maiden Yahda and the Spaniards which is worthy of retelling as MacInnes's book is classified as rare.

"Four war canoes, crossing the Gulf on their way to the Lions' Gate, were nearing the far point which we now call Point Grey. Suddenly the paddlers stopped paddling. They were astonished at seeing ships. There had been ancient tales of ships; and recently there had been rumors of their having reappeared. They were there now for all to see; two of them. Two great ships; and it was plain that even the smaller one would hold more than could be held by all four of the war canoes together, maybe twice as much. Each of the ships had two tall masts, but of different rig for the sails. The men in the canoes were grave at the sight, for they felt that no good thing was likely to come for the Indians out of ships from overseas. But Yahda was entranced. It was as if something greatly desired, but not believed, had all at once come true. And her spirit shone bright in her eyes as her arms reached out toward one of the ships; the one from which came on the wind a music trembling sweeter than any that ever she had heard before. She went all athrill to it. Then it was that the canoes were caught in a sudden, unknown tide; and things unexpected began to happen. The canoes were drawn toward the ship from which the music came. The canoe with Yahda in it was carried swiftly, in spite of the expert paddling of its crew. Soon it was close to the stern of the schooner **Mexicana**, from which a rope ladder hung down. The Commander, Don Cayetano Valdez, rose from where he sat on the deck with his superior officer, the Commander Don Dionisi Galiano, who had come over from the brig **Sutil** to compare notes of the coast survey, and while the time with a drink or two. They both looked down with interest at the canoes so queerly caught in a strong, narrow current, on either side of which no tide-rip or motion of the water was visible. A young Spanish sailor, who had been playing the guitar, rose also and looked at the approaching canoes, and then at the one with Yahda, so close now to the stern; and then only at Yahda. And Yahda, with outstretched arms, stood up in the canoe. Her hair was parted and pleated in two thick coils down her back; her prettiest shells were strung around her neck. Otherwise she wore only her summer kalikwhatie, which is a light petticoat woven of the silky inner bark of young cedar, colored with yellow and red. Then as the canoe swirled around the stern, this Yahda girl leapt like a panther at the rope ladder. She caught it and climbed quickly into the ship. That was how the trouble came. For it was the young sailor who helped her over the side on to the deck, and in doing that he gave her hand a squeeze that meant much all in a moment to both of them.

"Valdez gave a sharp order, and the rope ladder was hauled up out of reach of the Indians. But now the canoes seemed as if held to the ship in the grip of that cantrip tide. Then the Indians made as if to board the schooner and recover Yahda. She sensed what was in their minds. And she sensed the signs made to the Indians by the men in the schooner, and the meaning of the glance directed toward her by Valdez; who may have thought she was a slave attempting to escape. It all meant that she would be forced back into the canoe. Like a wild thing of the forest suddenly loosed from a cage, she darted along the deck to the prow. She turned and looked back at the young sailor, who had started to follow after her. One look was enough; she read the admiration in his eyes; she beckoned him to follow and straightway plunged overboard. The Spanish sailor followed and it seemed as if the tide took hold on the two of them. They were borne by it toward the shore at Kitsilano more swiftly than any fish can swim. But that same uncanny tide reversed against the canoes and held them back from pursuit.

"Now, if I were free to tell a story of this affair as I should like, then I would arrange a happy time for Yahda and the Spanish sailor for so long as they wanted to be together in the forest at Kitsilano; and never let an Indian or any interfering foreigner find them there. But in that which is written for schools one should tell the truth as it was, rather than as it should have been.

"Yahda landed in advance of the sailor; skilfully avoiding the great boulders lying along the shore. They are cruel hard to be dashed against, and that is just what happened to the poor sailor. In the twist of a third wave he was thrown against one of them just as he was making his feet; striking the wide of his head with such force that he sank back in the water, limp and stunned. Yahda went swiftly in to him, and, taking a firm hold behind his neck, dragged him safely to shore.

"Yahda knew much of what should be; and also of what would be. She knew what she knew in truer fashion than may be taught in any school. She was able to feel the way of unremembered

19

things, doing it by instinct, as we would say; and she was able to flash the way of new things, which is called intuition by those who believe in it, but for which the few who have the trick of it may have other names, or no name at all. When one can do that way in the natural run of affairs, then there is no need for the talk and palaver of logic. One knows what is what; and what to do instantly. Yahda knew well enough that this man she held was sorely hurt and likely to die; this lover who had come to her all in a twinkling minute out of the unexpected. She felt sure that Tolo Wahna [a medicine man] had a hand in the happening, but whether for good or ill, or for both good and ill delightfully together, that she could not tell. But as soon as she had her man well out of the water, she helped him to his feet, and led him in a daze across the sands. He sagged heavily against her before she had him where there was thick moss at the foot of a cedar tree. There she eased him down at full length with his head in her lap. Deftly she passed her little hands with their healing power around the wound on the side of his head. But it was a wound that would not bleed; or that was bleeding within. What next could she do? Her ears detected the sound of a stream near by, and she poled directly to it. She fashioned a cup of the big maple leaves and in that brought water back to the sailor. Although he was in a stupor, the water seemed to soothe and please him.

"Yahda lived through the hours that followed as if they were years, and as if they were all the real years of life worth having. It was in the time of the long twilight. She saw the slim yellow canoe of the new moon go westering down the sky. Over the Bay a flush of crimson lingered for hours. Then the blue night came with the large few stars; and the one sad golden star of summer that she looked to as her own. What happened that night under the cedar in Kitsilano we do not know; but the Spanish sailor moaned at times, and at times he laughed low and happily, muttering Spanish words of love and dreaming himself back home into a Spanish town. He heard a music of many guitars and bandurrias together; he heard the stimulating clicking of the castyanet; he knew warm women near him, and he smelled the new wine for the autumn frolic.

"Yahda listened to his words. It seemed in the sound of them as if memories came to her through a thin blue smoke of things that never were. And after that there was like the unrolling of vast, rich curtains of light, one shimmering behind the other endlessly, discovering new vistas and fashions of life, but coming never to any clearance of this from that. Yahda built a fire.

"Shortly after the sun had risen next morning, the two of them were found in the forest at the foot of the cedar tree by a landing party from the ships and by the men of the four canoes. The young sailor was dead. And from the look in the eyes of Yahda, the Indians knew that she was not there at all, but was beside herself or even farther away. For a certain sort of madness the Indians show careful respect; guarding and tending the body of one whose mind is absent. Yet in the circumstances the omens for a happy marriage and a lasting alliance with the people of the Squamish were not promising. Word of the strange happening, of the conduct of Yahda, and the death of the foreign sailor, would surely reach the ears of the Squamish Chief and his people; with swift growing additions quite untrue, but very effective for discredit. So it was thought better not to conceal but to construe. It was thought that by skilful interpretation the event might be shown as in some way favorable; as if Yahda at least were under special protection of spirits.

"The body of the sailor was buried as a sailor at sea off the Spanish Bank. He was said to have been a distant relative of the great Gabriola; belonging to a branch of that illustrious family fallen on hard days. Somewhere in Spain the wraith of him appeared before his mother; and she mourned and went forthwith to the church to pray for the repose of his soul; hopefully handing over her widow's mite for aid to that end. And a singing came of her prayers and her religion which worked to relieve the soul of that sailor out of a bad dream in the state that he was; whether you believe it or not."

No, Yahda is not part of **real** history, but today, on the Upper Levels Highway, there is a sign which tells the story of the meeting of the Spanish and British naval officers across English Bay at Spanish Banks. Yahda's name is not there but when you read that sign, think of little Yahda of the Capilano. And you might want to look more closely at the golden ship on the coat-of-arms of West Vancouver, and again think of Yahda. It will do no harm; rather, it will encourage an understanding that tales such as that of Yahda make the dry historical record seem just a little more human.

The Indians dwelling at Homulchesum and at Stuckale near Cypress Creek may have, during the following sixty-six years,

21

caught a glimpse of the great change in the white man's technology which saw sail gradually give way to steam and the ships of sail which got bigger and bigger. It is not inconceivable they saw in the distance, or heard from friends, of the black smoke-belching sidewheel trading steamer **Beaver**, owned by the Hudson's Bay Company, a ship which in due course would become a familiar sight to them until one day in 1898, reduced to the lowly status of a tugboat, the historic ship was wrecked opposite the mouth of the Capilano River. However, in 1858, that momentous year which witnessed the great gold rush to the Fraser River and the birth of the Crown Colony of British Columbia, the age of "high technology" arrived and the life of the native people would never be the same again. Through the First Narrows came the auxiliary steam sloop HMS **Plumper**, commanded by Captain George Henry Richards, RN, under orders to survey the waters Captain George Vancouver had first explored. As a result, the shoreline of what was to be the Municipality of West Vancouver was precisely etched out by thin black lines to become a navigational map. Five years later, the Pioneer sawmill was established at what became known as Moodyville, and later as North Vancouver and this was followed by Stamp's Mill in what is now Vancouver. To the fringes of Stamp's successor, the Hastings Mill, came a former Fraser River pilot by the name of John "Gassy Jack" Deighton who, with his Indian wife, her mother, her cousin, a yellow dog, two chickens, two weak-backed chairs and a barrel of whisky, opened a soon well-to-be patronized saloon, and from this humble commercial endeavor there arose the shacktown of Gastown which grew into the more respectable, namewise at least, Granville and eventually the city of Vancouver. West Vancouver's beginnings were more enlightening. They began with a lighthouse at Point Atkinson.

Tall and graceful ships of the winds, some with beautiful hand-carved figureheads, now made their way through the First Narrows to take on cargoes at the Burrard Inlet sawmills and these required navigational aids and pilots. In 1874 the sum of $4,250 was allocated for the building of a light at Point Atkinson and the contractor, Arthur Fenny, soon lamented he was unable to obtain the services of a carpenter "for less than $5.00 per diem and expenses." As a result the cost estimates soared to $6,202.95. The first keeper, Edwin Woodward, was hired at an annual salary of $800, out of which he was supposed to pay an assistant, but there is no record of him doing so. The building was described by W.A. Grafton, who handled the pilotage, as "a square tower sloping inwards to the top where the light was" and Beryl Gray, a West Vancouver writer, more romantically wrote in an article published by **The Vancouver Daily Province** in 1926, "it was a picturesque little wooden structure with a stone base." Woodward remained in charge until 1879 and during his tenure, on April 25, 1876, a son, James Atkinson Woodward, was born to him and his wife at the lighthouse, and thus we have a very important date in the Chronicle of West Vancouver for it heralded the arrival of the first white child in what is now the municipality. He died in February, 1954 and his ashes were scattered in the sea surrounding his lonely birthplace. The second lightkeeper, R.G. Wellwood, stayed on only for a year, quitting his job because, he bewailed, of the "wash, wash, wash of the waves on the rocks." He was replaced by Walter Erwin who remained on the job for thirty years and was one of the "sixteen men who once owned West Vancouver."

Loneliness and the remoteness from the rest of the world was, and is, a lightkeeper's lot up and down the coast, and one stormy night in 1883 this was brought home to Mrs. Erwin at Point Atkinson who became extremely ill. Somehow word reached Gastown of her plight, but because of the stormy weather conditions, not a seafarer dared to go to the rescue. Only Mrs. Susan Patterson volunteered. Alan Morley in his **Vancouver. From Milltown to Metropolis** gives us a vivid portrait of this woman who was to become famous as the "Grace Darling of Burrard Inlet": "Mrs. Patterson, a managing woman, was just the sort of hard-boiled angel of mercy Gastown needed. She tended the sick and injured 'never quailed from hardship, danger or disease' and could rout a drunken or brutal husband with a look and a word." With that description, then, it was obvious it would be Mrs. Patterson who would go to Mrs. Erwin's aid. Persuading two Indians to accompany her, she set out in a dugout canoe for Point Atkinson.

The paddles swing and dipping meet the lift of swelling tide,
Then lost to sight, engulfed between black billows brimming wide,
Until it seems no earthly hope their little craft can guide.

Drenched with the clinging salted spray, frozen with icy wind,
Rising and falling in the gloom that swathes of darkness bind,
They bravely battle with the storm the gleaming lamp to find.

On land the watchers, huddled, wait and offer fervent prayer —
But in the dugout, tossed like a cork, the woman shows no fear,
And searches strange abysmal dusk to see SKAY-witsut near.
[Thus wrote Nora M. Duncan in her poem **The Heroine of Moodyville (sic)**. SKAY-witsut was the Indian name for Point Atkinson.]

And then unfolded through the haze of quickly breaking day
A nestling cove with shining sands in golden welcome lay
That drew them to its sheltered beach beneath rock bastions gray.

The keeper waits with fearful heart to guide them carefully
O'er roughened trail; by thicket deep, by darkling forest tree—
Until with weary gratefulness the lighthouse door they see.

Thus soon our Mistress Patterson above the sufferer bends
And by her touch the healing grace, soft restful slumber lends,
As from her heart Doxology unto her God ascends!

Meanwhile in 1872, James Blake had pre-empted 160 acres on either side of what became Hollyburn Creek, and in 1877 Josias Charles Hughes took up 121 acres between Mr. Blake's property and the Indian lands, but Mr. Blake transferred his property at a later date to a Welsh deserter from the Royal Navy, John Thomas, better known as "Navvy Jack." Mr. Thomas put up a little home and lived there growing fruit trees, with his Indian wife and family, and operating a "by request" ferry service across the inlet, as well as working a gravel pit at the mouth of the Capilano River, selling his product to the now booming city of Vancouver.

In 1882 the government cancelled all pre-emption privileges on all unproved pre-emptions on both sides of English Bay to await the final right-of-way plans of the **Canadian Pacific Railway**, which was now beginning to head west to Burrard Inlet, and in 1886 these privileges were restored after the steel had been laid, and within a month a great deal of the land in what is now

West Vancouver had been taken up: J.P. Chapman selected Weston; J. McCormack, Dundarave; A.N.C. King, Altamont; P.A. Allen, West Bay; Stanley James, Brackenhurst; Murray Thain, the first harbor master, Sherman or Sandy Cove; Walter Erwin, Cypress Park; Nils Frolander, Point Atkinson; Captain Westerlund, Caulfeild; a man named Nelson, a framer at the Hastings Mill selected Eagle Harbor; a Mr. McInnis, Horseshoe Bay, while there is a record of a chap named McPherson establishing squatter's rights at White Cliff Point. Most of these pre-emptions rights were vacated.

Then there was Edward Collett who took up land at what is now Kew Beach where is located a great boulder which proved rather embarrassing to an ancient Indian chief. While over on Vancouver Island he promised his peers he could throw the rock from Cowichan over to Mount Strachan, which looms behind Kew Beach, but he fell short of his mark. Down through the years, West Vancouver has been blessed with having many wonderful characters in its midst, and "Holy Joe" Collett was the first of them. Mr. Collett had arrived in Vancouver the day after the Great Fire of 1886 which destroyed the fledgling city, and shortly afterwards went into the business of making charcoal to supply steam for the Fraser River salmon canneries. The base of his operations was called "Holy Joe's Cove." Holy Joe was often seen standing on street corners in Vancouver singing psalms and hymns at the top of his voice — hence his nickname — and then, when his throat was dry, he would head off to the nearest saloon to quench his thirst. In remorse he then went to the Salvation Army Citadel to be saved. One day Holy Joe thought it would make his work easier if he had a boat to convey his charcoal to the canneries, and so he set to work to build what became known as the truly remarkable **Holy Terror**. The material used was high-class flotsam from the beach, and it is said, "her lines curved in spots, as did the lines of the rocky shore." When the 60-foot ship was ready for launching, Holy Joe decided to go into town to celebrate, and on his return, after making his usual rounds, found the **Holy Terror** had burned to charcoal.

The name Holy Joe's Cove remained on the maps until 1913 when Quinton James Trotter acquired the 50 acres Collett had taken up and renamed it Kew Beach, from the "Q" in his first name and also in honor of Kew Gardens in London.

In this the earliest known photograph of the mouth of the Capilano River, West Vancouver's eastern boundary, it will be apparent that little has changed since that June day in 1792 when Captain George Vancouver sailed into the inner harbor. (VCA)

*Replica of Narvaez' **Santa Saturnina** arrives off Ambleside Beach. (WVML)*

"Piloto Commander Jose Narvaez" sets foot in West Vancouver. (VCA)

Edwin Woodward, first lighthouse keeper at Point Atkinson. (VCA) *Josias Charles Hughes who pre-empted Ambleside in 1877. (PA)*

*Dedication of Narvaez plaque at Ambleside Beach. Speaker is Reeve J. Edward Sears, with guard of honor from HMCS **Quesnelle**. (VCA)*

Mrs. Susan Patterson, the heroine of Point Atkinson. (VCA)

First Point Atkinson Lighthouse. (VCA)

Chapter Two

WEST CAPILANO

There was some good news and there was some bad news in 1891. First of all, the bad news. Navvy Jack Thomas didn't pay his taxes and was dreaming of heading for the Cariboo goldfields, and when he did pack up, James C. Keith, former banker, financier and above all, land speculator, picked his property up at a tax sale. Navvy Jack Thomas left his bones in the little miners' cemetery at Barkerville, but he is not forgotten. Navvy Jack gravel became famous in the construction industry in Vancouver and his name is perpetuated in Navvy Jack Point at the foot of 21st Street. The other bit of bad news came from an area close to what would be later known as Dundarave. There, a Vancouver tailor and part-time preacher, Francis Williams, had taken up a piece of land at the foot of 28th Street in the hopes that someday it might be developed into an estate. He didn't know it then, but he had been duped by a shyster salesman by the name of Mr. Brown who didn't happen to have title to the land when he sold it. Mr. Williams only found out in 1891 when he was forced to leave his home in what is now practically downtown Vancouver on account of a forest fire, loaded his goods and chattels on a scow and headed for his "estate." For a short time he, his wife, two sons and a daughter lived beside the small creek which flows through "his" property, rowing back and forth to work each day. When he got the news that would make anybody's day bad, he returned to Vancouver, no doubt a very disillusioned man.

The good news came on August 10 when Letters Patent were issued to provide for the incorporation of the District Municipality of North Vancouver, and in the subsequent election J.C. Keith was elected reeve. The population of the new municipality was only 300 and west of the Capilano River there was only the lighthouse keeper, possibly Navvy Jack, and maybe some squatters. It is also said that Sam Brighouse, one of Vancouver's most famed pioneers, built a fish processing plant at what would later be called Sherman.

It is, perhaps, the memory of Mrs. Susan Patterson's heroic mission of mercy to the Point Atkinson lighthouse that decided the District council, on February 15, 1892, to bring forth a money by-law permitting the borrowing of $40,000, at eight per cent interest for fifty years, to build a road from Deep Cove to Eagle Harbor. Known originally as the Lighthouse Road, it became officially designated as the Keith Road as J.C. Keith had taken up the debentures at par. It was not a mega-project, but it proved to be too big for the times. A major depression, not just a local one, was on the horizon and it was alleviated only by the great gold rush to the Klondike in 1898. Work **did** start on the road and a slash trail was cleared as far as Eagle Harbour, but construction stopped at the Capilano River and the slashings returned to nature.

Two Newfoundland fishermen, Captain Alcock and Captain Andrews, had established private wharfs for the use of fishermen at Fisherman's Cove, now Garrow Bay, and Peter Larson, later a well-known **hotelier** at Capilano Canyon began farming as well as a bit of logging at what is now Gleneagles. The land he was working was called "not particularly fertile," but the trees standing at the entrance to the golf course today speak, at least, of his honest intent. At Horseshoe Bay, in 1895, Edward "Scotty" Wishart and his partner, known only as Bill, began a small-scale logging operation, the first of many such hand shows which, in the passage of time, would leave their scars on the face of the primeval forests. The partnership didn't last long as it appears Bill had a strong aversion to work.

From out of this rudeness, however, there came in 1898, a passenger aboard Captain John Cates's new steamer **Defiance**, a man of impeccable family background — a gentleman and scholar by the name of Francis William Caulfeild. The **Defiance** would probably be bringing in supplies for the Point Atkinson lighthouse when she nosed into Skunk Cove and Mr. Caulfeild was entranced by what he saw. The following year he purchased a large piece of acreage and a close friend of Mr. Caulfeild's, H.A. Stone, describes Mr. Caulfeild's mood in his little book

31

A Short History of Caulfeild Village:

"This purchase entirely changed his mode of life, as thereafter he spent the greater part of his days at Caulfeild, abandoning the pleasures of English social life for the more lasting joy of peaceful endeavours amidst the wonders of nature. If we could share the thoughts of this kindly gentleman, then fifty-four years of age, whose extensive knowledge of the beauty spots of Great Britain led him to paint pictures of lovely Clovelly and other charming English villages, we can better appreciate his reactions at the sight of many Canadian towns and settlements he had just visited with their ugly straight roads, wanting in any form of beauty, and doubt not that his artistic soul had revolted.

"And so at Caulfeild his thoughts must have been, 'Here is a spot they shall not spoil. I will plan a village of good design according to the contours of nature. I will reserve the entire waterfront as a public park for the estate. I will lay the foundations of a village of beauty with wise restrictions.' And so he did!"

Laying out a village "according to the contours of nature" was, indeed, a unique way of going about town-planning and so were his initial "surveyors"; he used the paths followed by wild animals and the cows W.A. Grafton kept. Perhaps he was dreaming of a "Paradise" village which would be self-sustaining, but without direct transportation. Without that it could well have been "Paradise Lost." But in the long run, and with a great deal of hard work on his part, it became a beautiful reality, a true Paradise on Earth. To meet the prime need he built a wharf to handle not only Captain Cates's ships, which were the only link he had with the city, but small boats as well. He also built a house for the pilots who were rowed out to meet the ships entering and leaving the harbor. He built a little general store and post office, in front of which was an English-type cattle fence to keep Mr. Grafton's cows away and an ancient ship's anchor of unknown origin. With these developments there also came the change in name from Skunk Cove to Caulfeild Cove, and please, never, never spell it *"Caulfield"*! Finally, in 1909, with the installation of a water system from Cypress Creek, building lots were put on the market. The Caulfeild as we know it today, with its lovely, narrow twisting Piccadilly Lane and Clovelly Walk, was taking shape. It was not, however, until 1915 when Marine Drive was opened up that there was an "overland" route to his village and although he argued for many years for such a highway, when the surveyors arrived he protested with equal strength the route it was to take since it would slice right through his contoured village. Mr. Caulfeild won his battle and gracious homes were built by some of Vancouver's most prominent families, including Mr. Stone's "Stone Haven" at the intersection of Piccadilly and Marine Drive. Mr. Stone, who was managing director of Gault Brothers, a dry goods manufacturing concern, contributed generously to the founding of the Vancouver Art Gallery, and across Marine Drive from him lived Mrs. Julia Henshaw, scientist, world traveller and author, in whose home the Canadian Author's Society would meet to hear Mr. Caulfeild read his own translation of Homer's **Odyssey**. To fill out, at least partially, the cultural circle which developed in Caulfeild, we must not omit J.D.A. Tripp, the concert pianist and music teacher to whose home later would come such great musicians as Sir Thomas Beecham and Sir John Barbirolli.

Perhaps it is not out of place to jump ahead to the year 1927 when the little Anglican church, aptly called St. Francis-in-the-Wood, with its traditional "Lych Gate" out front. It was built, as Mr. Stone put it, "a building of simple beauty and solemnity." Even though it has been greatly enlarged, Mr. Stone's description still fits the scene where many fashionable weddings have been solemnized. For many years two of the most faithful members of the congregation were the much-loved and gentle Captain and Mrs. Frank Kettle. The Captain had served as second mate on the famed clipper **Cutty Sark**, had rounded the "Horn" and been shipwrecked on several occasions. He and his wife, Mary, came to Caulfeild in 1909 to look after the pilots and from 1920 to the 1940s lived in the old pilot house, a place which was sheer delight to small boys who marvelled at the great collection of ships in bottles, most of which were of the **Cutty Sark.** When the Kettles passed away, a memorial window was erected in their honor. It depicts **Charity** but their names are not mentioned, as the dedicators of the window said Frank and Mary were so humble they would be offended by recognition for the many works of charity they undertook. Next to the window there is a wood carving, the work of Mr. Caulfeild himself, based on the theme, "These men see the works of the Lord and His wonders in the deep."

Many of the homes in Caulfeild had their gardens carefully tended by an elderly Chinese, who also looked after janitorial

33

work in the church. One cold Sunday afternoon the rector, the author's father, went down to check on the furnace and to his surprise found a Buddhist shrine in the basement!

"There is a charm about Caulfeild that gets one. Once you have lived there, you do not leave it willingly. Should you have to go away, you are most likely to return." Thus wrote Mr. Stone, and with that we now turn back the years once again to meet Ontario-born John Lawson, another true gentleman, who has earned the title "Father of West Vancouver" by settling on the land once owned by Navvy Jack Thomas.

The Lawson Story reads almost like that of the opening of the Canadian West through the building of the Canadian Pacific Railway. John Lawson came out from Ontario to become a conductor on the CPR, serving on trains operating from the once bustling town of Donald, and it was here that he met Miss Christine Smith who was working in the railway company's boarding house. When the two decided to get married, they found it necessary to cross Rogers Pass to Revelstoke to make the arrangements, but there they found that a justice of the peace was lacking so they headed further west to Kamloops. Two miles short of their destination the "regular" broke down and they were forced to walk into town where the marriage ceremony took place. Their home was in Donald where their two daughters, Elizabeth and Gertrude and a son, Robert, who died in infancy, were born. Mr. Lawson continued to work for the CPR in Donald until the company abandoned the town in favor of Revelstoke, which was to be the new divisional point. It was this event which created the story of St. Peters "the Stolen Church", now at Windermere in the East Kootenay, which was brought down from Donald by Rufus Kimpton, who reasoned it was **his** church, a move which raised a hullaballoo by the Anglicans of Revelstoke who thought it was **theirs**. But to the Lawsons, such a theft was of no importance. They were staunch Presbyterians and what the "established church" did was of no concern. In Revelstoke, where the Lawsons now made their home, a son, Duncan, was born and from here their daughters were sent to high school at Parkdale Collegiate in Toronto, a school their father had attended. About 1903, the family moved to Vancouver and on November 20, 1906, Mr. Lawson attended a land auction sale in the O'Brien Hall where J.S. Rankin and Arthur J. Ford were selling land on behalf of the provincial government. Purchasers at that time were listed as J.S. Bain, Sitt and Williamson, Percy Webster, John Lawson, Professor Edward Odlum and F.C. Wade, who in 1912 was to be the founder of the Liberal newspaper, **The Vancouver Sun**.

On Easter Sunday, 1907, John Lawson trundled his family onto a "Columbia River boat", and with a scow loaded with household goods crossed the treacherous First Narrows to land at their new home at what once had been Navvy Jack Thomas's place. With the immediate Lawson family were Mrs. Lawson's two sisters, Margaret and Annie, Margaret's boyfriend, John Hart, a nine-year old cousin, Howard Hungerford, a canary and Margaret's dog. For years there was a popular legend that the **voyageurs** had the mind-boggling experience of ferrying a cow by the name of Brownie across the Narrows in one of the river boats, but many years later Miss Gertrude Lawson, a long-time teacher at Pauline Johnson School, set the record straight about the sea-going cow. In an interview with Wilfrid Bennett, a reporter for **The Province** and later a West Vancouver school trustee, she said the basis for the cow fable occurred two years later when the family cow, which had been brought over on a tugboat, wandered across the Capilano River and produced a calf. To bring Brownie and her calf back, Mr. Lawson loaded them both in one of the river boats and rowed them across the Capilano and along the shoreline for about a mile to the farm. Even with the updating of the event, Mr. Lawson's experience with **two** cows in a ten-passenger rowboat must have been a harrowing experience.

Shortly before the Lawson family moved in, James Ollason, who years later would be municipal clerk, made a journey into the wilderness from North Vancouver to the future Hollyburn. An account of this appeared in **The Daily Province** on June 30, 1926, and gives an insight into travel conditions at that time:

"Transportation in West Vancouver twenty years ago was run on what might be called the self service system. Taking the ferry on the Vancouver shore, then as now, one landed at Lonsdale Avenue, North Vancouver, and made use of such roads as there were. The road leading westward towards the Capilano in those days, although it may not have finally run up a tree, did really end in something like a squirrel track. So dense was the bush that three of us failed to find the bridge across the river and entered the West Capilano district for the first time in our experience over the shingle flumes. We crawled dizzily till we could

35

step off on to the old Keith Road. This journey was made at Christmas time in the year 1906 and the bridge across Brothers Creek was then being constructed. We crossed that stream on the stringers of the new bridge and were informed by Mr. Snider, the contractor, that he had a mile and three quarters of the road from the Capilano west to reshape. We traversed this stretch with much interest. The day was fine and although the view was limited by the walls of trees on either side, for which West Vancouver had since become so famous, was noticeably pure and refreshing. . . . A run out by boat on the old **Britannia** to Eagle Harbour, and a walk from there to North Vancouver by the old Keith Road, made a pleasant day's outing. If driving were preferable to walking, there was a steady old bay mare and comfortable buggy to be had at the North Vancouver Hotel and one may reasonably question whether scooting along the present highway at fifty miles an hour can give as genuine pleasure as we experienced driving lazily along over the turfy old Keith Road years before West Vancouver was born into the family of municipalities.''

After planting some holly bushes beside the stream which flowed through his property (hence the name Hollyburn) and fixing up part of the barn into a rough and tumble gymnasium for his family, Mr. Lawson began the process of parcelling his lands for sale. He was, above all, a land developer and not a land speculator, but it remains a mystery as to who his first clients were. To attract clients, he dreamed of a golf course, which was to be located just south of the present Municipal Hall. High taxes and high costs, even then, thwarted his plan. He was, perhaps, ahead of his time for golf courses years later would become the drawing card for real estate developments of then undreamed-of elegance.

Meanwhile, from the old village of Homulchesum at the mouth of the Capilano River reports were emerging of a situation that is all too familiar today, the question of Indian land rights, and the voice spreading these complaints came from Chief Joe Capilano, a friend of the Mohawk poet and story-teller E. Pauline Johnson. The chief, who allegedly usurped the name Capilano, went one day in 1906 to seek publicity for his cause from a Vancouver newspaper. According to Dr. James W. Morton, author of **Capilano. The Story of a River**, ''The exasperated editor finally told him to go and tell his troubles to the king. This facetious remark must have found a resting place in Joe's naive mind. The editor of the newspaper was amazed, not long after, to read in another journal that Chief Capilano Joe was about to leave for London to place his problems before King Edward VII." On July 3, in a blaze of glory, the Chief set out for London to see the king and in the British capital, dressed up in all his finest regalia, he became the hit of the Fleet Street scribes. Whether he actually met with King Edward is a moot point. He always claimed a meeting did take place, but his many critics, all white, by the way, said the meeting in Buckingham Palace was a figment of his imagination. The Chief, however, never backed away from his claim. He had met the king and that was that. When the Chief died in 1910 and was entombed in the little granite mausoleum above what is now Park Royal on Keith Road, his most cherished possession, a picture of "my friend", King Edward VII and Queen Alexandra, was placed alongside the casket.

For Mrs. Lawson, the idyllic setting of her Hollyburn home at this time had one big drawback, that being there was no Presbyterian, or *any* church for that matter, in the new community. She certainly would not be of the mind of the Kimptons of Donald who "stole" **their** church when they moved to Windermere by grabbing one from Vancouver. As a result, the family would board the rowboat, brave the treacherous tides of the First Narrows and head for church in Vancouver. It should be pointed out at this time that the First Narrows were much narrower than they are at the present and a combination of wind and tide could be extremely dangerous. Miss Gertrude Lawson later recalled, "Sometimes I didn't know whether to pray we would be drowned or saved. I was terrified many times by the force of the current. . . ." This hazardous voyage to Sunday services apparently did not last for long. In a sketch of the history of the West Vancouver United Church, Rupert Harrison, the present archivist for the District of West Vancouver, relates the next step:

"It was in Mr. Lawson's home on the waterfront at 17th Street that the first services were held. On Sunday, September 20, 1908, the Rev. W.A. Davis came over from Vancouver to conduct a meeting in that home. There were 33 persons in the little group, among them Presbyterians, Methodists, Baptists and Congregationalists. Pianist was Miss Elizabeth Lawson. . . At that meeting it was agreed that services would be held there every second Sunday. However, by the end of the following month these services had proved so popular that it was decided to meet regularly each Sunday afternoon.

"As the enrolment grew it became desirable to have some definite form of organization and so we find that on January 19, 1909, the Rev. George A. Wilson, as supervisor of mission churches, came over from Vancouver to assist in the formation of a Presbyterian congregation. At that meeting Messrs. John Lawson, John Sinclair, John Hart and John Teare were appointed a Board of Managers. Jokingly it was suggested that the congregation should be known as St. John's. It was not long before the accommodation in the Lawson home was inadequate and larger quarters had to be sought. With the help of the Hollyburn Ladies Aid, which had been organized on January 6, 1910, two concerts were held and with the proceeds a tent twenty-three by fifty feet was bought in the summer of 1910. This was erected on a wooden foundation on a piece of property provided by Mr. Lawson at the south-east corner of 18th Street and Marine Drive."

While the Presbyterian Church now had its base, bases of another kind were being developed, which, today, we call "economic." As early as the late 1880s and 1890s, Samuel Brighouse, one of the "Three Greenhorns" who are listed among the founding fathers of Vancouver, built a small fish cannery west of Sandy Cove, and another was located at Eagle Harbour. About 1900 Arthur Henry Sherman moved into the old Brighouse site and founded the Defiance Cannery, no doubt named in honor of Captain Cates's steamer **Defiance** which made the plant a port of call. A few years later, George Marr established a logging camp at what is now Dundarave.

This industrialization of West Capilano brought a next-door neighbor to the Lawson family who was to remain until November, 1917, — the McNair-Fraser Lumber Company, founded by James and Robert McNair who, in time, would be known as the "shingle kings" of British Columbia. After doing considerable research into the company, David Rees-Thomas deposited his manuscript with the West Vancouver Public Library. It is an important document in the history of West Vancouver and rightly deserves a role in this Chronicle:

"Initially, shingle bolts were hauled on horse drawn sleds [**from the company's timber limits in what is now the British Properties**] to the booming grounds near the foot of the present Sixteenth Street, whence they were towed to the Hastings Mill. In March of 1907, however, work was started on a standard gauge railway and it was completed within a few months. From its terminus on a pier at the waterfront near Sixteenth Street the line extended northeastward through the site of the present Odeon Theatre and through the middle of the 1200-block Inglewood to approximately the location of Eleventh Street, where it turned north. Upon reaching the level of Palmerston Avenue, the line again curved away to the northeast, crossing Brothers Creek [**then called Sisters Creek**] and its tributaries on a pair of long [**two hundred and three hundred foot**] trestles. There were two camps, the lower probably situated near Eleventh Street. The upper camp was located a mile and a half beyond the lower, on a site which later became that of the first home built in the British Properties. The grades ran from three to sixteen percent on the lower mile and a quarter of the line, while the upper stretch had grades as steep as twenty-two percent.

"The lower camp comprised a large stable, a cookhouse and a dormitory, all of cedar shake construction, while the upper included a blacksmith's shop, three bunkhouses and a combination cookhouse, stores and dining hall. The **Province** reported that the McNairs had a reputation for feeding the loggers well," a thing which these leaders of the very strenuous life much appreciate.

"The McNair Timber Company railroad was solidly built, much of it being constructed on heavy timber cribwork. Rather than use railway logging cars or trucks, the McNair's intended to trail the logs of cedar and fir between the rails. A 45-ton Heisler was ordered for this purpose. The two-truck locomotive, C/N **1103**, was built in November of 1906 and had 15 1/2 x 12 inch cylinders and 40-inch drivers. It was moved from Erie, Pennsylvania, to Vancouver on its own wheels, coupled into a train. Final delivery of the locomotive, by scow towed out through the First Narrows and across the inlet, was complicated by the fact that the pier to receive the engine was only partly constructed. The inexperience of the work crew under foreman James Mattison combined with the changing state of the tide delayed landing until after dark. "It was 9 o'clock at night," the **Province** relates, "when, by the light of lanterns, the locomotive, with an emphatic puff or two of its exhausts, steamed onto the temporary pier, thus closing operations for that night." By four the next afternoon, Monday, June 2, [1907], the Heisler had been transferred to the logging railroad proper and was making its way, slowly and cautiously, to the upper camp. There the crew took time for a well-earned meal. Subsequent events are described by the **Province**:

"...after supper, it was determined to try conclusions with a down-grade trip, and the start was made with several interested spectators in the cab besides the driver, and an expert from the engine company, who had control of the operations. Soon after starting, however, the brakes in some manner became locked and the locomotive began to skid down the rusty rails without moving a wheel. It had attained a speed of about seven miles an hour when the expert had to announce that he had lost control of the engine and to recommend those aboard to jump. This, fortunately, they did, escaping with nothing more than a shaking, and in one case, a sprain. With accelerating speed the huge locomotive sped down the track. It had probably got up to fifteen or twenty miles an hour when it came to a curve at the bottom. Here it left the rails and began to conduct pioneer agricultural operations in a soil in which small boulders and occasional stumps were frequent. The safety valve broke off and its pressure went down to zero in a second. Fortunately, in plowing into the comparatively free ground it did not meet with any irresistible obstacle, so that it is not so seriously damaged as it might have been!

Mr. Rees-Thomas noted "the engine was wrenched free of its front truck, which remained, inverted, on the rails. The stack was bent at right angles, and the remains of the headlight reposed upon a stump. The cab was badly battered, yet the engineer's valise remained within it. While it was to serve the McNair brothers no more, the tough little Heisler survived to be part of the lumber industry for many years."

"The wreck of the company's motive power must have come as a rude shock to the McNairs and perhaps more so to three other gentlemen," Mr. Rees-Thomas continues. "Not three weeks prior to the accident, an agreement had been signed between the McNair Timber Company and one David Grant, acting on behalf of a company about to be formed. On June 10, 1907, the McNairs formally entered into a partnership with Graham Fraser, a manufacturer from New Glasgow, Nova Scotia, Joshua Peters, of Moncton, New Brunswick, and Russell L. Fraser, a North

Vancouver engineer. The capital of the new corporation, known as McNair-Fraser Lumber Co. Ltd. was divided into 2,000 shares of $100 each, of which James and Robert McNair each held 500. Jim McNair remained president, chairman of the board and manager of the company, while R.L. Fraser became assistant manager. In September of the following year, however, James McNair resigned the presidency and chairmanship, and in December he sold his shares to Graham Fraser and one Henry H. McDougall, apparently without his brother's knowledge. The latter move, added to a family dispute over a 'church matter', led to a permanent rift between the brothers. James A., now a 'capitalist', went on to make and lose more than one fortune in the lumber business before his death in an automobile accident one foggy January night in 1942. Robert McNair retained his interest in the company until 1911. His holdings eventually included timber limits from Howe Sound to Port Moody, and at his death on August 30, 1932, he was remembered as one of the most successful pioneer lumbermen on the coast.

"Logging operations on the McNair-Fraser limits came to something of a standstill with the wreck of the Heisler, and it became obvious that something better than a geared locomotive was needed for the twenty per cent -plus grades on the line. The answer was to be found at Marshland, Oregon, in the camp of the O.K. Logging Company. John McNair (a cousin) was despatched to Marshland to learn all he could. The O.K. Company's machine was rebuilt by Willamette Iron and Steel from a Fouts Gripwheel originally operated by Henry Colvin. It was known as a "Walking Dudley", a name said to have been taken from that of an old logger who walked from camp to camp. The machine developed for the McNair-Fraser railroad incorporated certain refinements, most significant being the use of two bull wheels connected by diffferential gearing, while a single wheel was used by the original. A detailed description was given by Russell Fraser in **Western Lumberman** in August 1911:

"'The cable locomotive is mounted on two specially designed trucks. Each truck has four double flanged wheels with an independent axle on each wheel, two journals on each. The frame is built up of heavy eighteen-inch-I-beams and rests on the trucks at three points, two under the boiler and one under the tank end of the machine. The boiler is 76 inches in diameter by 138 inches high and carries 160 pounds of steam. It is placed at one end of the machine directly over one of the trucks. The engines are similar to those used on a 14 x 14 road engine. The power which drives the machine is transmitted through a differential gear similar to that used on automobiles, to the bull wheels over which the cables pass. This differential gear is necessary in order to equalize the strain on the cables while going around curves. The machine works on a standard gauge track and hauls itself along on two wire cables one inch in diameter. These cables are stretched along the track just outside of either rail and are held in place by means of hardwood pegs set in the ties. At the upper end of the track these cables are made fast to stumps. Then, coming to the machine, they first pass under guide shives, from there they pass to the bull wheels and are given four turns around each, after which they pass under guide shives similar to those already mentioned but located at the other end of the machine and from where they pass around tightening wheels placed at the outer end of the pier. The bull wheels around which the cables are wound are similar to a gipsy or ship's niggerhead, except that the diameter of the bull wheel is greater, measuring five feet across'.

"The Walking Dudley cost McNair-Fraser roughly $8,000, which proved to be a good investment. The cable, costing 15 cents per foot new, showed very little wear, even after two seasons of use. With a four-man crew (driver, fireman, chaser, and in dry weather, a greaser), the Dudley made four round trips in a ten-hour day, trailing ten to sixteen logs in each turn. The largest turn hauled to tidewater scaled to 34,700 feet. Still, logging on the 'Dudley Road' was not without incident. Frank Payson Colpitts, a West Vancouver pioneer, was interviewed by the **Lions Gate Times** in April, 1962. 'There were firs on Hollyburn that had five or six thousand board feet of lumber in them,' Mr. Colpitts recalls, 'and one cedar was cut that was said to be an 11,000-footer. But when she was on her way down the foreman would not wait to put an extra line on her at Lawson [?] Canyon. He signalled them to highball her through and the huge cedar crashed over the edge and plunged to the bottom. There wasn't even stovewood left'.

"The heat of friction on the trailed logs was so great that they were smoking by the time they reached water. It is not known whether a fire was ever caused by the Dudley, but the danger was always present. 1910 was evidently a bad year for fire in the woods north of Vancouver. The first of the season occurred in the vicinity of the McNair-Fraser camp on Sunday, April 24, but provincial fire warden Gladwin made good use of the 45 men in the camp and had the fire under control by nightfall. That year also saw 'Old Dudley' suffer the indignity of running out of control and off the end of the pier into the saltchuck. As the outfit weighed thirty-eight tons, it was no doubt a strenuous task to get it back on the track. The Dudley was off the rails on at least one other occasion, when it turned over somewhere between the lower camp and the waterfront, but on the whole it seemed to have been a successful piece of motive power.''

The writer of this treatise on the pioneer lumber company concludes with a sterile letter from the Registrar of Joint Stock Companies written in November 1917. In 1911 it had changed hands, and sometime before the letter was written (it was returned unopened) operations seem to have ceased. The obituary reads as follows:

"Sirs: Pursuant to section 268 (1) of the 'Companies Act' and amendments, you are hereby required to inform me whether you are still carrying on business or in operation; and, further, are notified that, as you have failed for a period of two years or more preceding the date of this letter to make, file, or send to me all such returns, notices or documents as are by the said Act required, you are under the said Act in default... I shall, at the expiration of...two months...., cause to the contrary not being shown, publish a...notice in the **Gazette** for one month that your name has been struck off the register, and on such publication you will be **DISSOLVED**.''

While the Dudley was ''walking'' up and down the mountainside, a considerable amount of house-building was going on in Hollyburn. Most of the homes were cottage style, but not that of John Lawson's brother-in-law, William Charles Thompson, who built at the foot of 20th Street where a high-rise apartment now towers. Mr. Thompson's home was four storeys high, including basement and attic, and had an imposing main stairway up from the entrance hall with a grandfather clock midway up. It also boasted a bay window of curved glass overlooking English Bay and hot water heating. While Vancouver and North Vancouver could boast electric power, West Capilano had, and for many years to come, only coal oil lamps to brighten the evening.

Mr. Thompson had come out from Inglewood, Ontario, to

43

join Mr. Lawson in the real estate business. It was a ripe time for such a venture. The province was on the verge of a boom. Richard McBride, "the silver-tongued orator of the West", who was premier of British Columbia, had said so many times. Wherever the sun shone, its rays fell upon an outpost of the British Empire. Everybody who was anybody was a true red, white and blue Conservative. Therefore, all was right with the world. Even the Dominion Government in far-off Ottawa had sensed the boom that was about to come, and in 1908 undertook the building of a pier at the foot of 17th Street. It is not known, of course, how many strings John Lawson pulled to get that pier, but in 1909 he, William C. Thompson, Robert Macpherson and John Sinclair formed the West Vancouver Transportation Company. The name is interesting, as even then it shows that people, like Mr. Lawson, were looking towards a District Municipality which would be called West Vancouver. Ferry service began on November 8, 1909 with the 35-passenger gas boat **West Vancouver** churning up the waters between Hollyburn and Vancouver. Thus began a tradition that would last half a century, and a record for safety in treacherous waters. Service "continued throughout the winter with only slight financial loss and no serious interruption in schedule," reported the **North Shore Express** on April 4, 1910. Skipper of the West Vancouver on its inaugural run was Captain A.A. Findlay, "a typical bluff old country sea-dog. A lady passenger once offered him a 10-cent tip. It was like asking Winston Churchill to accept a bribe." Miss Gertrude Lawson, with whom he boarded, recalls that he "always interspersed his conversation with 'as it were, as it were'. So I was sitting over there, as it were, as it were, and he was over here, as it were, as it were." The engineer on that inaugural run was Harry Lawson Thompson who served the "fleet" from the very beginning right up until the service ceased in February, 1947.

The promoters of the ferry system, who did not expect it to be a paying proposition, pinned their hopes on covering losses through the increased value of their landholdings, and in 1911 business seemed to be going so well they added another ship, the **Sea Foam**, sometimes called "the sturdiest of all the West Vancouver ferries."

The year of dreams came with the dawn of 1910. It came in with a real rush, a real estate rush, and so great was the stampede that much of the choice land had been sold by 1912. This put

44

the ferry service in jeopardy as the losses could not longer be subsidized by land sales. That year, 1910, also saw the formation of the first real vestige of "local government" through the creation of the West Capilano Improvement Association, a sort of ratepayers association.

All along the north shore, from the Capilano River to White Cliff there was electrifying activity as real estate salesmen talked in glowing terms to clients about subdivisions. A real estate firm, Irwin & Billings Co. Ltd. of North Vancouver, took out double-page newspaper advertisements to promote their holdings in Dundarave. With a plan of streets, all named after British prime ministers, Beaconsfield, Asquith, Rosebery, Palmerston, Pitt, Peel, Salisbury, Balfour and Gladstone, they offered waterfront lots at $4,500, with others going for as low as $450. The highlight of their advertisement was a drawing of the whole of the Vancouver area, resembling the modern aerial photograph, and a couple of highlights are worth noting. First, it mentions a proposed tunnel across the First Narrows, and secondly it shows a pier at the foot of Marr Avenue, now 25th Street, nothing that a contract for its construction had already been awarded. Here, the promoter's imagination ran a bit wild, for no such contract had been issued. The map also shows a proposed ferry service from Dundarave to Vancouver and to the beach at English Bay.

Behind this scheme lay the land of R.E. McNaughton, who, like John Lawson, would soon rank as one of the "Fathers of West Vancouver." He named his subdivision "Dundarave" after his ancestral home in Scotland. What Hollyburn did not have, Dundarave could soon boast, for one of the first business establishments in that area was the Clachan Hotel, operated by two sisters — Jessie and Helen Stevenson. It was a one storey building with a broad verandah on two sides and was located right on the waterfront, and was aptly named, for translated from the Gaelic it means "meeting place."

Adjoining the Dundarave subdivision, and using the same street names was Bellevue, "Vancouver's premier suburb." It was being promoted by The Alliance Trust & Investment Co. Ltd., and they offered a launch service to the site for prospective customers. In no way, was the Alliance Trust going to permit their clients to ride the **West Vancouver** and have John Lawson make a sale! "A lot in Bellevue is a joy forever; two lots is rapture. Be joyful by buying a homesite in Bellevue," they advertised. The "general

45

environment of Bellevue, would suggest to you, as it has to many others, that at no great future date this will be the West End of Vancouver. This is a point well worth your consideration."

Further west, Colonel Albert Whyte was marketing an ambitious development, at least so it seemed on paper, which he called White Cliff City. He was not a colonel in the field-rank sense, but rather gained his honorary title with a volunteer outfit in Tacoma called the Fusiliers. In every sense of the word, Colonel Whyte was an adventurer. A native of Ontario, his father gave him a five dollar gold piece and, at the age of 15 was told to "get out." He wandered down into the southern United States and became a water-boy in the Confederate army during the civil war, after which he went selling sewing machines. Ultimately he arrived in Tacoma, where, his niece Miss Dorothy Violet Whyte told West Vancouver archivist Rupert Harrison "he was responsible for the running out or expelling of the Chinese from Tacoma in 1886." On another occasion, Miss Whyte said, "he was immigration man at Point Roberts. . . keeping the Chinamen from running across the border and coming into this country" (presumably, the United States). He was a great fan of Robert Burns, and when his company, West Shore and Northern Land Company laid out White Cliff City he gave all the streets Scottish names. Before going broke as a result of the First World War he pursuaded the government to change the spelling of White Cliff to that of his own name and it has remained that way ever since.

While the real estate people were trying their best to make other people's dreams become a reality, there was one dream in what is now the British Pacific Properties that was going sour, but not for economic reasons. 'Tis said that behind every successful man there is a woman, but in the case of Harvey Hadden, a wealthy Nottingham textile merchant, a gentleman of means and taste, that concept, apparently does not apply, at least as far as Hadden Hall is concerned. Mr. Hadden visited Vancouver first of all in 1891 and spent about $60,000 buying up real estate in the fledgling city. Today those properties are among the most expensive in downtown Vancouver but, pity for him, he didn't keep them. Twelve years later he returned, but this time his eyes were not focussed on the "city" but on a 160-acre tract of land on the side of Hollyburn Ridge overlooking the Capilano River. The view from his holding was unsurpassed, as anyone who visits the

Capilano Golf and Country Club, which is located on the site, will know. It was here that Mr. Hadden built a glorious gentleman's home, a home that oozed of good taste with spacious rooms panelled in the finest polished cedar and with lovely gardens and little ponds.

Whether or not Mrs. Hadden ever saw the property is not known, but it is said, and this is only hearsay, that Mrs. Hadden thought she could see a wild savage Indian behind every tree, and refused to make Hadden Hall her home.

Hadden Hall eventually went for taxes to the Municipality of West Vancouver, fell victim to vandals, and in this Chronicle more will be heard of it.

Caulfeild pilot Captain George William Robertson with his wife and family, circa 1889. (WVMA).

Pilot station and boat house, circa 1906. (WVMA)

Francis W. Caulfeild, founder of Caulfeild. (VCA)

THE RED & WHITE STORES

Caulfeild store in later years. Note cattle guard in front. (WVMHS)

49

F.W. Caulfeild's home at 4699 Piccadilly. (WVML)

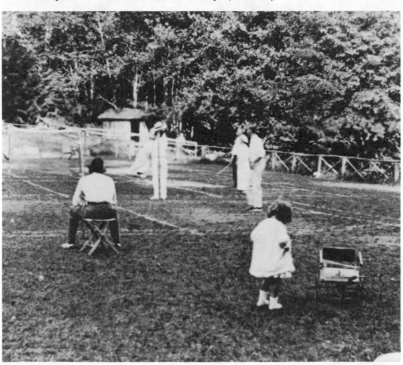

Playing badminton on the Village Green in front of St. Francis-in-the-Wood Church, circa 1915. (WVMA)

50

Caulfeild Cove, circa 1918. (WVMA)

Pilot boat moored in Caulfeild Cove, circa 1914. (WVMA).

Captain Frank Kettle. (WVML)   *Mrs. Mary Kettle. (WVML)*

Defiance Cannery, later known as the Great Northern, at Sherman. (WVMA)

The pretty little church of St. Francis-in-the-Wood, Caulfeild. (WVML)

The "Father of West Vancouver," John Lawson and his wife Christie. (PP)

John Lawson's home at Hollyburn, built by Navvy Jack Thomas. (WVMA)

John Lawson in buggy drawn by his prize-winning team, circa 1912. (WVML)

John Lawson with one of his horses at the foot of 17th Street. (WVMA)

After rescuing a deer from the water in front of his home, John Lawson became a sort of "deer-father." (WVMA)

Donkey engine and crew clearing land at Hollyburn circa 1910. (WVMA)

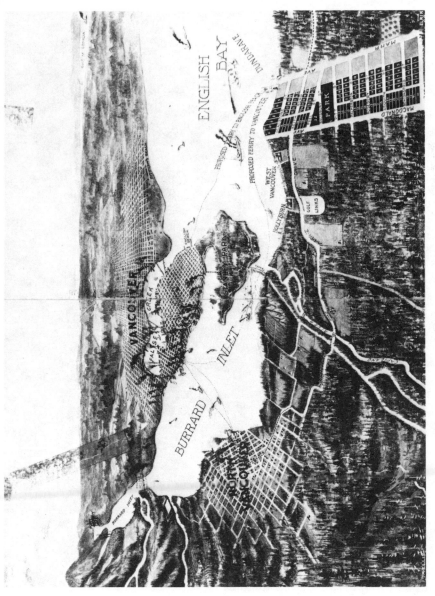

Plan of West Vancouver sub-division prepared by Irwin & Billings, realtors of North Vancouver, 1911. (WVMA)

Miss Gertrude Lawson.   *W.C. Thompson.*

Mr. & Mrs. John Harte.

Mr. and Mrs. W.C. Thompson and friend, Lily Woodward, in front of their bar in 1914. (WVMA)

Gracious home of W.C. Thompson, 2058 Argyle, built in 1909. (WVMA)

Clearing of Marine Drive, circa 1910, showing burned out stumps from fire which took place about 1884. View looks west from 18th Street. (VCA)

Clearing land for John Lawson's proposed golf course at NE corner 17th Street and Marine Drive. (VCA)

John Harte's home at 16th Street and Esquimalt, built in 1911. (WVMA)

W.G. Barker's first home at 22nd Street and Bellevue, 1911. (WVMA)

McNair Fraser Logging Camp, 1911, showing Walking Dudley at work. (VCA)

When the Walking Dudley walked too far. (WVMA)

"Our first passenger facilities." A logging railroad around 1910. (VPL)

Log booming near foot of Seventh Street in 1910. (VCA)

Chapter Three

FORWARD, WEST VANCOUVER!

At the beginning of the second year of the "boom"; West Vancouver was still very dependent on Vancouver and North Vancouver for just about everything. Unless the West Vancouver Trading Company at 17th and Marine had what was wanted in stock, it meant a long walk to the tram line in North Vancouver or a trip to Vancouver on the ferry. The West Vancouver Trading Company, which was to later house the post office which Mr. Lawson had originally set up in his home, was opened about 1909 by Messrs. Payne and McMillan on the site of the present Coronation Building. Mrs. Anne Eleanor Jones, in a series of historical articles published by the **Lions Gate Times** has left us a word-picture of the first landmark in West Vancouver:

"The old trading company handled everything from blankets to fishing tackle, lamps and groceries, and supplies came over on the newly-formed ferry service, landing at the Hollyburn floats."

The prices asked for goods in "those olden days" would make the mouth water today, but then, wages were much lower than now, and one can imagine that people were complaining about the "high cost" of things even then.

Education was another problem the residents of West Capilano had to face, and, again, it was either a trip into North Vancouver or Vancouver to go to school. In 1911, however, Mr. Lawson arranged to have Miss Mary M. Reid brought out from Erin, Ontario, to teach the seven boys and seven girls who made up the young population of the community. The school in which she taught was hardly a model one.

Prior to her coming, the children had to hike over the Keith

Road to attend classes in North Vancouver. All this changed, however, on account of nature's fury. The Presbyterian church held services in a tent on the corner of 18th Street and Marine Drive, and one day in February, 1912, the tent collapsed under the weight of snow. It was replaced by another with full height sides and a roof, and to help defray the cost, the building was rented to the school board.

Aside from the tent cave-in, February, 1912 was a "month of visions realized" for West Capilano. A petition was before the Legislative Assembly in Victoria calling for the break-away from the District of North Vancouver and the formation of the municipality of West Vancouver. It was signed by John Y. McNaught, Thomas A. Allen, Edward H. Bridgman, John Lawson, Jack Loutet, William Alfred Thompson and John Eades Ward, who were property-owners and residents and also members of the council of North Vancouver District, and by Charles Nelson, Samuel Gintzburger, John J. Hanna, Andrew E. Liddle, John Alexander and William J. Irwin, who were property-owners in that portion of North Vancouver District proposed to become West Vancouver. It was also a banner month for Premier Richard McBride whose office in Victoria seemed to be having a steady parade of would-be railway promoters, construction engineers and charlatans coming in and out, and now, everbody was waiting for the Legislature to resume sittings after the Christmas vacation and to hear what had been going on behind the closed doors of the premier's office.

On February 12, the Honorable Members of the Legislative Assembly were all in their places on the floor of the House, the galleries which overlook the Chamber were filled to capacity, as McBride, who was soon to be Sir Richard, Knight Commander of the Order of St. Michael and St. George, took his place in the front benches. It was to be, he knew, his finest hour. In time-honored fashion, he rose, bowed to Mr. Speaker, and began his oration:

"Mr. Speaker. With respect to the Bill which it is my pleasant duty now to submit for second reading, it is in effect an agreement entered into between His Majesty the King, represented in and by the Province of British Columbia, and Messrs. Foley, Welch & Stewart, a prominent firm of railway contractors, with an unchallengeable standing as railway builders, a standing that cannot be called into question. These gentlemen have been entrusted by the government of the Dominion with a major portion of the construction of the **Grand Trunk Pacific** line, and they have also carried to a successful conclusion contracts for the completion of large mileages of both the **Canadian Pacific** and the **Canadian Northern** systems. We are, therefore, not dealing with any strange combination, but on the other hand, with gentlemen of proven ability to carry out such works as they may undertake and such as is involved in the building of the Vancouver, Howe Sound and Fort George Railway...."

Thus was created the **Pacific Great Eastern Railway**, now known as the **British Columbia Railway**, or simply **B.C. Rail**. Under the agreement, Foley, Welch & Stewart "will, truly and faithfully, acquire, lay out, build, construct, complete, etc., a line of standard gauge railway from the City of North Vancouver and thence running north along the margin of Howe Sound, thence following the general course of the Squamish River and continuing north easterly to Lillooet, and by the most feasible route to a junction with the **Grand Trunk Pacific** at or near Fort George..."

While everybody cheered the premier's words, except possibly the Liberals, it was a great speech, but in the long run its effects would result in British Columbia nearly going bankrupt, and for two reasons then unknown, or at least not appreciated, that were lurking in the background. First, the premier was putting too much faith in Thomas Foley, Patrick Welch and Jack Stewart, and secondly, the world was heading at a furious pace toward global conflict. Few realized it at the time and those who did didn't want to talk about it too loudly. Trouble was brewing in the Balkans where ancient bitternesses, sometimes spurred on by rivalry between the Cross and the Crescent, were surfacing and the Great Powers were playing a dangerous game through secret treaties, promises and threats. With the assassination on March 18, 1913 of King George I of Greece, the road was open to the consequences of Sarajevo in July, 1914, the assassination of Archduke Franz Ferdinand of Austria-Hungary and his morganatic wife. It is necessary to consider the importance of these events, for immediately after the murder of George I, just a litte more than a year after McBride's speech, investors backed away in droves from anything but the manufacture of the tools of war. Another depression in British Columbia was to be felt as a result and soup kitchens would appear in Vancouver to feed the unemployed.

All that seemed so far away from West Capilano that it hardly seemed to matter what was going on in south-eastern Europe. Besides, who were these Bosnians, Herzegovinians, Slovens, Croats, Bulgars and Slavs, anyway? And, if Mr. McBride said the records of Messrs. Foley, Welch and Stewart were "unchallengeable", then it must be so, and that was all there was to it. What was important was the Bill, tabled as **2 Geo 5 Ch.60** in the British Columbia Legislature, which, on February 27, 1912 was approved, and, on "the Ides", March 15, received Royal Assent. This created the Corporation of the District of West Vancouver. It also gave the new municipality a $156,000 debt, its share of the District of North Vancouver's indebtedness.

An election was called for Saturday, April 6, with Arthur E. Liddle as returning officer and the results were astonishing to some. It had been expected by many that John Lawson, "the Father of West Vancouver" would be elected the first reeve, but instead, Charles Nelson, a pharmacist whose place of business was in Vancouver's West End, won easily. The results were: Charles Nelson, 103; John Lawson, 88, with one spoiled ballot. For council, James B. Mathers topped the poll with 147; T.F. Merrick, 141; George Hay, 134; Samuel Gintzburger, 100. John F. Warden, who was not elected, received 84 votes and there were five spoiled ballots. The school board vote showed John Lawson receiving 157 votes, William C. Thompson, 133; Charles Nelson, 123; Mrs. Annie Crane, 121 and T.F. Merrick, 115. Left out of the race was Robert Edwards who garnered only 75 votes. A later political analyst would look at those school board returns and say that West Vancouver was one of the first places to recognize women in public life.

The newly-elected council met for the first time at 4 p.m., Monday, April 8 "in the school house" at which time the fledgling municipal officers were sworn in, that is, all but Samuel Gintzburger. Then, "owing to it being Easter Monday, no further business be transacted and the meeting adjourn to Tuesday, April 9 at 4 p.m."

The school board met at the same time and one can only feel a bit sorry for Miss Reid as she now had five bosses to answer to. By the end of 1911 she had 21 students in her tent **cum** one-room school house, but by the end of the term in June, 1912,

67

there was a school population of 44.

When council got down to business on April 9 it did two important things. First, it established a committee to "make arrangements for a temporary meeting place for council until new quarters be secured", meanwhile, offering to pay $6 a month rent for use of the school house. They also agreed to "advertise for a suitable steamer to be chartered to run a ferry service between Vancouver and West Vancouver with accommodation for not less than 150 passengers." As far as the new quarters were concerned, Mr. Lawson informed council on April 16, "I beg to offer you a site to be mutually selected on my property at Hollyburn, West Vancouver, without charge and am willing to issue Deeds for the same unencumbered to the Municipality." At about the same time, the West Vancouver Transportation Company jumped in and made an offer for their boats. The minutes of the meeting for April 30 show it was the "opinion of council that the price asked by the West Vancouver Transportation Company is out of all proportions to the value of the boats, but that this council would be willing to enter into negotiations regarding purchase of their boats at a fair evaluation, although they will be of very little use in the ferry service being proposed". The negotiations proceeded quickly, no doubt because the owners were losing money and were anxious to get rid of their unprofitable venture. On May 14 council accepted an offer to purchase the **West Vancouver**, the **Sea Foam** and one scow for $6,500.

A by-law to purchase the little fleet was held on June 1, and, at the same time, the electorate was asked to approve a road and a school by-law. The results of all three were exactly the same: eighty-three in favor and one against. Now West Vancouver was in the transportation business through a "joint stock" company in which the reeve and councillors were the directors and the ratepayers its shareholders. The school by-law allowed construction to begin the following year of a two-room school at 13th and Duchess, to be called Hollyburn School.

While West Vancouver was unique until just recently, in having its own municipally-operated transportation system, it is also noted for having its own police force, the creation of which began on May 7, 1912 when John Teare was named municipal constable. This was followed by the appointment of Captain Frank Kettle as constable of Caulfeild and Richard Jones for White Cliff City, a territory which embraced Horseshoe Bay. All were appointed without salary and Constable Teare was to have jurisdiction over all the others. Later that year Constable Teare was granted a salarly of $75 per month, but he had to take on the duties of health officer, pound keeper and licence inspector in addition to his constabulary duties. His police duties were not particularly onerous as there was no crime problem to speak of, but the dawn of a problem was at hand when, during the year 1912, Ellsworth McMillan chugged over the Keith Road from North Vancouver to bring the first automobile into the municipality.

Although formally created on the Ides of March, that fatal day in history for Julius Caesar, West Vancouver that first year had its feet firmly planted, and could, indeed answer the clarion call of Samuel Gintzburger, who was no slouch when it came to wheeling and dealing in land. He took out a full-page advertisement in the **Daily Province** which screamed in bold type "Forward, West Vancouver!", adding this "is the order of the new Municipal Council" in which, of course, he was a member. He offered lots at $400 each, with easy payments, and warned people there was "a rush for homesites" so they had better join the action right away. Meanwhile, it was reported that real estate people in North Vancouver "were stuffing waste baskets with money" on account of the land boom there, but there is no record to say whether or not Mr. Gintzburger was doing the same with his Ambleside properties.

Late in 1912, following Mr. Lawson's gift of land for a permanent home for council, wagon teams began to move lumber up from scows beached just east of 17th Street to begin construction of the municipal hall, which was to cost $3,500 to build. Such an achievement was one that the "city", Vancouver, did not accomplish until 1936. While under construction, the councillors set up a tent beside the construction site, and when opened the new facility was said to be "of moderate size, but convenient arrangment. Its simple and tasteful exterior lines harmonize with the rural surroundings."

While Vancouver may not, or may *have been*, envious of West Vancouver getting its own municipal hall first, West Vancouver looked with envy on the "big city" and its neighbor, North Vancouver, for having a telephone system. About 1904 the B.C. Telephone Company strung a cable across the First Narrows but the first ship coming through brought it down. The company then turned to the water mains which brought North Shore water to the city and another attempt was made to link the North Shore by "some ingenious pioneer engineering." A football with a light line to it was dropped into the north end of the water main and the ball was pulled out on the south side with the telephone line attached to it.

Thus, by 1912 it was, theoretically speaking, possible to make phone calls from West Vancouver to Vancouver and the challenge of such an opportunity was met by Mr. Lawson and his wife. They canvassed the area to sign up a minimum of 56 subscribers required by the phone company before an exchange could be established. Finding the petition still short four subscribers after his campaign was completed, Mr. Lawson offered to take the additional phones himself. However, it was not until September 5, 1914 that an exchange was established in the back of the West Vancouver Trading Company store.

John Lawson's big day came on January 18, 1913. Charles Nelson did not seek re-election to a second term as reeve, so the battle was between Mr. Lawson and George King. With a 180 to 144 win, John Lawson, the new reeve, was carried home in triumph from the polling station on the shoulders of his supporters, headed by a parade carrying broom torches to light the way.

Water, schools and the **Pacific Great Eastern Railway** were among the pressing problems of the day, but there was also the matter of "pollution" and one is not quite sure that the complaints brought to council about a "Chinese laundry" polluting the creeks was really directed to protect the environment from pollution or to protect the environment from the Chinese as, at this time, the Asiatic Exclusion League throughout the province was extremely active. In fact, one of the first orders of council after incorporation was to keep Orientals from working on any civic project.

The key issue, however, was water and while the ratepayers were pressing council for action, fast flowing water created a problem on Keith Road, the municipality's land-link with North Vancouver. A new span was under construction, but, so goes the story, the foundations had not been completely excavated before the cement crews came to pour the concrete. Hence, in the winter of 1917-18 when the Capilano River began its annual high water run-off, the east abutment was undermined and away went the bridge foundation. If Colonel Robert Thompson Lowery, the West Kootenay editor who was known to be a liberal taster of beverages other than water had been around, he would have stood up and cheered. In an editorial in his New Denver **Ledge** he proclaimed that "water is the greatest curse the world has ever known", citing how it carried typhoid, causes ships to sink and drowns sailors, creates havoc during floods and, he concluded, the only safe liquid was booze and he had never heard of **that** causing the havoc of water.

Obtaining household water supplies was a chore for the pioneers of West Vancouver and this was reflected in an article in the **Daily Province** of June 30, 1926:

"Many difficulties were experienced by the first settlers in West Vancouver in the matter of water supply, each house builder having the trouble and expense of installing his own water system. These little plants have fallen into disuse years ago, though some relics of the early days from 1912 to 1915 may still be seen, such as old wells, elevated tanks and pumps of various types. Wells in West Vancouver were never very much of a success owing to the great depth of the clay hardpan. Very few of the diggers had sufficient patience to dig through the hardpan to the artesian supply which undoubtedly exists in the seams of rock below. Most of the wells were dug in the clay, but not through it, so that they acted merely as storage tanks for soil water, usually running dry every year about a month after the dry season had set in. During the dry season of 1914 and 1915 campers and others who were not adequately supplied with water had to move back to the city in a hurry. To make the best of a bad situation the council put on a team and wagon to haul water from Pipe Creek near 31st Street, and deliver it free to residents who were in need. In sections where water was scarce, the quiet and peace of the day would be disturbed by the clang of the bell and the sturdy housewife sallied forth with bucket in one hand and the washtub in the other to obtain the day's supply of aqua pura from the water wagon."

Another vexacious question was the railway and its proposed routing along the waterfront. West Vancouver, rightly so, claimed that the railway would spoil the waterfront and interfere with the ferry landing, while the company maintained this route was the best and cheapest. The argument went on and on, and finally council won at least a sort of victory. Messrs. Foley, Welch and Stewart agreed to move back from the waterfront, but only

71

a bit, and an agreement was reached to use Bellevue Avenue for the right-of-way. Construction along the North Shore officially began on August 13, 1913 from the foot of Lonsdale. The date has no symbolism as August 13, 1913 was not on a Friday.

On November 13, 1913 there began what appeared to be the beginnings of a "Smith takeover" of West Vancouver schools. Following the 1912 school by-law the road was open for the building of a two-room school house called Hollyburn School. Following the resignation of Miss Reid, Miss Lillian Smith was named principal of the new school with Miss Eva Smith as her assistant. After a year, Miss Lillian Smith became principal of a new school at Dundarave, and her position was taken up by a Miss Beatrice Smith.

The first classes for the "Dundarave School" were held in the Conservative Hall, later to be called the Dundarave Hall, and as a meeting place it was a rival to the Clachan Hotel. In due time the Conservative Hall would serve as a meeting place for the Anglicans, the Presbyterians, the cabaret-goers who knew it as The Palms, and as a community hall.

Built by W.J. Irwin, it became the focal point for education in the western part of the municipality because parents in the area complained about the distance between their homes and the new school at Hollyburn. As a result, another two-room school house was built at the site of the present Altamont Hospital but while construction proceeded, the Conservative Hall served the purpose of a school house. Miss Lillian Smith was named principal of the new school, and she was succeeded by Miss Beatrice Smith at Hollyburn. In late 1915 Miss Lillian Smith left the Dundarave School and was replaced by Miss Eva Smith.

It was in 1912 that Mr. and Mrs. William Millard, who had arrived in Dundarave from England in 1911, accompanied by their young daughter, Ethel, opened their home to the growing number of Anglicans in the community. They had been holding services under canvass at a camp at 24th and Bellevue, the property being owned by a Mr. Wyatt. Like Mr. Lawson's Presbyterians, the congregation soon outgrew the holding capacity of the Millard home, and on April 13, 1913, using students from St. Mark's Theological School in Vancouver as student ministers, services were held in the Conservative Hall. That fall, the Venerable Archdeacon Francis Heathcote, later to be known as The Right Reverend Sir Francis Heathcote, Bart, D.D., Bishop of New Westminster, organized a vestry and appointed parochial officials. It marked the beginnings of St. Stephen's parish.

Construction of the **Pacific Great Eastern Railway** was, by the fall of 1913, well underway, but it was not until years later that the general public realized what was really going on. The sub-contractors to Foley, Welch & Stewart, it was alleged, were cheating the firm blind. Costs for removal of gravel were charged at the same rate as for blasting and because of the economic situation caused by the Balkan situation, Sir Richard McBride released to the railway company the funds slated for the Horseshoe Bay-Squamish construction, although no work on that stretch of the railway had even been started. He did that, he said, so the railway north of Squamish could be built and create jobs for the unemployed. In its negotiations with Messrs. Foley, Welch and Stewart, the municipality had made one strong demand that being the line from North Vancouver through to Dundarave must be completed by January 1, 1914, and that demand was met, but only by a hair's breadth. On New Year's Day, the **Daily Province** sent a reporter over to the North Shore to cover the start of rail service:

"On New Year's Day," the anonymous reporter wrote, "promptly at 10 o'clock the train of two steel combination coaches left the station at Lonsdale Avenue and in 16 minutes the conductor called "Dundarave!" The train, with its passengers who were guests of the Company, sped swiftly along the well-ballasted road bed which skirts the north shore of the Inlet, passed the historic Indian mission, crossed over Capilano River, and thence along a number of cuts and fills to the present western terminus. At the doors of the Indian dwellings, and on the side of the tracks, squaws and braves of other days stood in speechless amazement and their eyes sparkling with delight, for a railroad through their property means dollars in their pockets. No more will these inhabitants of this village have to plod their way along the dusty road or paddle their dug-outs along the shore. Now they can board a train and be in the centre of North Vancouver in a few minutes..." This was the first run of the **Pacific Great Eastern Railway**, a name which men would soon corrupt the initials **P.G.E.** to mean **Past God's Endurance**, but, at the time, the reporter sagely editorialized, "the whole world is looking toward this spot." The train was in charge of conductors G.S.

Middleton and H.Y. Noble, with H.A. Hall and J.A. Edwards at the throttle.

During the construction period Mrs. Sarah Millard operated a cookhouse at Dundarave for the workers and her daughter, Ethel, for many years a primary school teacher at Pauline Johnson, recalled her mother charged "25 cents a meal" and they were very good.

On August 4, 1914, the Great War, the "war to end all wars," broke out in Europe and men everywhere, including those toiling on the railway, hastened to the "call of the colors." The first man to go from West Vancouver, according to Cromar Bruce's little tabloid newspaper published in 1919 and called the **West Van. Courier**, was a Mr. McUrtie, an employee of the Vancouver post office "who was a regular passenger" on the ferries. He was "the first to put on khaki and the last to return."

First West Vancouver municipal council, 1912. Back row, left to right: W. B. Carter, engineer. Councillor George Hay, Councillor T.F. Merrick, Councillor Samuel Gintzburger, Clerk G.H. Peake. Front row: Reeve Charles Nelson, Councillor J.B. Mather. (WVMA)

Clearing land for first municipal hall on property given by John Lawson (WVML)

Municipal Hall, completed in September 1912. (WVMA)

Shack built by Stuart McIntyre at Haywood and 15th Street, 1912. (WVMA)

The Slater Home, 1700 Marine Drive, later known as Hampton Court (WVMA)

Looking up Marine Drive from 13th Street, 1912. (WVMA)

Hollyburn general store, corner 17th and Marine, 1912. (WVMA)

First Hollyburn school class, outside Presbyterian Church which was used as a school house. Photo taken September 1912. (VWMA)

"The Walled City," the cannery at Sherman. (WVML)

Sub-division ad for Strath Gordon, at top of 22nd Street near location of present Hillside Secondary School, 1912. The Vancouver World, May 18, 1912.

Dundarave Castle on the shores of Loch Fyne, Argyll, Scotland. (WVMA)

The Clachan Hotel, Dundarave, 1912. (WVMA)

Col. Albert Whyte, founder of Whytecliffe. (PP)

Pioneer residents Emily and William John Nesbitt. (NS)

Chapter Four

WAR AND PEACE!

With the outbreak of war in 1914 against the Central Powers of Europe, there was a wild outburst of patriotism and solidarity behind the Empire and the flag and council fell in step. By resolution, they demanded a register of "all Austrians and Germans be kept" and, at the same time agreed that the jobs of all men working for the municipality who had entered His Majesty's Service be kept open for them on their return. A **P.G.E.** construction building, now called the Ambleside Hall, and at time of writing a shelter for buses of the West Vancouver Transportation fleet, was turned over to the Red Cross to be a centre for their activities.

While the "Beat the Hun" theme was uppermost in everybody's minds during the terrible first war year and the following years, the steady growth of the municipality did not diminish. It was during the bitter year of 1915, in fact, that West Vancouver embarked on an ambitious program to resolve the all-important water problem which had faced the pioneers since the beginning. In a special West Vancouver edition of the **Daily Province** in 1926, James Duncan spanned the years to bring his readers up to date:

"Late in the summer of 1915 the question of water supply was brought before council and a contract was entered into with the Cotton Company for the installation of a system. This was to include an intake on Brothers Creek and about twenty miles of feeder and distribution mains. The mains were changed from steel, which were originally intended, to wood stave pipes and the contract included the supply of about sixty hydrants and other accessories required for a gravity system. The changed prices of material and labor on account of the war, and the difference between the cost of steel mains and wood stave pipes, made it possible for the council, at a later date, to cancel $35,000 of the original $150,000 bond issued which reduced the annual charges to about $9,800. With about 200 consumers and the financial obligation as outlined, the Brothers Creek plant began to supply water July 1, 1916. During construction W.R. Carroll, C.E., was municipal engineer and the writer appointed as inspector of works. The first twenty miles of mains still form the larger part of the system in the eastern end of the district. As they extended over a large area, it later became the object to give supply from these in all directions without increasing the capital expenditure. This has been largely done by the installation of small diameter steel pipes, paid for out of revenue. Strange as it may seem, since 1916 the length of the pipe in the ground has increased to twice the original mileage, but the capital account, and, of course, the fixed charges still stand at the initial figure, though the numbers of service connections increased from 200 to 1200. Soon after the Corporation began the business of supplying water, it became apparent that without a considerable storage capacity we would be in a precarious position during the dry season, which usually lasts through July, August and September. The entire flow in Brothers Creek would drop occasionally for a period of ten weeks to one-third of a cubic foot per second, which quantity under the high head or pressure prevailing, was not sufficient to fight a prolonged fire and keep up the domestic supply at the same time.

"After considering various schemes, an agreement was reached with the City of Vancouver whereby water should be supplied from their Capilano mains at Keith Road bridge. A six-inch pipe was installed in 1919, the cost of the pipe and necessary values being only a little over $3,000. This afforded an inexhaustible supply and the line is protected from injury, either wanton or by frost or other extreme weather conditions. Up to 1920 the Brothers Creek plant had been operated chiefly for the purpose of fostering the growth of population. The service was given at a low rate and the fixed charges were levied on the whole municipality, but forces which were to bring a change were already at work. In the spring months of 1920 the provincial authorities pointed out to our council that as certain areas in Caulfeild, Whytecliff, etc., had installed waterworks without municipal assistance, it was unfair that they should be contributing towards the fixed charges for the Brothers Creek plant which served an area of not more than 2,000 acres in the south-east part of the district. Reeve Vinson and Councillor Leslie, who was waterworks chairman, seriously considered the whole question, with the result that a higher scale of rates were put into effect, and the waterworks finance reorganized. An area which the works could supply with water was laid out on a map, and the entire fixed charges were collected from the area which got the service. In other words, the waterworks became a local improvement. These changes were followed by a period of building activity in 1921, so marked that the revenue from the water system grew rapidly, the plant reaching a stage which permitted the laying aside of a reserve fund.

"This prosperous condition has continued, and if future councils can resist the temptation to take too much out of the waterworks, and will permit a fair proportion of the revenue to be spent on development and maintenance, there is no reason why it should not continue as a municipal asset of the greatest value.

"Long before the east end of West Vancouver had a water system, Mr. F.W. Caulfeild had employed Messrs. Harmon & Burwell to design and install a modern system in D.L. 811. This was completed in 1909 from the reservoirs on the north line of D.L. 1240 down to and around the settled area, with hydrants and all accessories. The supply was drawn from Caulfeilds Creek. The following year a five-inch pipe was installed to draw a supply for the reservoir from Cypress Creek also. This was taken from a point at the head of Cypress Falls. The works were well designed and had the additional virtue of having plenty of water in proportion to the demand. The cost of installation was about $11,000, which was quite a large expenditure for one man.

"A proposal was made in 1916 that the municipality purchase the system, but an agreement was not reached. In 1923, the Caulfeild estate signified a willingness to sell and the writer, with Mr. Harmon, acted as valuator, the purchase price being set at $4,600. The local improvement principal was applied to Caulfeild, as had been the case in the east end of the municipality. About 1911 a mile of three-inch and two-inch water supply pipes were installed at Horseshoe Bay by the West Shore and Northern Land Company. The supply was drawn from a small stream to the east of the railway station. The pipe lines are still in use. Some change in the ownership of the lands created a doubt as to who owned the waterworks, and the years from 1918 to 1924 were occupied with arbitration. In May, 1921, the property owners of the district sent a formal petition asking that the municipality take control of the works and operate them for the benefit of the community. In 1922, under municipal management, a small syphon was installed at Whyte Lake to increase the supply sufficiently to meet the needs of the district. In 1921 water notices had been posted in D.L. 1494 on Nelson Creek and in 1923 plans were drawn and filed at Victoria for a supply from that creek. This will meet the demands of the western end of the municipality for a number of years to come..."

By 1915, Sir Richard McBride was a broken man. Scandal upon scandal had been piled on his head, largely over his beloved **Pacific Great Eastern Railway**, and the opposition Liberal Party, which heretofore had not shown much gumption, was having a field day. Health problems also beset the premier, and it is sometimes alleged he took to drink. Publicly it was Bright's disease, an ailment of the kidney, which was affecting him. Perhaps it was a combination of all the above, plus a broken heart, that led him to resign his office on December 15. West Vancouver saw him only once as premier and this the occasion for one of his last official functions in office. It was the official opening of Marine Drive, and he looked old, tired, and if you looked closely, haggard from all his troubles.

As we have already seen, the District of North Vancouver had set out to build the "Lighthouse Road", or Keith Road, in the very early days, but it was never finished. As one of its first objectives in 1912, the council of West Vancouver began to lay the foundations for a main east-west street to be called Marine Drive and at a meeting of council held January 19, 1914 a notice was given to introduce a by-law "to expropriate land necessary for Marine Drive in Indian Reserve". Beyond 13th Street and the stretch covered by Marine Drive at that time, the Keith Road remained nothing but a survey line, or at best, a trail which wound through the dense forest towards Howe Sound.

All this changed when Sir Richard McBride officially opened the new highway on August 11, 1915. All of the Vancouver newspapers, the **Daily Province**, the **Evening Sun**, the **News-Advertiser** and the **World** turned out to cover the event. Despite his handicaps, Sir Richard, "the silver-tongued orator", could still mesmerize an audience. He was eloquent. He was patriotic. He was proud of being the first British Columbian to be elected to the high office of premier of his province. This native son of New Westminster, above all, was enthusiastic and his speech at the opening reflected the feeling of "damn the torpedoes, full speed ahead." It came from his heart. It was a great event and it deserved a great speech. The **World** reporter wrote:

"With simple but distinctive ceremony Premier Sir Richard McBride at 1 o'clock yesterday afternoon turned the lock with a silver key presented to him by Reeve G. Hay on behalf of the municipality of West Vancouver and swung open the gates on the westerly bridge over the Capilano River, with which action he declared the Marine Drive officially opened. The simple ceremony was followed by a more auspicious ceremony at a point on Marine Drive about two miles east of Cypress Park where the premier addressed the gathering. It was West Vancouver's red-letter day, one which marked an historic day in the municipality's history. At a cost of about $300,000 it marked the opening of one of the finest drives on the Pacific coast for not only does West Vancouver share this splendid thoroughfare, but the city and district of North Vancouver. The latter has its end of the Marine Drive completed and in good shape almost to Deep Cove, and they recently completed a $18,000 bridge across McCartney Creek to make more accessible the features which lay adjacent to the North Arm. Fully 150 automobiles attended yesterday. Each carried from five to seven passengers. The auto parade was made under the direction of the Vancouver Auto Club and from the starting point of the line-up on Robson Road before the ceremony to the arrival and enjoyment of the hospitality of the Cypress Park people, there was not a single incident to mar the day's proceedings. The programme was carried out in an excellent manner. Premier McBride reflected an optimistic outlook for British Columbia, based upon its wealth of natural resources and good roads to open them up. It was, however, punctuated with the stern realities throughout which the empire is passing. Owing to Germany's preparedness Great Britain would be obliged to raise the greatest army the world has ever seen to win, but from what the premier had seen during his trip to the front there was nothing surer than ultimate victory in store for the Allies. Sir Richard brought back with him stories of the great bravery and courage of the Canadian soldiers.

"The premier touched very briefly on his railway policy except to intimate that it would be prosecuted as soon as finances were available. The connecting up of Vancouver with the Peace River country would assuredly materialise but the Second Narrows Bridge and the P.G.E. must, like other things, remain in future's background. Perhaps never in the history of the North Shore had there been more fraternity shown between the cities and the municipalities adjacent to Burrard Inlet than at yesterday's proceedings. Vancouver was represented by Mayor [L.D.] Taylor [who, by the way, was owner of the **World**] and members of the city council; Jonathan Rogers, president of the board of trade; President Blackmore and Secretary Ford, of the Vancouver Auto Club, and Deputy Chief of Police McRae; New Westminster, by H.G. Robson, president of the board of trade and Sheriff Armstrong, president of the New Westminster Auto Club; North Vancouver city by Mayor [G.S.] Hanes and members of the council; G.H. Morden, president of the board of trade, and Chief of Police Davies accompanied the council.

"The site chosen for the speech-making was admirably chosen. The platform was built on the roadside, where the vista was uninterrupted, wide and beautiful. A most fitting location, it was on the seashore for the opening of a marine drive. Although there were many prominent personages present, Reeve Hay was forced, on account of time, to confine addresses to the premier, Mayor Hanes and Reeve Bridgman, representing the other two municipalities on the North Shore. The president of the Vancouver Auto Club made a few congratulatory remarks. Preliminary to calling upon the premier, Reeve Hay expressed his gratification at the number who accepted West Vancouver's invitation. He said that four miles of the Marine Drive had been completed at a cost of $250,000 and he hoped that the day would soon arrive when they would be able to continue it to the western extremities of the municipality. The construction of the road so far was greatly assisted by $50,000 which they had received from the provincial government.

"Premier McBride recalled with what insistence the North Shore representatives had advocated the construction of the road, and it was on account of their insistent demands that the government ultimately gave the grant. Sir Richard paid a glowing tribute to the road and its builders by claiming it had no superior on the Pacific coast. The government's policy in the last few years was to encourage and advance the construction of railway and trunk road building, and in this respect the report of the minister

88

of public works has shown an expenditure on trunk roads of $40,000,000 in recent years. 'I will not bother you,' he said, 'with what has been spent on railways. It would run into a good lot'. This road, he said, with coming developments throughout the province, would ultimately prove a business thoroughfare as well as a scenic driveway. It was a striking example of the good roads movement instigated by the advent of the motor car. While municipalities had run into debt with progressive policies in the last few years, Sir Richard had no criticism to offer. Rather, he commended them for the developments which had been effected which, if they were left in abeyance, would not likely materialize for 10 years hence. . . . Following the few remarks of the other speakers the party proceeded to Cypress Park where lunch baskets were opened and their contents spread out on tables under the beautiful shade trees. The officials of the Cypress Park Land Co. provided cups, coffee, tea and ice cream and a very eventful day was brought to a successful and delightful close. In a few after-dinner remarks, Premier McBride stated that within ten years he looked to see Marine Drive connected with the head of Howe Sound and Squamish. The two new bridges which span the Capilano River are splendid illustrations of superior design and workmanship as well as the one in the district of North Vancouver. The Capilano bridges, which are constructed of re-inforced concrete, were built by Messrs. Naylor Brothers at a cost of about $48,000. The largest one is 335 feet long, with 180 feet of approaches. When completed the new Marine Drive will be about 30 miles in length and for a considerable distance asphalt pavement has been laid."

With the opening of Marine Drive to Caulfeild, West Vancouver, even though it was still in the coal lamp era, began to think it was well on its way on the road to attaining the ultimate in status, that of being a place of excellence. The attainment of that goal was still a long way off but the necessary drive needed to reach the pinnacle was there. The municipality, of course, had a natural charisma which everybody could see as they drove their gas buggies along Marine Drive or took the **Pacific Great Eastern Railway** out to Whytecliff (**nee** White Cliff). There was, unfortunately, absolutely no town planning to give the community any aesthetic form. Lots of various sizes were put haphazardly on the market leaving, for one thing, that puzzling jog on 15th Street. It was a community whose industrial base was harvesting timber from the slopes of Hollyburn Ridge, yet few of the residents were engaged in the logging business. If there was another base for West Vancouver, then that had to be real estate. For the most part the municipality was, even as it is today, a bedroom to Vancouver. There were a few impressive homes, although for the most part they were what we would call cottages. Muddy streets were the rule rather than the exception and drainage was by means of ditches dug along either side of the streets into which young kids were prone to tumble, and when wind and high tides combined, the waves battered against Argyle and Bellevue Avenues. West Vancouver's weakness was that it didn't have any electric power. Evening meals were "romantically" intimate candlelight dinners, or more commonly, served under the *unromantic* glow of coal oil lamps. Its strength, however, came from the number of clubs and organizations which flourished, and over the next decade these would number more than forty. All this was taking place in a world which seems misty to us as there was no local newspaper to chronicle what was going on in the community. We can imagine the little telephone exchange's "hello girls" were kept very busy plugging in calls into their switchboard as important club business was transacted.

The telephone in the olden days was a wondrous machine, but as it clung, unstylized, to the wall it looked as ugly as sin. It had a long-necked black mouthpiece, a pair of shining bells above that, and on the right of the brown mahogany base was a crank used to call the Operator who would nasally reply: "Number puleeze." On the left side was the ebony receiver. One of the problems of the machine was there were often several people using the same line, and these were called Party lines. If somebody were on the phone when another subscriber wanted to use it, he or she was told politely (in most cases, anyway) that the line was busy, but a real busybody would keep on listening in to pick up the latest tidbit of gossip. One common conversation from the Ambleside area might well have been the noise emanating from the John Nesbitt farm on Clyde Avenue. Mr. Nesbitt, who had come to West Vancouver in the fall of 1912, raised a few head of cattle, grazing them on the swamp lands that are now Ambleside Park, the west end of which later served as the community's first garbage dump. In addition, he kept chickens, peddling both the milk and eggs around town. It was the roosters which were the bone of contention, and numerous complaints reached the council chamber about them crowing at the wake of dawn. Mr. Nesbitt did his best to answer the complaints by simply chopping off their heads and then enjoying a hearty chicken dinner. But a chicken farm without roosters, as everybody knows, will not succeed so Mr. Nesbitt promptly got some more roosters, probably hoping in vain, of course, that the matter would rest. But roosters will be roosters, and so there was almost a continuous flow of complaints to council resulting in more executions and more chicken dinners.

With convenience in mind rather than deliberate town planning, the future course the commercial districts of West Vancouver would take were being established. Dundarave, in 1914 got its long sought-after $40,000 pier, but the ferry service did not last long as the pier proved to be too exposed for the skippers to take a chance on making a safe landing. In anticipation of this service, however, the owners of the Clachan Hotel extended their premises upward by one storey and in the same spirit of progress a string of shops began to emerge along the Marine Drive frontage between John Alexander's (later David Morgan's) real estate office and the Conservative Hall. It covered one long block, except for a later grocery and confectionery store built by a Mr. Robinson, who, it was rumoured, was a retired hangman. Perhaps because of this rumour, some of the kids in the mid- 1930s were afraid of him and preferred to buy their candy from Mrs. Robinson or their son, Bob. It was in 1916 that the pier came to its own, with the start-up of the annual Dundarave Regatta, an aquatic event which, for years, drew the best swimmers in British Columbia to the competition.

If John Lawson was called "The Father of West Vancouver", then the honor of being known as "The Father of West Vancouver Schools" must fall to a gentle little Englishman of the old school, George E. Brealey. In his precise handwriting, he has left us a memoir dealing with the development of the school system in West Vancouver. "Pop" (we **never** dared to call him **that** to his face for fear of being hauled off "to the office"), wrote: In August 1915, Mr. G.E. Brealey appeared on the scene and remained as Principal in West Vancouver for exactly 21 years. By strange coincidence, this exactly tallied with my length of service in England. I arrived one morning in late August from Marpole, then named Eburne, on the 8 a.m. ferry, **Sonrisa** or **Doncella**, and found my way to school. Schools opened in the last week of August in those days. At Christmas, Miss Lillian Smith left Dundarave Hall and my assistant, Miss Eva Smith, was transferred there... In January, 1916 the School Board appointed Miss D.M. Jones, BA, to a class at Caulfeild in a room at a private house, but in 1917 Mr. Bailey leased a plot of land south of Marine Drive at Cypress Park and the Board erected a one-roomed school which still stands (1941) with a woebegone appearance. Miss Jones and her pupils were transferred to this new school house in March, 1917. In the previous August (1916), owing to the congestion at Hollyburn School, a third division had to be formed for which temporary quarters were obtained in the old fire hall which adjoined the Old Hall [Ambleside Hall] which was used for concerts, church services, ratepayer and other meetings... We had no need of movies, etc. in those days as we got no end of amusement at the ratepayer's meetings. Two rivals, East End and West End meetings, [were] usually crowded and hecklers provided a "Barrel of Fun".

The spirit of logging had been around ever since 1904 and the demise of the McNair-Fraser Company with its Walking Dudley was, like all logging outfits, inevitable. The "greatest show on West Vancouver's earth" was about to come, but that the logging industry was alive and well is reflected in the minutes of council. On December 26, 1916, the municipal clerk was "instructed to notify Mr. Ritchie [James Ritchie of the Cypress Lumber Company] that he will be held liable for any damage caused to the surface of Marine Drive by his drawing shingle bolts across same." In August, 1917 the company was back in the news again when it sought permission to build a flume "under the bridges at Marine Drive west of 27th Street." There was another shingle mill on Inglewood, just west of 17th Street, known as the Vedder River Shingle Mill, but the big news came on February 12, 1917 when the Capilano Lumber Company sought approval from council for its proposed railway right-of-way down the west bank of the Capilano River. Up to this time the company had been leasing a flume, described in 1906 as being "one of the longest flumes in America", which had been built by Indians and Japanese, some of who had lost their lives on the job, for the Burrard Inlet Flume and Boom Company. The proposal the company had in mind was a mega-project for its time, but it was not completed until after the war in Europe was finished.

The war was, of course, on everybody's mind. How many West

Vancouver families had their menfolk in the blood-soaked trenches is not known, but it can safely be said there was hardly a family who did not agonize over the reports which filled the newspapers each day of the savagery with which the battles were raging. In the end, five would not return. John Lawson's son, Duncan, was "over there" and Mr. Lawson himself dropped a few years off his birth certificate and enlisted but the lost years caught up with him and he was sent back home to tend to his real estate business. Everybody on the home front was buying Victory Bonds and in as many ways as possible, was pulling his or her weight to support the boys overseas, except for one group on which council focussed its attention on January 2, 1917. At that meeting the councillors brought to the attention of the provincial government "the advisability of putting in force a poll tax, the proceeds to be applied to the Patriotic Fund. This action is recommended owing to the fact that it is impossible at the present time to collect anything from the large number of foreigners who are enjoying the protection which the Empire affords." And when the conscription debate was on in the House of Commons in Ottawa, council voted to "heartily endorse" compulsory military service. (At the same meeting, the councillors saved the municipality the sum of $20 by selling off the police motorcycle for $100 and purchasing in its place a bicycle costing $80. The saving of $20 was applied to the funds of the Public Works Department.)

By March, 1918, a branch of the Great War Veterans Association, the forerunner of the Canadian Legion, British Empire Service League, had been established in North Vancouver to meet the needs of the home-coming battle-scarred veterans in regaining their position in civilian life, and for its part, council, under Reeve V.V. (the initials stood for Valient Vivian) Vinson, set up a special committee to welcome home the veterans.

There had been many tragic shock waves throughout the municipality and, indeed, throughout the world since the Kaiser's armies crossed the Belgian frontier in that fateful month of August, 1914, but on October 21, 1918 council was shocked to record in its minutes the death, on the Douai-Cambrai Road in France, of 21-year old Duncan Lawson. Three weeks later, the "war to end all wars" was over. Three mighty kingdoms had crumbled in the dust, millions were dead or wounded, and as a result of the Armistice signed on November 11, a great sigh

93

of relief swept over the land.

Official recognition of the end of hostilities, as far as West Vancouver was concerned, did not take place until July 19, 1919 when the West Vancouver branch of the Great War Veterans Association, which was formed in March, 1919, sponsored a Peace Celebration, at which peace medals were given to all the school children. Prior to that celebration, council, at the request of Vancouver city council, passed the following resolution which urged the Dominion Government to expel all undesirable interned aliens as a "menace that will, sooner or later, have a demoralizing effect upon the country and mitigate against the rehabilitation and repatriation of the thousands of men who have suffered and who have bled to make this country possible."

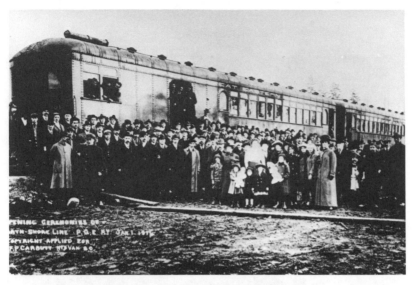

*Crowds welcome first **Pacific Great Eastern Railway** train at Dundarave, January 1, 1914. (WVMA)*

End of Track, at Dundarave, January, 1914. (WVMA)

Mrs. Fenner and family cutting wood supply for Clachan Hotel, 1913. (WVMA)

Water well and wood pile at Clachan Hotel, 1913. (WVMA)

The Conservative (Dundarave) Hall built in 1913. (WVMA)

B.C. Squab "ranch" at Jefferson and 23rd Street, circa 1913. (WVMA)

View of Lawson Avenue (now 17th Street) looking north from Government wharf, showing John Lawson's real estate office on the left and the trading company store in distance, circa 1913. (WVMA)

View north-east from 14th Street and Bellevue Avenue. Note rails for P.G.E. Railway, buildings on Marine Drive, and "Baby Mt." (Sentinel Hill) in distance. (WVMA)

Marine Drive under construction, circa 1913. (WVMA)

Construction site of Capilano Bridge, August 1914. (WVMA)

Looking south at workers excavating east abutment over Capilano River, August 1914. (WVMA)

Temporary bridge on 6th Street between Clyde and Duchess Avenues for transporting equipment and materials to bridge site, 1914. (WVMA)

Gordon Road (now 22nd Street) showing first St. Stephen's Church, 1914. (WVM & HS)

First church wedding in West Vancouver united John Lawson's daughter, Elizabeth and William Pitman, 1914. (WVMA)

First real estate office in Dundarave; originally that of John Alexander, 1914, then David Morgan and latterly Pery T. Masterman. Finally first Bank in Dundarave, circa 1948. (WVML)

Southwest corner of 14th Street and Argyle Avenue, 1914, showing bakery rig and ferry office. (WVMA)

M. Godfrey's home, 1366 Inglewood Avenue, 1914. (WVMA)

Garthorne's cottages, 22nd Street and Marine Drive, 1914. (WVMA)

Larson Bay, Gleneagles, circa 1914. (WVMA)

Clachan Hotel, Dundarave, circa 1914. (WVMA)

View of 14th Street looking south from Jefferson Avenue, circa 1915. (WVMA)

Miss Dorothy M. Jones clearing homesite, circa 1915. (WVMA)

Capilano Bridge, Keith Road, circa 1915. (WVML)

Marine Drive bridge over Capilano River, 1915.

Mr. and Mrs. Nick Williamson in their McLaughlin auto, 1915. (WVMA)

107

Ceremonial gateway to welcome Sir Richard McBride to West Vancouver on the opening of Marine Drive, 1915. Note sign "Pacific Highway". (WVMA)

Reeve George Hay speaking at official opening of Marine Drive, August 11, 1915. Premier Sir Richard McBride on the left. (WVMA)

Blacktopping Marine Drive, circa 1927. (PA)

Pacific Great Eastern Railway *overpass at 31st Street, 1915. (WVMA)*

Swimming at foot of 14th Street. Old Ambleside Hall on right, 1916. (VPL)

Horseshoe Bay, August 1916. (VCA)

J.J. Hanna home, corner 22nd Street and Mathers Avenue, circa 1916. (WVMA)

Ex-Reeve Charles Nelson's home, 23rd Street and Marine Drive, 1916. (WVMA)

111

Pacific Great Eastern Railway accident at "Y" between 24th and 25th Streets about 1915. (WVMA)

Ex-Reeve David Morgan's home, 2600 block Nelson Avenue, 1916. (WVMA)

Marine Drive, looking west from 24th Street, 1917. (WVMA)

Failure of east abutment of Marine Drive bridge across Capilano River in flood of December 31, 1917. (WVMA)

Garthorne's grocery, 25th Street and Marine Drive, 1918. (WVMA)

Dundarave Pier and Clachan Hotel, 1918. (WVMA)

Horsehoe Bay from foot of Nelson Avenue, 1918. (WVMA)

Looking east along Marine Drive from 25th Street, circa 1918. (WVMA)

Entry into Peace Parade, July 1, 1919. Note "West Vancouver No. 6" which was a look into the future. (WVMA)

Peace Parade, July 1, 1919. Left to right, Effie Wenmoth, Molly Haine, Florence Thompson, Unknown, Bert Thompson, Ethel Millard. (WVMA)

View of West Vancouver shoreline (Ambleside Beach) in August, 1919. (PA)

Swimming at Dundarave, circa 1920. (WVHA)

Shield's Vedder River Shingle Company mill on the east bank of Lawson Creek, Inglewood Avenue and 18th Street, circa 1919. (WVMA)

Chapter Five

A FLICK OF THE SWITCH

War is senseless, but what happened after the Armistice was signed in the forest of Compiegne, France, made even less sense. The men who had slugged it out at Vimy Ridge, Passchendael, the Somme and other blood-soaked fields were, just about, members of a lost generation. Many of them had joined up right after leaving school and had entered the forces without any trade or experience in business life. Others had been jobless before the war broke out as the result of the depression which hit British Columbia in 1913, and when they returned to their homes they found little or no provision had been made by any level of government for their return to civilian life. They were frustrated, some even broken in mind and body because of their ordeal. The only bright hope seemed to lie in a proposal to settle the men on farms, as had been done following the Boer War, but after the boys had seen Paree, few were interested in settling down on the offered land and many of those who did soon became disillusioned with farm life and drifted, jobless, back to the city. The onus seemed to have fallen on the men themselves to do something about the situation, and this they did by rallying around the Great War Veterans Association. This active and understanding organization, however, was stymied more often that not by governmental indifference to the plight of the veterans. It is a tragic story and for many in West Vancouver at the time the usually accepted description of the 1920s as being the "Gay Twenties" was nothing but a hollow mockery of the truth. It should not be surprising, then, to find in the minutes book of council, as late as January 24, 1921, the notation "since cases of want and suffering exist in the municipality owing to the unemployment situation" it was moved that a Relief Department be established with the municipal engineer and chairman of the public works committee of council being placed in charge. Lucky, indeed, was the man who could get a job with the Capilano Lumber Company on the west bank of the Capilano River where the British Pacific Properties are now located. In 1919 the Memphis, Tennessee-based company had put into operation their mega-project, the sixteen mile-long railway whose shadowy remains can still be seen near Keith Road and the Capilano River. James W. Morton, in his book **Capilano. The Story of a River** describes the operation:

"By February, 1919, ten bridges had already been built, one ninety feet high and 400 feet long, and as many more would be required before the full sixteen miles, including spurs, were completed. They had started off in a small way, most of the grading being done by hand labor, but by 1919 the valley echoed to the puffing of steam shovels and the pounding of pile drivers.

"The camp was probably the most modern in the province. One hundred and twenty employees lived in buildings similar to railroad cars, forty feet long, fourteen feet wide. Each had ventilators, a toilet and a shower bath and sink, with hot and cold running water. There were clothes hangers and a locker for each man, steel sleeping bunks and woolen mattresses, a laundry and a drying room. Each building was steam-heated and electric light was furnished by the Delco system. The two dining cars had a capacity of sixty each, and instead of the usual benches, individual stools were provided for the lucky loggers who worked for the Capilano Timber Company. A warehouse and root house for storing vegetables made it possible to order a month's provisions at a time—and the owners promised to install refrigeration at an early date. There were even fifty pigs kept in sties at a convenient distance from the camp...

"For 1919, it was plush and expensive, though the timber was believed to be of very high quality. At various times there were said to be 200 to 600 million feet of it, seventy per cent of which was cedar, fifteen per cent fir and the balance spruce and hemlock. G.G. Johnson [the manager] predicted that the 'quality will excite the admiration of Vancouver millmen.' It was said the limits of the company contained the largest percentage of big trees of any in B.C. The spar tree for loading and yarding was 125 feet high and on top of it was a block weighing one ton.

"Perhaps this was considered a huge investment in 1919 when

a much larger proportion of the B.C. forests was closer to tidewater than it is today, yet the valley was a comparatively easy region in which to construct a railroad. It was a great glacial saucer of good grade, the largest construction expense probably being the bridges or trestles across ravines which angled back into the mountains from the river.

"There were sixteen miles of railroad, including spurs, which looped outward from the mainline on both sides of the Capilano. Along the western side of the valley it ran at one per cent grade and well up from the river since it was forced to pass over the height of land at the Second Canyon. . . . the railroad by-passed [a cliff] running over the rocky plateau just a hundred yards to the west. From here it twisted and turned up small valleys, over the great trestle at Houlgate Creek and then southward almost in a straight line just below the present British Properties, over a portion of Rabbit Lane, past the most eastern limit of the Capilano golf course, and below Capilano Cemetery. South of Keith Road it swung gradually eastward around the present [1970] Trapp property, angled over the river to the east bank and then across the deltaic flats to the booming grounds at the foot of Pemberton Road. In 1919, seventy logging cars and two geared engines, a Climax and a Heisler, towed out 75,000 feet of logs daily and the company hoped to treble this within the year. The price of shingles, logs and lumber was steadily rising and the markets of the eastern States and Japan welcomed the beautiful cedar of the Capilano Valley."

It was, however, not a profitable undertaking in the end, for several reasons. It cannot be established exactly when the railroad ceased operations, but it was gone within the decade. "By 1934," Dr. Morton writes, "most of the majestic cedars in the valley had been felled, their great drooping limbs amputated, and the dismembered trunks hauled, torn and bruised, to the booming grounds in North Vancouver. The valley was almost as naked as it had been in the post-glacial period ten thousand years earlier."

With the demise of logging operations in West Vancouver, the community was left with only the old Defiance Cannery, whose name was changed to the Great Northern Cannery after its purchase about 1920 by Francis Millerd from Arthur Henry Sherman, but as will become apparent, there were side benefits to the scars left on Hollyburn Ridge by the timber companies.

In mid-June, 1919, the fire department, which was entirely volunteer, erected at a cost of $62 a fire hose tower beside the ferry slip and just in time, too. A fire broke out nearby and a row of three or four stores at the foot of 14th Street went up in smoke. The children who were attending school at Ambleside fire hall received not only an actual fire drill but the rest of the day off.

Again, in the meticulous handwriting of Mr. Brealey, we find an equally meticulous account of the rising school population in West Vancouver.

"In December 1918 the Cypress Park school was closed and Miss Jones and her pupils were transferred to a newly completed two-room school on 27th Street known as the Dundarave School [on the site of the present Altamont Private Hospital]. This school was built at the sole expense of the Department of Education, which at the same time made a two-roomed addition to the north side of the Hollyburn structure converting it into a four-room school. The division which had been located at the fire hall was brought back to it. Signs of growth themselves in spite of the war; and temporary measures, owing to the war, were resorted to in the years immediately following the conclusion of peace. The Cypress Park School was re-opened under Miss Laura Crewson in August, 1920. A room, detached from the main building, was erected on the Hollyburn School site in 1920 making it into a five-roomed school. Miss Eva Smith took charge of an intermediate division in the hall of the United Church from August 1920 'til 1921 when she was made principal, assisted by two lady assistants of the newly erected three-room section of the 22nd Street school. Mr. [W. Moore] Jackman was the Board's energetic chairman at this time and a by-law was passed this year (1921) for a complete eight-room school on 22nd Street. Miss Smith resigned after one year and in September, 1922, G.E. Brealey, with [W.A.] Davidson, Mr. [Charles E.] Burbridge and Miss [Mabel] Macfie as class teachers there. In January, 1923, owing to building operations they were transferred as follows: Mr. Davidson to the Masonic Hall at 17th and Bellevue; Mr. Burbridge to the Basket Factory Building in Lawson's orchard, 17th Street, and Miss Macfie to the temporary building on the 22nd Street school ground".

"In Whytecliffe," Mr. Brealey continued, "in September, 1921, a one-roomed school in a rented private house was opened with Miss Ethel Millard in charge. In 1923 the Capilano Timber Company built a one-roomed school near the city intake, and in March, Mrs. Mary Bruce was transferred from Cypress Park to take charge. Later it became a testing ground for new appointments and here Mr. [Dan] Kirk, Mr. [Hugh] Brown, Mr. [Reg] Hamilton and Mr. [John] Allan commenced their duties under the West Vancouver School Board. Pauline Johnson School was completed and opened in September, 1923. It was named after the poetess of the Capilano, Pauline Johnson. This is especially appropriate by reason of the fact that the Capilano River forms the eastern boundary of the municipality for a considerable distance. A fine portrait of the poetess presented by the Vancouver Pauline Johnson Chapter of the Imperial Order of the Daughters of the Empire [IODE] hangs in the principal corridor of the school. At the official opening A.E. Lord, school inspector, was present as the representative of the Educational Department, Mr. Brealey becoming its head and the supervising principal of all the schools in the municipality, six in number. The building, of which Mr. Hugh Hodgson was architect, was thoroughly modern and followed the Seattle type of school. Mr. Hodgson just previously had served two years as assistant architect to the Seattle School Board.

"In September, 1923, high school teaching was commenced by Mr. F.J. Patterson assisted by Miss Mahaffey in two rooms at Hollyburn School. This left only two rooms at Hollyburn for elementary school work, as the annex was used for woodwork under Mr. Ball, the first instructor in this subject. Miss Jones supervised needlework for senior girls. In the autumn of 1924 two rooms were added to the south side of Hollyburn making available four rooms for high school teaching. This was accomplished by structural alteration, absorbing the two wide lobbies on the south front. At the time the Dundarave Hall was rented to receive the overflow from Pauline Johnson, and here Miss Etta Crewson had a division of Grade 8 pupils. In February, 1925, a second annex was added at Hollyburn, but one was still used as the Woodwork Centre. In September, 1925, a two-room annex was added at Pauline Johnson and in 1933 they were moved to the Inglewood grounds to form the library there."

Time has a habit of running away with itself, and so this Chronicle must go back in time a bit, like the favorite comic strip character of the 1920s and 1930s, **Alley Oop** did with his "time machine", to set the course towards West Vancouver's goal, to wit, excellence. A lot of things today are taken for granted, such as being able to throw a switch and becoming dazzled by all the benefits of the electrical age, but there was also something in those days which may seem now to be a bit of an anachronism, that being the complete devotion to the British Empire, on which the sun never sets. We now call it the British Commonwealth of Nations, a phrase which does not call for, nor does it need, a continual display of flag waving. In 1921 a group of ladies in West Vancouver, dedicated to "One Flag, One Throne and One Empire", formed, in memory of Duncan Lawson, a chapter of the Imperial Order of the Daughters of the Empire. It was, with all its regal patriotism, a down-to-earth organization that, over the years, through its sponsorship of the Girl Guides and the Brownies and other endeavors in good times and bad, left an indelible stamp on the growth of the community.

The spine of West Vancouver was emerging from the "trilobite" era into full growth and strength, despite the anxieties of the troubled era so often masked by the trite phrase "Gay Twenties." As we look back on those times, perhaps we can be thankful that West Vancouver was not mesmerized by the euphoria released by the end of the war which so captivated and ensnared many areas. For instance, West Vancouver maintained a balanced budget, which at the best of times, is not an easy thing for a council to do, and in the dread 1930s, which loomed ahead, the municipality did not have to suffer the humiliation, as North Vancouver endured, of going into receivership. If the I.O.D.E. spelled out a spiritual association with the Empire, then, at the same time, there was an outpouring of what may be called another form of spiritual grace. There were two of these graces, both highly visible, which came along in 1921. On July 21, Archibishop Adam Uriah DePencier inducted as rector of St. Stephen's Anglican Church the Rev. J.P. Dingle as the first rector of the parish. As early as 1915 the parishioners had purchased a lot on the corner of 22nd and Fulton and had erected a hall, which after the new church was built in 1927 became the parish hall. In the same year that St. Stephen's was formed, the Roman Catholics of West Vancouver, who like members from other denominations worshipped in private homes, founded St. Anthony's parish with Father Brabender as priest. It was built on land given by Archbishop T. Casey, helped with a generous donation made by Father Bedard of St. John's Missionary House in Vancouver and by a "friend in Toronto."

Graces usually come in runs of three, and so the third grace, the one that would lead West Vancouver truly to the promised land of excellence, came in 1922 with the long-awaited introduction of electric power in what had been the coal oil-lit world of the pioneers. Gordon Robson, who was appointed municipal solicitor for West Vancouver in February, 1917, reflected on the behind-the-scenes maneuverings which brought about the dawn of the incandescent bulb in an interview with archivist Rupert Harrison in 1980:

"I was fortunte to play a part in bringing electricity to West Vancouver," Mr. Robson, who was later a police magistrate in West Vancouver, said. "It resulted in enormous growth to the municipality immediately after it was installed. As a matter of fact, shortly after it was installed West Vancouver had more electric ranges and boilers per capita than any other place in British Columbia. The Municipality had been trying for seven years to get the B.C. Electric Co. to come into West Vancouver and service the District but to no avail. It was considered that we might erect our own power plant and operate it [at Cypress Falls] but this was deemed not to be feasible. It sounds rather egotistical but it is not meant that way. I had a great friend who I had known intimately for many years. He came from New Westminster, as I did, and he and I were, at this time, living in a suite together in Vancouver. He was Chief Inspector for Gas and Electricity for the Province of B.C. and appointed by the Dominion Government, which, amongst its laws, enacted that a company producing electricity could not sell electricity to a foreign country unless it was willing to supply the local demand. A letter was drafted and sent to the B.C. Electric requesting that they sell the Municipality power. The company made a mistake by writing back, stating that they would not sell power to the Municipality. My friend and I considered this letter and sent it to Ottawa. From Ottawa there was dispatched one of the high officials in the Department and he met with me and said that they would go along with us in our desire to have power and hoped we could make an agreement with the B.C. Electric but warned me that it had to be a reasonable agreement or they would not back up the Municipality. Following that I had several meetings with Mr. Walker, a high official with the B.C. Electric, and we hammered out an agreement which, in my opinion, resulted in the very fast growth in the Municipality from then on. The ordinary practice of the B.C. Electric at that time was that, if a person required power and several poles were needed, the applicant had to pay for the poles. To have such an agreement in West Vancouver would retard the growth enormously. Under the new agreement a specified area was defined which was approximately in a line drawn north from the waterfront in the vicinity of West Bay northward for a considerable distance, and eastward to the Capilano boundary of West Vancouver and down to the water again. The agreement provided that if a person was living within that area, even though the Company might have to run poles for three quarters of a mile or more, that person was entitled to be connected for a flat charge of $5.00. Although the agreement contained a guarantee of so much revenue to the B.C. Electric within so many years we were never called on to pay it.''

And so, the lights came on. Street lighting, then, became a concern of council and this was duly addressed, although not without a great deal of controversy as to who should have it first. Such is the nature of Man. Another nature of Man, so basic in unwritten law — that of remembrance — became apparent on May 30, 1925 when the Grand Lodge, A.F. & A.M., laid the cornerstone of the war memorial which faces Marine Drive and is close-by the tree-lined McDonald Creek. No finer setting could be found than the one Baron Byng of Vimy, Governor-General of Canada came to on July 5, 1925 to unveil one of the most beautiful, yet simple, monuments of Remembrance to be found anywhere.

Around that archway have stood medal-bedecked men who had had service in the Northwest Rebellion in Canada, the Northwest Frontier of India, the Zulu campaigns leading to the Boer War, the First World War and men who served in the Second World War, in the North Atlantic, the Battle and Defence of Britain, North Africa, Italy, Northwest Europe, the South Pacific, Hong Kong, and of later date, the United Nations' efforts in Korea, The Congo, Suez, the Gaza Strip, Viet Nam and Cyprus.

They shall grow not old, as we that are left grow old:
Age shall not weary them, nor the years condemn
At the going down of the sun and in the morning
We will remember them.

But we, who have grown old and remember, must remember

Regimental Sergeant Major A.O.S. Freemantle. His Christian name was Oscar, but nobody knew him by that name: he was *Rattlesnake Pete*, a name given to him during the First World War when he trained young recruits. Like a rattlesnake, he gave one warning, and then he struck. Rattlesnake Pete, not a hair on his head, stood proud and erect, medals from campaigns that not even the history books mentioned, clinking on his chest as he stood proudly to attention during the singing of **God Save the King**. He was the ultimate personification of all that the archway of remembrance stood for. When the Second World War came around in 1939, Rattlesnake Pete was among the first to try to enlist, but he made a proud mistake. He went before the recruiting officer with all his medals up — Northwest Rebellion, Zulu and Boer, plus First World War, and was politely thanked for his patriotism. With all his battle records aside, Rattlesnake Pete attained a glory that lay beyond Batoche and Mafeking. He made the **Guinness Book of World Records** on two occasions by winning the Irish Sweepstake twice in a row and for capturing the world pipe-smoking championship by puffing away on a Boer pipe using one eighth of an ounce of tobacco, lit by a single match, for one hour and fifty-seven and three-quarter minutes. The old war horse finally charged his way into Heaven in 1950 at the ripe age of 90. **R.I.P.** He was someone to know and someone to respect, particularly when you remember being called out as an A.R.P. runner during the Second World War in the midst of a blackout and told to deliver a package to RSM Freemantle and then, in the dark of night, being instructed to go, forthwith, to the store to pick up some mixer, and then, when he was inspecting A.R.P. high pressure hoses, he was standing over a join when the darn thing burst, sending him to a most undignified landing. RSM Freemantle pulled himself up, his beady eyes glaring and nobody, but *nobody*, dared to even smile and one could see that even in his eighties he was still the *Rattlesnake Pete* of yesteryear.

A year after the Memorial Arch was dedicated, June 28, 1926, Branch 60, Canadian Legion BESL was organized at a meeting in the upstairs room of the ferry building, but it was not until June 30, 1930 that, through the use of volunteer labor and on land donated by the municipality, the Legionnaires got their own hall.

That same month there was cause for a big celebration, the

opening of the last link in the highway through West Vancouver to Horseshoe Bay. In a special section of the **Daily Province**, on June 30, there flowed forth a stream of eloquence that would have dazzled the mind of a cliche king: "Marine Drive Winds Way Amid Scenes of Beauty" read the headline.

"Mere words can not describe nor pen picture the beautiful scenes unfolding before one's eyes as one travels along this new reach of highway. Forests of towering cedars reach skyward, carpeted below with the multitudinous wild flowers of the forest, roses, tiger lillies, bleeding hearts, honeysuckle and heather growing in profusion in the crannies of rock here and there along its length." It also moved the then well-known Canadian poet, A.M. Stephen, who lived at 22nd Street and Gordon Avenue, to compose an ode:

West Vancouver

O come where the West Wind lingers
  With hand that is loathe to part
And the music flows when its fingers
  Press light on the wildwood's heart!

From the drum of the rockly ledges
  Stretched stark o'er the dim ravine,
In the pipes of the whispering sedges,
  It calls with a joyance keen.

As a flute-song, low and tender,
  It wanders by the streams
Where the alders, tall and slender
  Sway softly wrapped in dreams.

A winnowing wing of the coolness
  In glades where the white desire
Of trilliums holds the fullness
  Of Spring's primordial fire.

It knows when the dryad's laughter
  In the deep, green gladness rings,
It knows and it follows after
  Where the dark-branched cypress swings.

128

O sweet, where the dog-wood gleaming
  Shines bright as a woodland prayer,
Its voice, through hushed aisles streaming
  Stirs life in the gloaming there.

And the plumes of the elder glisten
  Bent low by their pearls of dew,
While the choirs of morning listen
  To the love-note strange and new!

Oh come where the West Wind tarries
  In the land of the sunset fire!
You will know that the song it carries
  Is born of a world's desire.

That edition of the **Daily Province** brought out an issue that had been simmering on the back burner for years, that being a bridge across the First Narrows, or Lions Gate as it was now being called, and now, said the newspaper "it is rapidly approaching realization." So far, no decision had been made as to whether it would be a suspension bridge or a cantilever span. Three firms were "in strenuous competition" for the project:

"The cables, according to the plans, will be supported on steel towers. The bridge has been designed to provide ample right-of-way for pedestrians and at the same time to permit three automobiles to pass on the roadway, which is to be of concrete. It is proposed to carry the bridge from a small gully, east of Prospect Point, to a point on the Indian reserve east of the Capilano River, and to carry the roadway on the North Shore straight from the long sloping approach to Marine Drive, where it will branch in the form of a "Y" to serve east and west bound traffic. Three tentative plans, prepared for the Dwight P. Robinson Co. [of New York] by Dr. J.A.L. Waddell, have been submitted. Two were for the cantilever bridge—one 900 feet long, and second 1,000—and the other for a suspension bridge of 1,200 feet. The maximum clearance in all cases was 168 feet above extreme high water. Provision is made in the plans of both cantilever bridges for four lanes of traffic, two 48-inch water mains and gas mains. Arrangements can also be made for electric cars. The estimated cost will be $2,500,000, but the company [Dwight Robinson] is prepared to spend as much as $3,500,000 and the financing will be arranged entirely in Canada. It has been suggested suitable decorative work be included in the plans, including two large lions of durable material at the piers at both ends, and that the words "Lions Gate" be enscrolled in large letters on the centre of the bridge."

There are a lot of other interesting tidbits in the **Daily Province** supplement which are worth noting: A new trail to Black Mountain has been cut from Horseshoe Bay; a sports field is now being laid out at Ambleside Park. The young folks of St. Stephen's parish are organized, there being a company of Girl Guides, a troop of Boy Scouts and a Wolf Cub pack; a party recently ascended Hollyburn Peak, 4700 feet, for the first time by saddle pony; Pacific Stages Limited are now running a sightseeing bus from Vancouver to Caulfeild via Second Narrows bridge. With the opening of the new stretch of Marine Drive, they will continue to Whytecliffe; the building permits for 1926 to May 31 total $199,685 which is more than the combined totals of North Vancouver and North Vancouver District; the Christian Science congregation which has been holding services in the Dundarave Hall has decided to erect a church and a site has been purchased on 20th Street; the Horseshoe Bay Hotel advertised "modest rates" and "the beach directly in front of the hotel has been cleaned of large rock which now makes it ideal for the kiddies to wade, while a new float with springboards and other amusements has been erected for the more experienced swimmers."

The issue also heralded the advent of Rockcliffe Park, "a name chosen by three judges, Messrs. Burd [Frank Burd, managing director of the **Daily Province**], [Robert] Cromie [publisher of the **Sun**], and [Major General] Victor Odlum [owner] as the most suitable name for the new Amusement Park at the terminus of the Marine Drive extension from Caulfeild to Whytecliffe."

Known for many years as the Odlum Estate, and on his death, given to the University of British Columbia, General Odlum, soldier, newspaper publisher, diplomat and scion of a distinguished family, in fact one of the earliest investors in West Vancouver real estate, was Prof. Edward Odlum, Rockcliffe was a quiet retreat. The man behind the scheme was realtor W.W. Boultbee, who, the **Daily Province** said, had already spent about $100,000 on the development.

"Comprising an area of twenty-five acres, it is a promontory jutting out into Howe Sound between White Bay and Cliff Bay, and is clothed with a magnicifient stand of timber. The undergrowth has been cleared and in the park land, beneath the fir and cedars, kiosks and shelters with stoves for the convenience of picnickers will be erected. A parking ground, with a capacity of 250 cars has been cleared and laid out. At White Bay, on the south side of the park, a boathouse has been constructed with storage for sixty boats at the sides, while the centre will be used as a bathhouse, lockers being provided. On the roof will be a promenade deck and lounge. A service station for autos will be built at the entrance to the parking ground, while on the tip of the promontory, sixty feet above the waters of the Sound, a tea-room, with a dance floor space of 32 by 67 feet has been constructed. A huge rock fireplace adorns the centre of the room, the building being surrounded by a ten-foot verandah, from which a wonderful view of the Sound may be had, south, west and north."

Like so many at-the-time-wonderful-things, Rockcliffe, no longer an endowment of the University of British Columbia, has changed, beyond all recognition, and, down the road from Rockcliffe, so has another one-time landmark Nick Kogas's Parthenon which stood on a rocky bluff overlooking the sea, just as the Temple to Poseidon, just south of Athens, does. As beautiful a concept as Kogas' Parthenon was, it was made of perishable wood, not marble, but some of the replicas of great Grecian art enhance the present Municipal Hall.

The newspaper also gives us an insight into the beginnings of the West Vancouver Public Library, of which the municipality can be proud. It has books for every taste, but, what about the taste provided by Miss Jemima Peattie, who occupied the site before the library was built? She had a tiny confectionery store but from her bedroom-kitchen-living room she turned out the most magnificent apple puffs the world has ever tasted and sold them for a nickel a piece to the **Daily Province** carriers who had their "shack" next door.

"On the first of May, 1926," the **Daily Province** reported, "West Vancouver's Public Library (West Vancouver Public Library Association), was moved from its old home in a small wooden building, on the corner of Fourteenth Street and Bellevue Avenue, to more modern and convenient quarters at the corner of Fourteenth and Marine Drive in Gemmill's drugstore. Members visiting the library during the day were very appreciative of the more convenient situation, the well-lighted interior and nicely arranged shelves. A large shipment of books—210 volumes, 100 fiction, 50 non-fiction, 60 juvenile—were placed on the shelves on opening day. The Hollyburn Public Library Association was formed five years ago, by a small number of pioneer residents who realized that a public organization was needed to care for the rapidly increasing demands for reading matter. Mrs. Field was appointed librarian (her son, Patrick, became reeve of West Vancouver). Her small private library of 250 volumes was purchased and housed in her store. The Municipal Council of 1921 gave generous assistance to the newly formed association, a grant of $250 being made to the board for purchasing books, paying affiliation fee, rent and fixed charges for the year. The councils of 1922 and 1923, appreciating the value of the library to the community, also made small grants. In 1924 and 1925 monetary assistance was refused and the library has been self-supporting for the last two years. Its early success was chiefly due to the untiring efforts of its board, consisting of Mrs. [R.C.] Proctor, Miss [Marion] Almas, Messrs. [W.M.] Jackman and [Richard] Ford and Mr. James Porter, who was chosen president, and held that office for four consecutive years. From the start the library was affiliated with the Provincial Travelling Libraries, and part of its fixed charges is a sum of $50, payable annually at Victoria, in return for which a shipment of books is received three times a year. These books are largely non-fiction and juvenile. New fiction is purchased by the board, and a number of reprints, or two or three of the latest copyrights are added monthly. Under the direction of the board and the courteous and obliging librarian, Mr. G.M. Gemmill, the library has made steady progess and its present turnover is about 220 books a week.... The board has considered for some time the possibility of securing a permanent home for the library, with a comfortable reading room with magazines and papers. This could be effected in two ways: Either by the municipal council assuming control of the library, and changing its status from a public library association to a municipal library, or by the hearty co-operation of public-spirited residents with the members in raising a fund large enough to procure a reading room and to equip it in a manner that would be a credit to the muncipality.''

A "mild adventure" could be experienced by riding down the Capilano Timber Company flume on the west side of the river as it passed through the canyon. (VCA)

Rodger's boat rentals at Horseshoe Bay, circa 1920's. (WVMA)

Hollyburn general store and B.C. Telephone exchange on 17th Street and Marine Drive, circa 1920. (WVMA)

Dundarave Regatta, circa 1920. (WVMA)

Brothers Creek water system intake, circa 1921. (WVML)

Assembled crowd at dedication of Memorial Arch, July 5, 1925. (WVMA)

Baron Byng of Vimy, Governor-General of Canada, speaking at dedication of War Memorial on July 5, 1925. (WVMA)

Regimental Sergeant Major A.O.S. "Rattlesnake Pete" Freemantle. (PP)

West Vancouver veterans of the Fenian Raids, 1866, at a Memorial Day celebration on June 4, 1922: Left to right, Councillor W.H. Kinney, J.H. Grady, Col. Albert Whyte and A.A. Almas. (WVML)

West Vancouver's memorial to the fallen of two World Wars. (WVMA)

A peaceful setting behind the War Memorial. (WVMA)

138

Garrow Bay and Whyte Island, showing home of Mr. and Mrs. Thomas Garrow, 1927. (VCA)

Out for a drive in 1922 along Marine Drive, with Sherman cannery in the background. (VPL)

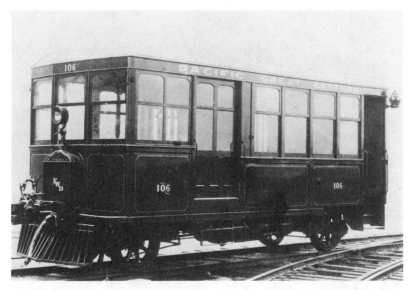

Pacific Great Eastern Railway motor coach No. 106, 1927-28. (WVMA)

Fishermans Cove, 1927. (VCA)

West Vancouver's first apartment building, Appleton Court built at 17th Street and Fulton Avenue in 1928. Tenants had free radio! (CC)

View looking west on Marine Drive, just east of 14th Street in 1929. (WVHS)

Hollyburn Pavilion, site of current post office, 17th Street and Bellevue Avenue. (CC)

Constable Thomas Snelgrove on police motor bike, circa 1928. (NS)

143

Baby Mountain, now known as Sentinel Hill seen from Prospect Point with West Vancouver No. 5 ferry passing mouth of Capilano River. (WVMA)

Chapter Six

FUN AND GAMES

On April 9, 1926, **Volume I Number I** of the **West Van. News** rolled off the press, and with Harry Hodgson sitting at the editor's desk (he was soon to be joined by Captain Francis Lovegrove who later took over the paper by himself) the municipality formally entered the journalistic scene. Previously it had been served by papers from North Vancouver, such as the **North Shore Press** and the **Express**, although in 1919 Mr. and Mrs. Cromar Bruce, members of a distinguished Vancouver newspaper family, started the **West Van. Courier** and in 1922-1923 there appeared the **West Van. = Guard**. Not much is known about these two little tabloid-sized newspapers as only a few copies, perhaps six at most, have survived, but now, with the **West Van. News** on the streets we get, for the first time, a continuing peek in the life and times of the community. While thumbing through the old files in the West Vancouver Municipal Archives one soon becomes aware of the great amount of recreational activity that was going on. A sampling of the various organizations which had sprung to life amply reflects the diversity of interests at the time when the municipality had just emerged from the coal lamp era: the Horseshoe Bay Boating and Yachting Club, West Vancouver Musical Society, St. Anthony's Social Club, A.O.T.S. (As One That Serves, sponsored by the United Church), the Anglican Young People's Association, the Orange Lodge, the Masonic Lodge, Women's Benefit Association, West Vancouver Baseball Club, the Scottish Society with its inevitable Burns Night, the Dundarave Horseshoe Pitchers, the Scottish Daughter's League, West Vancouver Archery Club, a Choral Society, the Board of Trade, West Vancouver Tennis Club, Cricket Club and Senior

Baseball Club, and the West Vancouver Prohibitionist group who launched a "dry by 1929" campaign.

While there was no independent Parks Board until 1943, a fine network of parks was being developed across the length and breath of the municipality, some were well established and it was said at the time that West Vancouver "excels in the beauties of nature." Administration of the fourteen areas of parkland, most of which were undeveloped, came directly from council. These parklands included Ambleside, a large area on Hollyburn Ridge, Inglewood, a 20-acre plot between the high school and 20th Street, Irwin, a four-acre site at Dundarave, West Bay, Sherman, Trestle, just west of West Bay, Cypress Falls, Point Atkinson, Caulfeild and Klootchman, which had been donated to the municipality by Francis W. Caulfeild, Memorial, Nelson Creek and Altamont.

The idea of utilizing the lure of a golf course as a means of selling real estate, which John Lawson had thought about in the early days, and then abandoned it, was still very much alive in 1926 when two developers launched ambitious schemes, one for an eighteen-hole course at the old Hadden Hall site, and the other a nine-hole set of greens at Larson, which soon would be known as Gleneagles.

The Hadden property had reverted to the municipality for taxes several years before, and was now in a sorry state of repair. Vandals had wrecked the interior, the once beautiful gardens had returned to nature, and not long after, some careless skiers lit a fire in the wrecked building and it burned to the ground.

The special West Vancouver issue of the **Daily Province** in June, 1926 noted: "The council is now negotiating with a private company to sell them 200 acres in the northeastern part of the municipality (Hadden Hall) for an 18-hole golf course, the estimated cost of which will be $150,000." A further story in the same issue sheds a bit more light on the project, but does not mention the name of the "private company," but it was J. Haydn Young and Associates.

"The estate forms a small plateau on the north-east side of Hollyburn Ridge and is park-like in appearance," the story stated. "It has been examined by experts, who state it would make an ideal golf course. The council was recently approached by the representatives of a private company who wished to buy the estate with this idea in view... Negotiations are still proceeding, though

146

there is a strong feeling on the part of many of the citizens of the municipality that the course should be developed and owned by the municipality."

The promoters lost no time in getting a membership list drawn up, and on August 27, the **West Van. News** carried an advertisement inviting membership in a "Proposed North Shore Golf Course", calling for one dollar to accompany the application and tentatively set the entrance fee at $100.

A week or so before the above announcement was made, a rival appeared on the scene, and it seemed a "golf war" was about to break out.

Peter Larson, who had developed a farm on the 204 acres he had taken up in 1902, was now getting on in years, and when General R.P. Clark, a well-known Vancouver realtor and developer, offered a reported $100,000 for the property, the deal was made. On August 13, 1926, the **West Van. News** announced a "New Resort for West Vancouver."

"A golf course will be constructed of nine holes to commence with," the paper stated. "The best part of the waterfront on a charming little beach will be reserved for the use of residents. The whole of the area will be developed along uniform and well-planned lines. It is intended to make application to the **Pacific Great Eastern Railway** for permission to rebuild Larson Station, which is on the property, so that the station also will be in keeping with the general scheme of architectural beauty which will be a feature of this resort. The location commands wonderful marine views. From Eagle Harbour on the south to within a few yards to Whytecliffe on the north, an ever-changing vista of beauty delights the eye. There are a number of beautiful trees, a fine maple grove near the main entrance being one of the features. Excellent sea-bathing can be enjoyed here. There is a good water supply from a stream which runs through the property and which is never dry. The developments will be proceeded with just as soon as possible."

The fee structure for the "Gleneagles Golf and Country Club" was announced in the **West Van. News** on September 13, 1926, with prospective members being asked to pay $50 upon application and a further $100 on or before May 1, 1927.

Many prominent Vancouver people were among the initial purchasers of land at Gleneagles and on January 7, 1927, the **West Van. News** was able to report "work on the Gleneagles Country

Club is going on apace. Mr. Vernon, golf expert, is supervising the laying out of a splendid golf course. The grounds are being cleared and graded and it is hoped the course will be open for play by Dominion Day. On the grounds, when everything is completed, will be a fine club house, tennis courts, bowling greens and a miniature golf course. At Larson Bay, situated on the property, there is a good anchorage and in addition the Bay will have attractions in the way of boats and facilities for swimmers."

Captain Charles J. Archer, who was local agent for General Clark, set out an exciting progress report in a Letter to the Editor which appeared in the **West Van. News** on June 17:

"As a member of the Gleneagles Golf and Country Club, I would like to draw the attention of residents of our Municipality to the splendid progess which has been made to date. The course is almost ready for play and opening games will take place 1st July. This enterprise is a credit to the Municipality and is resultant from the efforts of a few interested citizens who appreciate the attractions and beautiful setting and possibilities of the chosen location. In writing this letter I am desirous of suggesting that for community reasons, the membership representation from West Vancouver should form the dominating influence which will ensure its permanent establishment as a West Vancouver Golf Club for West Vancouver residents. A very attractive feature of the membership condition is that the family of a member are entitled to all playing and general privileges of the Club. This has been specially provided for in keeping with the policy adopted to encourage a pleasant family recreational atmosphere. . . ."

And so, on July 1, 1927, play got underway at Gleneagles and on March 16, 1928, the **West Van. News** carried a front page story to say that A.J. Finnie of West Vancouver had scored the first hole in one. "The feat was recently accomplished at the seventh hole while playing with his father, J. Finnie and was verified by Mr. Jock Glen, the professional at the links." The same item mentioned that many improvements had been made and many "lost ball" patches had been cleared.

As for the Hadden Hall golf course, that had to wait until it was announced that the British were coming.

Another major recreational activity in West Vancouver is skiing on Hollyburn Ridge and for the background to that sport, we must turn to an undated manuscript written by Gerry Hardman:

148

"One of the first organized groups was the forerunner of the present Varsity Outdoor Club, formed in 1920, known then as the "Outdoor Club." They first built a cabin on Grouse Mountain, however, in 1922 it was destroyed by fire. As a result, they took up temporary headquarters on Hollyburn Ridge in Naismith's [sic] [Nasmyth] old board and batten cabin at First Lake where they remained for about two years prior to moving back to a new cabin on Grouse. The purpose of this Organization was to conduct trips for University students and friends and promote an interest in hiking, mountain climbing, snowshoeing, etc., on a recreational basis. These outdoor enthusiasts, together with B.C. Mountaineering Club members and others, were responsible, in part, for the extension and improvement of trails to Hollyburn Peak, Black Mountain, Mount Strachan and even a rough trail to the Lions.

"Shortly after the Outdoor Club returned to Grouse Mountain there appeared on the Hollyburn scene a Swedish gentleman by the name of Rudolph J. Verne, at about the same time, 1925, three of his countrymen joined forces with him in a sort of loose partnership and started a Ski Camp at the old Naismith (sic) Mill, making use of the bunk houses and other buildings that were still in a reasonable habitable condition. These three were Oscar Peterson, Olaf Anderson and Andrew Israel. At times, they had others working with them, Axel Sneis, in those days a skier of some renown, Harold Enquist, later to pioneer on Mount Seymour.

"One winter's operation at the Old Mill site convinced them that this location was not suitable for a Ski Camp or Lodge. In the spring of 1926 a start was made to move to the present location of Hollyburn Lodge, known in those days as Hollyburn Ski Camp at First Lake. The Naismith (sic) Mill Buildings were dismantled and the salvaged lumber was skidded by stone bolt pulled by a team of horses over what is now the Fire Access Road (Fred Burfield's Road) as a route. This operation was difficult due to the poor condition of the new tote road, the horses had a bad time, particularly during wet spells when everything was a sea of mud. The Ski Camp was finally ready for occupancy in the late fall of 1926. As you may expect, conditions were rather primitive. At that time there were no other cabins in the vicinity so overnighters slept in the main building on Hemlock or Balsam boughs on wooden bunks, 50 cents per night. Heat was provided in the bunk rooms both for warmth and cooking, on air-tight heaters which had a habit of going out just after you hit the sack and with the supply of wet wood on hand, refused to start in the morning. 1926/27 was a long, cold winter!

"At this point," Mr. Hardman continued, "I should return to the man who was first to see the possibilities of the Ridge as a recreation area, R.J. Verne. His main objective was to promote the growth of skiing as a sport. Prior to this time skiis were somewhat of a curiosity, however, he had unlimited enthusiasm and drive, and soon gathered around him a small group of equally enthusiastic people. Out of all this came into being the Hollyburn Pacific Ski Club. This club was formed at a special meeting of a few ski enthusiasts at 615 West Hastings, Vancouver, B.C., on the 2nd of March, 1927, upon the initiative of R.J. Verne and was officially recognized by the C.A.S.C. on April 15th, 1927. As a matter of further interest, this club was the first Ski Club on the Pacific Coast of North America.

"The first competitions were held at and around the Hollyburn Ski Camp area on April 15 to 17, 1927. The list of charter members consists of some fifty people, some, while not as active on the Ridge as they once were, still maintain an interest in the goings on. To name just a few, Ralph Morris, the first Club captain, together with Al and Eric Twist of the Pioneers Cabin, Harry Collins, Abe Knight and many others. All these people were the pioneers of Hollyburn Ridge as a recreation area. They started the log cabin 'building boom' of the late '20s and early '30s and what we have today is due in no small part to their efforts."

It is interesting to note a section of the Rules and Regulations laid down by the club in 1927: "In the club's opinion, cross-country skiing should receive first consideration and should at least be on even terms with jumping. The club in its desire to bring cross-country racing in Canada back to its proper place is particularly fortunate in having within its radius the finest territory for cross-country skiing in the Dominion."

There were other forms of fun and games going on as well during the late 1920s and 1930s. In May, 1926, J. Howard Fletcher, a future reeve of West Vancouver, opened his Hollyburn Theatre with "five vaudeville acts" and a "Great War Play" entitled **The Dark Angel**, and in March, 1927, the old Ambleside Hall was converted into the municipal garage, with its activities shifted

150

over to the Hollyburn Pavilion which stood on the site of the present post office at the foot of 17th Street. To cite all the activities that went on in that hall would fill a book in itself but one cannot idly skip over the political meetings held there, especially when James Porter, the long-time chairman of the library association was present. For the speaker of the evening it was nothing but disaster to be confronted by Mr. Porter. He was deaf and carried with him wherever he went a huge ear trumpet, made with sheet metal and a rubber hose, and he would often stand beside the speaker with his ear trumpet pushed up against the lecturer's mouth so he could hear, but that was not always satisfactory. If Mr. Porter missed a point the speaker had made, he would roar "Whatja say?" and, of course, the speaker by this time was completely frustrated and had forgotten the point he had made.

To anyone raised in West Vancouver during these years, May 24, Victoria the Good's birthday, was the high day of all high days, unless you happened to be a boy who was "volunteered" by his teacher to dance, in public, around the maypole at Ambleside Park. It was the day that ushered in summer, therefore, could summer holidays be far behind? There was a great parade, starting from 20th Street down to Ambleside Park. It was all very exciting; there were no fancy commercial floats, just kids all dressed up in costumes their mothers had spent hours in making, and for those who didn't get all fussed-up, there was the chance of hopping aboard the red fire truck, and perhaps, if they were fortunate enough to sit beside the driver and turn the handle of the shrieking siren to become almost a hero. Merchants along the parade route tossed out free candy, but above all, it was a school holiday.

If you lived, like this writer did on 22nd Street and attended Pauline Johnson School, you almost felt you were going through an "Iron Curtain" once you left the Pauline Johnson-Hollyburn School boundary at 19th, and no doubt the "Hollyburn bums", as we called them, felt the same. We from "P.J." felt we were the master race, although there were harrowing experiences to go through to defend that belief, particularly when the results of inter-school relay race results were announced. "Them bums" from Hollyburn had a formidable array of runners on their roster, topped off by the Breeden brothers, Wally and Stan, plus Joe "Buffalo" Mathias, grandson of the famed Chief Joe Capilano.

151

Most years we of P.J. were humiliated by their success, but not *every* year. Oh, what joy there was in the western part of West Vancouver when one year, I forgot which, two of our superb athletes, Norman Lidster and Reid Mitchell, led the good guys to victory. Oh, how we lorded over the Hollyburn kids that day, even going so far as to call them "bums" to their faces and to say "we have a brick school and yours is just made of wood," and of course, they would reply with "Sticks and stones may break our bones, but names will never hurt us." Curiously, this inter-school name-calling, and feelings suddenly stopped when we passed from Grade VI into the hallowed halls of junior high school and then we all, after a week or so, began to look down on those "children" from elementary school.

On May 24 we had pomp and pageantry, which, we thought and did believe, rivalled or surpassed New Westminster's ancient celebration which was held on May 1. The May Queen, who came from Hollyburn and Pauline Johnson on alternate years, was gorgeously dressed, as were her princesses, flower girls and pages. They arrived in state at Ambleside Park in a horse-drawn landau, escorted by kilted members of the Seaforth Highlanders' Cadet Corps. Then, after riding in state around the park, the Queen was escorted by the reeve (for ten of those years by J.B. Leyland) to the dais where the previous year's Queen waited to hand over her crown. All stood to attention as high school principal J.R. "Jimmy" Mitchell, the long-time master of ceremonies, led off the coronation ceremonies by leading, in an off-key voice which boomed over the loudspeaker, the singing of **God Save the King**. There was the maypole dance, and another to the tune of **Pop Goes the Weasel**, followed by sports events, and a banquet which was not for the kids, who lined up outside where ever the dinner was being held, just to admire the lovely regal party regally enter the hall. Next day, these young ladies were just girls, and if they had pigtails, it was not a matter of near-regicide if they screamed blue murder when you dared to dip their hair into an inkwell or glue-pot.

Alas, the May Day celebrations now belong to history, but they deserve **en masse** treatment as this Chronicle travels down memory lane.

There was an article in the **West Van. = Guard** in June, 1922, under the heading "Hollyburn School Sports" that could be an "opener" for the pageants yet to come.

"...The kindness of Mrs. Young, of Fourteenth Street, provided ice cream cones by the dozen, a recognition of the hearty support given by the school to her daughter, Irene, as a candidate for position of May Queen of the North Shore, which secured for her the scarcely less coveted position of first maid of honor....Principal Brealey called for three cheers for the Trustees and for Mrs. Young, whose ice cream had not chilled enthusiasm. The pupils then sang **O Canada, Shall School Acquaintance Be Forgot?** and **God Save the King**, and the children filed out to receive each a bag of sweets and fruit. The girls in addition had a playground scramble for nuts showered by the Principal; and the school session of 1921-22 closed with pleasant memories."

The crowning of the May Queen of the North Shore was held in North Vancouver and up until 1930, West Vancouver was represented, although the **North Shore Press** gives us little or nothing in its columns about West Vancouver entrants to the celebration. In 1930 a meeting was called by the Parent-Teachers' Association from both Hollyburn and Pauline Johnson Schools at the Fortune Cup Inn, to discuss the possibility of having a local May Day celebration.

The outcome of that milestone meeting was the naming of six-year old Mavis Whipple, a student of Hollyburn School as the first "Miss West Vancouver." The big, three-block long parade, was led by the General Gordon School Band from Vancouver and it was noticed that among the players was a West Vancouver youth. His name is not recorded, but from that "spotting" there arose a demand that West Vancouver form its own school band. The little star of the show was accompanied by attendants Diana Chapman, of Dundarave, Pat Hodgson, of Pauline Johnson, and Bunny Whipple of Hollyburn. There were three flower girls, Eileen Russell, Jean McLeod and Doreen Kearns, and Companies I and II of the Girl Guides formed the guard of honor. Decorated cars occupied by Reeve Leyland and members of council led a section of decorated bicycles and then followed, according to the **West Van. News**, "a wonderful array of motley garbed children" and others not in costume. Parade judges were Dr. E.A. Henry, Mrs. F. Eatock and Mrs. W.B. (Sabina) Small. Sibbie Small! No Chronicle of West Vancouver would be complete without paying tribute to this lady, who, down through the years, worked so hard on behalf of the May Day Committee, and also for the

Imperial Order of the Daughters of the Empire and the various organizations that sprang up during the hard days of the Depression of the 1930s. In fact, there was scarcely anything going on in West Vancouver during those years that Mrs. Small was not involved up to her arms in helping.

In connection with this first and only "Miss West Vancouver" pageant there was a "Most Beautiful Baby" contest. This was held for only three years, and the winners were Mavis [Fletcher] Garrison, Albert Fletcher and Hazel [Fletcher] Mudry.

In 1931, sponsorship shifted away from the P.T.A. to become more of a community celebration, and twelve contestants lined up for the competition to be the first May Day Queen of West Vancouver. At a ceremony held in the Hollyburn Theatre, Reeve Leyland drew the winner's name from a hat. She was Peggy Barker, of Pauline Johnson, and her maids of honor, May Armstrong and Jean Hill, came from Hollyburn School. The remaining girls, Enid Clements, Margaret McLellan, Adelaide Lopatecki, Keitha Adams, Patricia Bibbs, Jean Warner, Janet Thompson, Dorothy Jackson and Olive Childs formed the Queen's honor guard which was supplemented by four flower girls, a herald and crown bearer, Mavis Whipple, the former Miss West Vancouver. For some reason, seven-year old Mavis was declared to be too young to fill the position of crowning her successor and this honor fell to Mrs. John Lawson. Following the Ambleside Park ceremonies, the Queen and her attendants left to place flowers at the War Memorial and then went to leave flowers at the North Vancouver General Hospital.

By this time, the West Vancouver Schools Band had been formed through the efforts of Mrs. M. Masterman and other members of the school board, along with J.A. Condon, Tom Russell and others. When the boys and girls made their **debut** at the 1931 festivities, they were under the baton of J.A. Condon, an interim bandmaster until Mr. Jordan was available.

The newsletter of the West Vancouver Museum and Historical Society, called **History-onics**, for October, 1985, was devoted entirely to the story of the May Queens. It was researched by Georgie (Edington) Wilson, and covers the years in which May Day was **the** event of the year.

"Jean Warner," Mrs. Wilson writes, "one of the Honor Guard of the year before [1931] was to see a few changes in her entourage. Instead of an honor guard of nine, she had one of six,

154

a more manageable number if only during the parade when the guards walk on either side of the royal car. It is to be presumed that the queen came from Hollyburn and the maids of honor from Pauline Johnson, but with a royal party of nine, how was the guard of honor divided between the two schools? Another change was the addition of a page, young Norman Jackson. He must have caught the eye of the reporter as his costume was described in detail. He was, said the **West Van. News**, clad in a yellow satin suit of the Louis XIV period and carrying the key to the city on a yellow satin pillow. The presence of two queens necessitated two vehicles, and enabled a nice distinction between the reigning and non-reigning queen. From somewhere in the West End a carriage was borrowed, for which Shelley's 4-X Bakery provided a team of matched white horses. In this assemblage the reigning queen, Peggy Parker, rode in the parade to Ambleside Park. The Queen-Elect, Jean Warner, rode in a convertible all bestrewed with paper flowers. Both were, of course, accompanied by three maids of honor. After her crowning, Queen Jean rode away from the park in the carriage, (driven by Mr. Little resplendent in top hat and cutaway coat), while retiring queen Peggy departed in the convertible.

"Now that there were two queens, it was possible to have each outgoing queen crown her successor and this became the practice. The crown itself was not passed on, indeed the only accoutrement to be used year after year was the key to the city.

"The maids of honor in this second year were Jessie Ritz and Kathleen Bernard. Kathleen was better known to her contemporaries as Bubbles and that is how she signed the parchment roll. She was to marry James Sinclair, one of her high school teachers, and thus became the wife of one of Canada's more distinguished cabinet ministers. When her daughter Margaret married, she also became the mother-in-law to a prime minister [The Right Honorable Pierre Elliott Trudeau].

"There was one change in the entourage for Queen Joan [Parker in 1933] —the addition of a second page. Norman Jackson, serving a second year, was joined by Reid Mitchell. Already in this third year, it had been established that each year would be a new experience. The dresses for the royal party were changed each year, to be expected with changing fashions. But the review stand was also redesigned. In 1933, the new feature was a canopy over the queen alone. For the first time, the official picture contains a visiting queen, with her two maids of honor. She may have been from the North Vancouver celebrations, although the North Vancouver celebrations were also held on Victoria Day. A queen-to-be can be seen in the guard of honor, although Dale Eriksen was not to reign until 1935. And making a first appearance was Isobel Russell as crown bearer. She was to appear in a royal party no less than five times. In 1933 she is crown bearer, and in 1935 a flower girl. This reverses the usual order as flower girls were generally taken from grades one and two and crown bearers from grades three and four. She was later to appear once as a guard of honor and twice as a maid of honor.

"The two previous queens had both served as a guard of honor before becoming queen. Queen Margaret [Curry in 1934] has the distinction of assuming the throne without any previous involvement. It does seem to be a distinction. In her own court was Dale Eriksen, now Mrs. Dan McGowan, as maid of honor and with her eye on the throne. Two sisters, Dorothy and Louise Messinger are guards of honor, but it is a younger Messinger girl, Mary, who would be queen in 1942. The crown bearer, Gladys Wilson, was also to be queen, her turn coming in 1938. Some girls seem drawn to such activities, although the luck of the draw would determine which became queen. The Fletcher family, of beautiful baby fame, was to have its first representative in this year. Doreen, who served as a flower girl, led off a wave of Fletcher appearances, five in the 1930s and three more in the 1940s.

"There was not so much opportunity for the male side. Reid Mitchell did serve a second year as page. There must have been some problem in head office as his father, Jimmy Mitchell, had to double up and serve as both master of ceremonies and committee chairman. As for the platform, the idea of the canopy was well received. In this year, it was also included, but enlarged so that it covered the queen and both her maids. In the official picture, there are definitely three thrones. Last year the maids of honor might have been sitting on plain chairs, but not this year.

"By going from maid of honor in 1934 to queen in 1935, Dale Eriksen created a problem. Both queen and maid of honor appear at two May Days, one at which the queen is crowned and the other when she crowns her successor. With Dale as queen, retiring queen Margaret was left with but one maid of honor. She was replaced by a young lady named Delwyn Beatty, but there is no information on why or how she was chosen. Perhaps she

156

was the fourth choice in the popular election by students the year before. Equally possible, she was picked at random when the committee suddenly realized that they were a maid short. Obviously, it is better if the progression is from guard of honor to queen, and there were two future queens among the guards—Norma Minions for 1936 and Ruth Parnum for 1937.

"Queen Norma's (Minions in 1936) reign was to see a change in the queen's entourage with the addition of a sceptre bearer. This suggests a change in the queen's regalia—there is no need for a sceptre bearer unless a sceptre has been added. For most May Day celebrations hereafter, the sceptre and the sceptre bearer were to be part of the ceremony. Like the crown, each sceptre was made for a particular May Day, and it would seem, became one of the mementoes which she took away after her reign. No one would have known, but this was to be the last year for the crepe paper dresses. For Georgie Edington, it was one year too many. Paper or no paper, her beautiful green dress stood up to the rigors of the crowning ceremony, but not the events that followed. In this year, at least, there was a royal tour of the municipality, and during the tour, Crown Bearer Georgie had to sit on Reeve Leyland's knee. To her chagrin, during the tour, her dress split up the side. Perhaps it was this that persuaded the committee that all participants should wear cloth. Again, among the guard of honor is another queen-to-be. Lois Minkley had to wait three years to reign. Jimmy Mitchell no longer had to wear two hats as a teacher from the high school had been recruited as May Day committee chairman. It is probably not a coincidence that Jimmy was principal.

"Also taking part in the 1936 coronation ceremonies were Anna Sparks, Doreen Kerley, Dorothy Messinger, Jessie Wrisberg, Barbara Edwards, Margaret Payne, Diana Chapman, Mary McLeod, Gordon Sangster, Beverly McCulloch, Peggy Thompson, Beryl Scott, Donna Dalgleish and Gordon Thompson.

"Ruth Parnum was elected the 1937 May Queen. This year there was a change in the entourage—in dress but not in number. As mentioned the paper dresses were no more, but that change would not be too noticeable to the audience. But they would have noticed the change in the pages. Gone are the satin breeches, the satin shirt and the big floppy satin hat. Now the pages are miniature judges in long black gowns, white gates away collars and powdered curled perukes. It may have been an easier outfit to get little boys to wear, but somehow it does not seem appropriate for either a page or a coronation. Former crown bearers Isobel Russell and Gladys Wilson are among the guards of honor.

"The entourage was unchanged when Gladys Wilson became May Queen in 1938, but on the stage there were now six thrones. Someone had decided that the retiring queen and her maids should have something better than just chairs. The new thrones are a little smaller than the old ones. At that, there are not enough thrones to go round as there are five West Vancouver queens on the platform. Queen Gladys and retiring Queen Ruth had been joined by former queens Norma, Dale and Margaret. Six queens if one wishes to include Mavis Whipple who made her last hurrah on this occasion. Seven if one is clairvoyant and knows that maid of honor Lois Minkley is scheduled for promotion. Pages on that occasion were Ian Macdonald and Albert Fletcher.

"When Lois Minkley was crowned in 1939, there was again the need for a fill-in when a maid of honor became queen. Dorothy Nelson was named to take the role of retiring maid of honor. Someone must have realized that the garb of the pages was inappropriate and had them re-named Chancellors. For that title, the black outfits, legal as they look, is quite fitting. And, after a surplus of queens the year before, this year there was not a single extra one on stage. But there was a new committee chairman, Alec. J. Gleam.

"Jean Fiddes was chosen May Queen for 1940, and for some reason, there was no sceptre bearer, and the same happened in 1941. Again, there were no visiting queens, and for the first time, no "Sibbie" Small as matron. Isobel Russell, for the second time, was maid of honor. She would not appear again, so next year, a "retiring" maid of honor must substitute for her. Doreen Garrard, older sister of the renowned opera singer, Donald Garrard, took her place.

"When Helen Jackson was crowned in 1941, Mrs. Small had been replaced as matron by Ruth Thompson, and J. Edward Sears had replaced J.B. Leyland as reeve. Thus it was that for the first time, a May Day coronation was held without Mr. Leyland being on stage. That year it was said the stage was austere beyond description. Drapes had replaced the lovely trellis backdrop with its own greenery. The top of the drape was fringed and adorned

158

with three-crown cut-outs. Right in the centre was a little sign reading God Save Our King and Queen. The artificial grass that had always covered the floor and the steps had been replaced with artificial brick.

"The Senior Home Economics class took over the catering job for the 1942 May Day banquet which was held in the United Church hall. It was a junior high school girl who ascended the throne that year. Mary Messenger received the crown from retiring queen Helen Jackson. Maids of honor were Dorset Stephenson and Sheila Gracey."

The "spirit of May Day", in 1943, in the minds of some, had to be tempered with the realities of the war, but Captain Francis Lovegrove, an old military man, took the opposite view in an editorial in his **West Van. News**:

"Some doubtless will think that in this time of the greatest war in all history the celebration should be cut down or not held at all on account of the expense. We can only again remind them, and it ought to be a sufficient answer, that May Day is for the children. We humans grow old very fast, and not many child memories remain with us at maturity. The children of today cannot help but carry to manhood and womanhood a number of unhappy memories. They will scarcely be able to forget fathers and brothers and sisters who went away with a brave smile and never came back, of mothers weeping for their dead, of lack of many of the good things that made life enjoyable and of their puzzlement for the reasons of so much misery. Why not, therefore, give them a few happy memories to set up against some of the blight of their young lives? Help them to recall the white-gowned May Queen sitting on her throne and surrounded by her entourage of youth, the Maypole dancing on the green in which perhaps they took part, and the races they lost and won. Such is the spirit in which we should keep the May Day celebration this year. Let us all be children for the day with the children and so be better able to face the stern time of stress and inevitable loss which is so fast approaching."

As Captain Lovegrove had hoped, the festivities which saw Dawn Smith crowned "was one of the most successful in the history of the event. . . The parade was larger and better than has been the case for years. . .and about 5,000 people assembled in the park to view the interesting program." Queen Dawn's attendants were Marilyn Murphy and Mavis Fletcher.

It was just two weeks before D-Day on the beaches of Normandy that Ruth Steen became the 1944 May Queen, and because it was the "first really wet May Day" the coronation was held in the Inglewood auditorium late in the afternoon. Ah!, but there was good news that day. For the first time in 12 years of defeat, West Vancouver beat North Vancouver in the great relay race. As a result of the weather, the parade was put off until the following Saturday, and then Queen Ruth and her maids of honor, Diana Cruickshank and Norma Wiles, rode in state along Marine Drive.

After five years of war, nobody had really got used to peacetime living when Irene Empey in "fine although scarcely sunny weather" was crowned before 7,000 people, "the largest on record." With her attendants, Joan Orrey and Nancy Andrews, she opened the Children's Dance, which must have been, according to the **West Van. News**, quite an event:

"To the children the great event of May Day, apart from the May Queen celebration and sports, is their own dance in the Auditorium, as was amply shown on Friday night when 1105 of them attended to spend a happy evening of fun and dancing. May Queen Irene and her entourage officially opened the proceedings, and the fact that with so many present dancing space was necessarily crowded in no way detracted from the merriment and enjoyment of the youngsters."

As was the time-honored custom, the sound of bugles announced the arrival of May Queen Judy Vyvyan for her coronation as Queen of the May for 1946. It was a larger than ever parade that year, starting off at Dundarave, and this year the banquet was held in the Youth Centre, with toasts being raised to "The King," "The May Queen," "The ex-May Queen" and "Out of town guests." Grandstand seats cost twenty-five cents. Queen Judy's attendants were Reta Gardner and Barbara Kelsey.

It had now been 17 years since Mavis Whipple was crowned "Miss West Vancouver", and now, as Queen of the May, Donna Richmond, with maids of honor Ann Gilmour and Veronica Waller, assumed the mantle of office, and that was the year "West Vancouver wuz robbed." The **News** tells what happened:

"The annual road relay race between West Vancouver and North Vancouver High Schools was won by the latter after a stirring finish in 17 minutes and 36 seconds. Only 10 feet separated the two runners at the tape, and the final result might have been different had not a youngster on a bicycle got in the way of Joe Lidster, West Vancouver's last runner, just as he was making his final dash for the finish line in the last few yards of the race."

The occasion also provided a ceremonial opening of the Horseshoe Bay Community Centre. After the coronation ceremony at Ambleside Park, the royal party headed west, where, flanked by a Seaforth Highlanders cadet corps escort, Queen Donna cut the ribbon, after which Reeve Tom Brown said "it was eminently fitting that the new hall should be opened by Queen Donna, the children's queen."

After an inauspicious morning of cloud and intermittent drizzle, which made the sports at Ambleside Park somewhat unpleasant for both competitors and the many onlookers, the sun burst forth a little before noon and from then on the municipality's Eighteenth May Day was celebrated in really summer weather. All the pageantry of yesteryears was repeated during the crowning of Maureen McKeown who was flanked by maids of honor Wendy Rathbone and Edna Arnet.

The 1949 May Day celebrations brings up an interesting question, one that has been debated down through the years and is still going on: What ever has happened to our weather? On the day when Daphne Lidster was crowned queen, and Ann Louise Ritchie and Sherrill Macdonald made up the royal party it was cloudy and threatening in the morning, but that bad omen didn't last through noon, as just in time for the celebrations to begin, the sun began to warm up the decorated platform. That celebration reflected the progress West Vancouver was making. With the opening of the Ridgeview Elementary School, the royal court had to be enlarged to include representatives from Pauline Johnson, Hollyburn, the Junior High, Gleneagles and the new school.

To herald the crowning of the 1950 May Queen, Barbara Thomson, the last surviving distress rocket from the now defunct West Vancouver ferry system was exploded in the air and there was another noticeable reminder that West Vancouver was on the move with the transferring of the hotly-contested North Vancouver-West Vancouver road race to Ambleside Park because of the heavy traffic conditions along Marine Drive. Beverley Platt and Deanna Palmer were the maids of honor for the occasion.

Behind all the glitter of West Vancouver's annual May Day celebrations there was always a real community effort, a spirit, if you will, that has always been the backbone of the municipality. When the 1951 fiesta came around there were no less than 15 organizations represented on the organizing committee, and as Reeve J. Howard Fletcher put it, "they are really on the job." Chosen that year were Joanne Smith, queen, and Elinor Burrows and Joan Gilmore as maids of honor.

Three grade sevens were selected in a draw ceremony, held by Reeve Fletcher, to have the honor of being the Queen of the May for 1952. They were Fay Warren, with Sally Newbury and Wendy Farmer as maids of honor, and the annual banquet this time was held in the new senior high school auditorium.

For the next two years, steady downpours forced last-minute schedule changes, with the crownings being held in the school auditorium and the track and field events, as well as the maypole dancing, put off for several days. In 1953, Queen Candy Carroll and her maids of honor Patsy Watts and Lynne Warburton, were forced to take cover after the rain began shortly before noon, and in 1954 Ann Johnston and her two maids of honor, Georgia Harris and Jocelyn Searle, proved that it took more than a little rain to break with tradition. In fact, Queen Ann added a bit to the tradition herself as she had been a flower girl four years before.

The weather turned out fine for Susan Porter as she and her entourage, Mary Kaffka and Carolyn West, smiled down from her throne before some 5,000 spectators in 1955 and, "once again," said the **West Van. News**, "the adult audience was amazed and moved by the dignity and composure of the young May Queens and their very young attendants." The weather "co-operated without reserve" for the 1956 celebration which was hailed "as the finest May Day in years". The queen that year was Wendy Welsh, with Judy Kaffka and Iris Dougherty maids of honor.

Nancy Porter reigned over the 1957 festivities, and not to take any chances with the weather, arrangements were made for a special weather report to be broadcast at 8:30 that morning. It turned out to be a day like the old ones were, when May Day unofficially launched the start of summer and the opening of the swimming season. For Queen Nancy and her maids of honor, Marilyn Tearoe and Marilee Boughen, it was a day to remember.

History was the theme of the 1958 celebrations, and just a few days before Dell Galloway ascended the throne, the British

Columbia Centennial Stage Coach, bound from Victoria to the old gold town of Barkerville, passed along Marine Drive, its six horses still feeling somewhat seasick after a rough crossing on a Blackball Ferry from Nanaimo.

Like just about every community in the province, West Vancouver picked up a local historical theme to focus attention on May Queens of the past. With her maids of honor, Joanne Miller and Bonnie Jean Lewis, Queen Dell planted twenty-eight cherry trees at Ambleside Beach. Each of these trees honored a past May Queen, and for the occasion, eighteen of them were on hand to witness the event.

> 1959: Shirley Black, queen; princesses, Alana Thomas, Verena Unger and Sally Campbell.
>
> 1960: Nancy Griffiths, queen; attendants, Lynn Rickard, Marsha Greig, and Julie Hammond.

For the 1961 celebrations, the **Lions Gate Times** paid particular tribute to some of the people, not just the organizations, who down through the years had put the celebrations together, tasks that deserve a queen's crown.

"All the service clubs of West Vancouver work together with the May Day Society each year," wrote **Times** reporter Maureen Read, "but it is the little individual in the background who carries some of the burdens year after year. Mrs. Sibbie Small, one of the May Day originals, is officially the Society's treasurer, but we all know she is the backbone of the organization. Mrs. R.J. Patterson, another original with Mrs. Small (they worked in the first May Day in 1930) is an ardent gardener and active Duncan Lawson [IODE] member. She has always had the responsibility of collecting the flowers and decorating the May Queen's stand, cars, and so on, for more years than she cares to admit. Then there is Mrs. A. Evans. Her title? Second vice-president. For years she has personally managed the May Queen party, petal throwers, entourage, banquet and maypole dancing. The job entails weeks of work, but she handles it with the ease of a professional. Mrs. W. Green makes the lovely white satin capes each year for the new May Queen and her three maids of honor. Mrs. R.A. Thompson annually makes the Queen's crown.... Mrs. F.A. Titcomb personally makes the flowers and assembles them into bouquets for all the guards of honor, flower girls, sceptre bearers and crown bearer. Mrs. T. Leigh and Mrs. A. Parkinson of the Lions Gate IODE have the guards of honor and the flower girls under their wing. Mrs. J. Armstrong and Mrs. J. Hewett have had the mammoth job of training and organizing over four hundred girls for maypole dancing. The mothers of Hollyburn School have been training the petal throwers. All the IODE chapters of West Vancouver— Duncan Lawson, Lions Gate, Hollyburn and British Pacific, put many hours of voluntary effort into May Day. Again this year, as in past years, the three May Day balls are efficiently managed by the mothers and fathers of the youngsters who attend the dances.''

With all that teamwork behind her grand entry to the throne, Diane Patterson, with her entourage, Lynda Gisby, Carol Clark and Sally Knowlton, became the 1961 Queen of the May.

Like her predecessors, Queen Diane has a plaque-marked tree in her honor at Ambleside, and so does next year's Queen, Suzanne Loehrich. Her coronation had a special attraction. Just a week before the West Vancouver Boys' and Girls' Band, under the direction of Clifton C. Bryson, had won the ''Marching and Playing-Fancy Drill'' competition at the fourth annual International Band Festival held in Abbotsford in the Fraser Valley. Her maids of honor, by the way, were Michlen Scott and Kathy Hunt.

Those who went to school, say in the 1930s, will remember the visits of the school inspector, and how everything had to be spotless and the teacher pleaded for good behavior from his students. One such inspector— they are now called superintendents— was William Gray, a rosy cheeked fellow with rimless glasses who would slip into a classroom, listen to the teacher for a few minutes, and then inspect the kids' copy books. Well, in 1963 his granddaughter, Margery Edith Gray, became the 34th Queen of the May, with Meta Stevenson and Clare Hetherington. Queen Margery and her attendants gave up their exalted rank the next year to Queen Helen Babalos and maids of honor Barbara Parker and Patricia Heiliger.

A television interview came with being named the 1965 May Queen, and Dougal Craig had the honor of being the first West Vancouver queen to appear before the cameras on a Channel 8 women's program. As far as is known her maids of honor, Elizabeth (Liza) Greene and Elaine Paget did not share that distinction.

The next year, 1966, was marked by another British Columbia centennial celebration, this time to commemorate the union of the Crown colonies of Vancouver Island and British Columbia, with Victoria becoming the capital, much to New Westminster's disgust. Reigning over the celebration was Queen Louise Smith, with her princesses Cathy Anderson and Karen Ross. The West Vancouver Band which, as usual, took part in the ceremonies, was now under the baton of Leonard Whitely who had recently returned from the band of the Princess Patricia Light Infantry.

Never before had there been 13 bands in a West Vancouver May Day parade, but in the 1967 Canadian Centennial Year, "May Day watchers" could well and truly say that that parade was the biggest and best. More than one hundred entries made up the parade which took 12-year old Patricia Dawson to her place of coronation.

The "spirit of '67" continued into the next year and the 1968 queen, Jill McGregor, and her entourage turned on their charm, like their predecessors had done down through the years. But this year there was something special and it wasn't just the rain.

In addition to receiving her crown, Queen Jill was witness to the signing of documents which "twinned" West Vancouver and the Montreal residential suburb of Verdun. Negotiations between the two communities for "twinning" had been launched in September, 1966 through the Union of Municipalities of the Province of Quebec in collaboration with the Canadian Centennial Commission, but for various reasons implementation of the agreement did not take place until May 20, 1968 in West Vancouver, with another formal signing on June 24 in Verdun.

An official party from Verdun arrived on May 19, a day which was designated as Ambleside and Tiddly Cove Day in recognition of the spoofing of **Vancouver Sun** cartoonist Len Norris. That evening, as Mayor J. Albert Garipey of Verdun, the city's general manager and representatives of the Verdun Catholic School Commission, the Lions Club, Verdun Richelieu Club and the Knights of Columbus crossed the Lions Gate Bridge, a series of bonfires along Ambleside Beach were lit to give the visitors a "fiery welcome." After the signing and the crowning of the Queen, the party left for Eagle Harbour where Parc Verdun was dedicated (a similar park, Parc West Vancouver, was dedicated in Verdun).

"Best ever" is more than just a cliche used to describe each May Day. Each year did seem to get better, but two things remained constant: the pageantry and the enjoyment shown on the faces of the children during the festive days. The 1969 May Queen,

Marilynn Vince, was described as "the spirit of springtime personified" as she received her crown as her princesses, Terri Taylor and Nancy Burns, watched. "Biggest and best ever" was a phrase used to describe the 1970 pageant when Queen Susan Nixon and her princesses, mounted the flower-decorated stage at Ambleside Park. In 1971, the traditions of 42 years of pageantry continued with Kellie Burnett and her princesses Anne Marshall and Donna Swanson, as the beautiful members of the royal party. Leslie Grundle was the 1972 May Queen and nobody realized it at the time but the 1973 Queen, Joanne Clarke, and her princesses, Elizabeth Hunter and Shelly Fraser, would be the last in a long line of West Vancouver May Day celebrities.

The end has come. **Finis**. But in the minds of thousands, the Queens of the May will not be forgotten:

1930: Mavis Whipple.
1931: Peggy Barker (Mrs. W.A. Allen).
1932: Jean Warner (Mrs. D.G. Armstrong).
1933: Joan Parker (Mrs. R.R. Morrin).
1934: Margaret Curry (Mrs. Jack Martin).
1935: Dale Eriksen (Mrs. D.D. McGowan).
1936: Norma Minions (Mrs. E. Hamilton).
1937: Ruth Parnum (Mrs. David King).
1938: Gladys Wilson (Mrs. G.T. Gibson).
1939: Lois Minkley (Mrs. Harry Strevel).
1940: Jean Fiddes (Mrs. W.W. Douglas).
1941: Helen Jackson (Mrs. H.W. Hall).
1942: Mary Messinger (Mrs. J.R. Allan).
1943: Dawn Smith (Mrs. B.A. Langley).
1944: Ruth Steen (Mrs. Ruth Buck).
1945: Irene Empey (Mrs. Irene Kelsey).
1946: Judith Vyvyan (Mrs. M. Lockett).
1947: Donna Richmond (Mrs. B.J. Shepard).
1948: Maureen McKeown (Mrs. G.N. Tickell).
1949: Daphne Lidster (Mrs. Ronald Grisdale).
1950: Barbara Thomson (Mrs. Douglas Rogers).
1951: Joanne Smith (Mrs. Roger Tait).
1952: Fay Warren (Mrs. Roland Neault).
1953: Candy Carroll (Mrs. Glen Rustad).
1954: Ann Johnstone (Mrs. C. Brousson).
1955: Susan Porter (Mrs. J.B. Wright).
1956: Wendy Welsh (Mrs. G.D. Marshall).

1957: Nancy Porter.
1958: Dell Galloway (Mrs. P. Walton).
1959: Shirley Black (Mrs. P.J. Bonner).
1960: Nancy Griffiths (Mrs. K. Archer).
1961: Diane Patterson (Mrs. D. Williams).
1962: Suzanne Loehrich (Mrs. P. Melhuish).
1963: Margery Edith Gray.
1964: Helen Babalos (Mrs. Makris).
1965: Dougal Craig.
1966: Louise Smith.
1967: Patricia Dawson.
1968: Jill McGregor.
1969: Marilyn Vince.
1970: Susan Nixon.
1971: Kellie Burnett.
1972: Leslie Grundle.
1973: Joanne Clarke.

With such a magnificient view, it is no wonder that people took to Hollyburn Ridge for a day of skiing. (WVMHS)

*The Hollyburn Ski Lodge was **the** place to go. (WVMHS)*

Vancouver Ski Club cabins on Hollyburn Ridge. (WVML)

Reflections on a summer afternoon on Hollyburn Ridge. (WVML)

Peggy Barker, West Vancouver's May Queen in 1931 rides to her coronation with crown bearer Mavis Whipple. (WVMHS)

Riding in a horse-drawn "state carriage" May Queen Peggy Barker goes to the coronation of her successor in 1932. (WVMHS)

A scene re-enacted over many years was the crowning of May Queen Joan Parker in 1933. Reeve J.B. Leyland is at the microphone. (WVMHS)

Tree planting was one of the traditions May Queens followed year after year. Here, 1933 Queen Joan Parker is assisted by Reeve J.B. Leyland. (WVMHS)

May Day Parades always sparkled with the gaily decorated bicycles ridden by the children. (WVMA)

No West Vancouver May Day celebration was completed without the school children dancing around the traditional maypole. (WVMA)

175

Chapter Seven

THE BRITISH ARE COMING

Victoria-born Alfred James Towle Taylor, engineer and investment entrepreneur, was tough and practical, but over and above those qualities, he was dynamic. He was not the type of man to sit idly by and dream impossible dreams. Such things clutter the mind, and his was too sharp for that. In his mind he saw a vision—not a dream—of West Vancouver finding its true role as being a place of excellence through a prestigious residential area on the eastern slopes of Hollyburn Ridge, in the same general area where, years before, Harvey Hadden had built his ill-fated Hadden Hall. Before that vision could become a reality, many obstacles had to be overcome but with his well-known attributes of enthusiasm for an undertaking, backed by the strength of his tremendous drive, "A.J.T.", as he was known to his associates, was the man, if there ever was one, to topple obstacles where ever they might be found. The biggest obstacle to his grand design was money, vast sums of money, not only for the development of the land but for a bridge across the First Narrows as well. One without the other would be impractical. There were forests of trees growing in British Columbia but among the many species to be found the money tree was not one of them. In 1927 he packed his family off to England where he set up an investment house in London's Rabbit Lane, and there, in the capital of world finance, he began to preach the glories of British Columbia, and in particular, his faith in the slopes of Hollyburn Ridge.

At home, Councillor J.T. Watt, a real estate man by profession, was busy thumping the drum on behalf of the municipality. He had told the **West Van. News**, in its first edition the year before, that West Vancouver's "growth was phenomenal and remarkable," adding that "the population has increased five or six times in as many years" and, in a comment, the editor stated one thing was lacking: an apartment house. There was, he said, "a golden opportunity in West Vancouver for the builder or capitalist awaiting," a remark which planted the seed of action in the mind of Charles Appleton who, in 1926, built the municipality's first apartment, a two-storey and basement building on the site of the present Municipal Hall. In this Chronicle we have listed several "Fathers" and so Mr. Appleton's name must be entered into the roster as the "Father of Apartments" in West Vancouver.

At the same time Appleton Court became a landmark, the Scottish Society, in honor of the Diamond Jubilee of the Canadian Confederation, erected a landmark that was to remain for many years. In 1927 the Capilano River, which forms the eastern boundary of the municipality, ran as free as the whims of nature had decreed from the beginning of time. Its final dash to the sea was unpredictable and it made its own rules. During its annual spring run-off caprice the swollen waters of the Capilano danced as a child of nature through two channels. The eastern channel, though dry for most of the year, became the boundary between the District of North Vancouver and West Vancouver. This double channel had made it necessary to construct two bridges across the river when Marine Drive was built. It was over the eastern channel, now diked off, that the Society erected a sign made of "huge peeled logs" that stood as a "welcome" to West Vancouver as one crossed the "frontier" from east to west.

At the same time as the Scottish Society was busy erecting its sign, the provincial government proclaimed Marine Drive would henceforth be known as the Pacific Highway. It was an arbitrary decision on the part of Victoria and West Vancouver council would have nothing to do with it: Marine Drive it had always been, and Marine Drive it would remain. Period. The name Pacific Highway was never heard of again.

In December, 1927, another landmark made its appearance with the opening of West Vancouver High School at Inglewood School, with F.J. Patterson as principal. Until it closed in 1978 to become a Y.M.C.A. centre, the halls of Inglewood had echoed to the footsteps of many young people who would, in the passage of time, become distinguished scientists, business leaders, doctors,

178

university professors, entertainers, politicians, and, above all, good citizens.

For those students who lived at West Bay there was a bit of confusion as to the name of the place they called home. They said they lived at West Bay, but the Post Office Department in Ottawa thought differently and established a post office in the Black Cat store called Wadsley, and everybody was hopping mad about it. A petition was taken up to have the post office keep the old and established name, and a person signing himself "Old Ebor" fired off a letter of complaint to the **West Van. News**, which appeared on November 28, 1928. He said anybody from Yorkshire would recognize the name and would not be amused. The only Wadsley he could find in any gazetteer he had checked was Wadsley Mental Asylum at Wadsley Bridge near Sheffield. "I would like to live at West Bay," he wrote, "but would never have my English mail addressed to Wadsley." As far as the Post Office Department was concerned, they stuck to their guns but few residents of West Bay ever said they lived in Wadsley.

The day after "Old Ebor" had his letter published, a rumor of long-standing was confirmed by the **Pacific Great Eastern Railway**. The line, which had been in trouble ever since it was created by Sir Richard McBride in 1912, had been taken over from Foley, Welch & Stewart on February 22, 1918, by the provincial government, and now figures showed it was costing the taxpayers of British Columbia $300,000 a year to operate the North Shore branch. At noon on November 29, 1928 trains stopped running, but the company made it clear they were not abandoning the line. The company then asked for a release from its contract with the municipality and offered to contribute $105,000 toward road construction in West Vancouver which would be met by a $140,000 grant from the provincial government under its Secondary Highways Classification Scheme.

There was one thing that West Vancouver could feel proud about during the 1920s and that was its financial position and the fact that the careful watch on spending had kept things in line. As far back as 1922, at least, that had been the policy. In his inaugural address that year, Reeve V.V. Vinson had said, "Our finances should be guarded and every effort made to keep well within our limits. . . . There is so much that this district requires for its development that in our anxiety to meet these requirements we may overstep our finances and in doing so do our

179

district more harm than good, and my advice is: Look before you leap.''

Reeve Sydney Gisby, on January 24, 1924 had the same warning for his councillors: ''...every member of Council should adopt the policy of keeping the expenditures of the municipality within its income.''

Again, in 1925, Reeve Gisby declared: ''So far as finances are concerned, you are in the most fortunate position of any Council since Incorporation, of commencing your duties with a surplus in the Sinking Fund account and with no bank overdraft, and it is my earnest wish that you maintain that good financial position that we are in, but in order to do so, you will have to keep expenditures within your income.''

It fell to Reeve V.V. Vinson and his council to feel the impact of that most fearful day for the world, Tuesday, October 29, 1929, the day which came to be known as Black Tuesday when the stock markets crashed to usher in the Great Depression. It was fortunate that West Vancouver's finances were in good order. Even at that, watchful diligence of the ledger books was more vital now than it had been before. When J.B. Leyland assumed the office of reeve in January, 1930, he demanded the ''utmost economy must be used in all departmental expenditures, and estimates of revenue should be conservative and monies spent for essentials only until such time as the anticipated revenues are reasonably assured. In this policy of economy there is no intention of prejudicing future developments, but rather an endeavor to improve our financial status before twelve months have passed.''

Perhaps Mr. Leyland had an inkling into what A.J.T. Taylor was up to in London. Ever since he had set up his investment office in Rabbit Lane, A.J.T., like Richard the Lion Heart, had been on a crusade to attract British investors to his promised land, the flanks of Hollyburn Ridge. His persuasive talk had already attracted the attention of two very influential London financiers, W.S. Eyre and the Right Honorable Lord Southborough, PC, GCB, GCMG, GCVO, KCSI, who represented the Iveagh Trust, the richly-endowed investment fund established by the Guinness Brewing Company. It was His Lordship who brought the Earl of Iveagh, a member of the family who had control of the Guinness brewing empire, and his two brothers, the Honorable Arthur Guinness and Lord Moyne, into the picture. A package was put together, but before anything was signed, Mr. Eyre wanted to make a personal inspection of the lands on Hollyburn Ridge. With A.J.T. Taylor he boarded a West Vancouver ferry, and quickly realized that the Taylor vision was a practical one.

Prior to the British taking an interest in the 4,700 acres of tax sale land on Hollyburn Ridge, several other would-be developers had appeared on the scene, and among them were Colonel Albert Whyte, who had lost his Whytecliffe properties during the pre-war depression, and Pat Burns, the Calgary meat processor. Senator Burns nearly reached an agreement with the municipality over the property, as the then municipal solicitor, Gordon Robson, told archivist Rupert Harrison:

"The agreement culminated in an agreement between his lawyer, Mr. [Arthur] McEvoy, and myself. It covered a certain area which included the site of the present golf course among other acreages. After the two solicitors had agreed to the agreement, Mr. Burns refused to sign it, I believe because he was advised that he was too old at that time to enter into such an agreement. I was sent to Calgary by the council to interview Mr. Burns as to the reason for not signing it. When I arrived there he didn't want to see me, and kept putting it off, day after day, even sending me for a ride down to the Turner Valley oil fields to kill time. Finally, I suppose, he thought, 'I'll get rid of this pest', so I had an interview with Mr. Burns in person, and he still re-iterated his decision not to sign the agreement. I brashly suggested to him that out West we had always believed that Patrick's word was as good as his bond. He flushed, but made no comment. However, when I returned empty-handed Mr. Burns paid my fees and all my expenses so the trip didn't cost the municipality anything... It was fortunate for the Municipality that this agreement fell through because otherwise there would have been no British Pacific Properties agreement and no First Narrows Bridge."

Mr. Robson was at an important meeting between Reeve Leyland, Councillor William Dickinson, Mr. Taylor and Mr. Eyres, whom he described as being "one of the most charming men I ever met. He had no sides. He was just a friendly human being."

"In discussing the matter," Mr. Robson recalled, "the Guinness man had referred to the fact that they intended to construct a golf course and Reeve Leyland told him 'If you are not

181

prepared to spend more than a million dollars on the Club House and Golf Course we are not interested in that phase of the matter.' He retired to consider his position and in the meantime, the three of us were all shaking, wondering what was going to happen. He came out and said he was prepared to accept Reeve Leyland's conditions. He then wanted to go over more of the property. We said that we would see he was guided around. He refused. He said that he wanted to see it by himself. So he went. Their deal called for a certain number of acres and we didn't have title to meet that much land. So we went to the Provincial Government and got them to give us, at no cost to the municipality, certain acreage which, together with what we had, made up the required acreage.''

A company, known as the British Pacific Properties Limited was formed, and in 1931 it acquired the necessary land. In truth, now, the British had come!

A much humbler development was also taking place at Horseshoe Bay, with the arrival in 1931 of Dan Sewell. Tom Sewell tells the story:

''In winter Horseshoe Bay rolled up its sidewalks and just a few pioneer families lived there year-round. A waterfront property had caught Dan Sewell's eye, the only one with a private beach. It was owned by a Mr. Thorpe who had acquired the property from the well-known Roedde family, printers from Vancouver, who had built their summer home there. Also sitting on the site was a lodge which Mr. Thorpe had moved onto his property from its former location on Bay Street where Troll's now stands. Money was short, but Mr. Thorpe was willing to sell. A deal was made. Without further ado, Dan moved his family into the former Roedde summer home and renamed the relocated building Whytecliff Lodge... Whytecliff Lodge offered visitors accommodation upstairs, a dining room catered by Eva Sewell on the main floor and the convenience of a store.''

'Those were lean years,' Tom recalls. 'We started business in a primitive way. We knew how to drive nails, so between us we built our first floats and boats and went into the marina and inn-keeping business.'

''Always willing to try something new, Dan started to experiment with a new way to catch salmon, by using a herring strip as bait on a rod and line. This was unheard of as all saltwater fishing to that time had been done by trolling from a rowboat with plugs and spoons tied to simple hand-held lines of strong twine. When a fish bit, the fisherman simply wound the string onto a wooden holder and hauled in his catch. Particularly strong opposition came from the plug and spoon suppliers, who saw a threat to their business and claimed that herring strip would bring unwanted dogfish and cod into prime salmon fishing grounds. Dan persevered and their fears were unfounded. Casting for salmon with rod, line and herring strip quickly caught on. Within a short period of time, traffic to Sewell's became heavier and Dan was credited with introducing the method to British Columbia waters.

"Dan's original rental 'fleet' of clinker boats was built of cedar and copied from designs of boats he liked. Heavy to row, these boats had the disadvantage of not being able to take their occupants very far out into the Sound. Dan Sewell was about to try another first. In 1933 he took a Briggs and Stratton engine, the type which was being used in household appliances such as washing machines at the time, and installed it in one of his boats. The first 3/4-horsepower, air-cooled 'putt-putt' was born. Manufacturer Stratton even came all the way from Milwaukee to have a look. So here was former building contractor Dan Sewell with one of the first power boat and sports fishing operations on the coast. In the highly competitive rental and fishing market which stretched right the way out from Vancouver, along West Vancouver's shoreline, the word soon got around. News of the excellent fishing at Sewell's spread across North America like wildfire through the thriving vaudeville theatre in Vancouver. Top-billed entertainers would play Vancouver by night on one of their tours and then motor to Horseshoe Bay to fish during the day. Whether in a dressing room in California, Maine or Florida, these troupers would be reminded that 'if you play Vancouver, be sure to fish at Sewell's.'"

The signing of the agreement between the municipality and the British Pacific Properties, which also called for the building of a bridge across the First Narrows, now popularly called the Lions Gate, after the twin-peaked Lions mountain behind Hollyburn Ridge, did not bring immediate prosperity to West Vancouver. The problems related to the unemployed were causing great concern to all, and although few "tin-canners" from Vancouver made their appearance in the community, there were cases of extreme hardship within the ranks of the citizenry. In June, 1932, a

Welfare Association, chaired by the Rev. F.A. Ramsey, was formed and to its ranks came many dedicated men and women, most of whom were in dire need themselves. When the Co-operative Commonwealth Federation, the C.C.F. Party, was formed in Regina in 1933, one of its first elected members to the British Columbia Legislature was Mrs. Dorothy Steeves who represented the North Shore. She worked tirelessly for her hard-pressed constituents in both North Vancouver and West Vancouver. Christmas in 1932 had all the prospects of being a bleak holiday for those unemployed with children, but the Association canvassed the whole of the municipality for "a toy for every child" and that objective was attained. That Christmas, 153 food hampers were distributed, and by New Year's, it was found an additional seven would be needed. In March, 1933, the Association staged a Poverty Frolic, a repeat of the Christmas dance billed as the Snowball Frolic. Both were successful in raising much needed money. The workless were also encouraged to set-up home gardens and free seed was distributed.

When Reeve Leyland opened his 1932 term of office on January 21, he told his council: "During the past year municipal bodies throughout the country have faced a serious situation, caused by business depression and unemployment, and the financial horizon today is still such as would only justify the most careful consideration and economy in all expenditures... We find that West Vancouver occupies an enviable position among municipalities of this province, and this claim can only be maintained by a continuation of the careful policy adopted by the 1931 council." Again, a year later addressing a new council, Mr. Leyland pointed out "In view of the increasing cost of social services, the possibility of further reductions in government grants, and the cost of unemployment, the greatest economy must be exercised if we are to avoid increases in taxation if we are to balance our budget. May I suggest that the Capital and Maintenance expenditures in revenue producing departments be curtailed as much as possible in order that tax-payers may receive as much benefit as possible from these revenues?"

Although no miracle had occurred, and the problems of the unemployed still loomed like a bad dream that wouldn't go away, Reeve Leyland, in 1934, made an inaugural address to council that was not filled with doom and gloom.

"Notwithstanding the difficult times through which we have

184

passed," he said, "West Vancouver has progressed rapidly during the last few years, and our own progressiveness will in itself bring with it many serious problems. These problems can be handled satisfactorily by careful planning and far-sighted vision on the part of council and it is certain to be, if the same enthusiasm and co-operation that has existed in the past is continued in the future. We have reason to maintain our faith in the destiny of this municipality as becoming one of the most attractive residential areas in Canada."

There are a lot of things to remember about those trying Great Depression years in West Vancouver. Some of the things that were going on might well have been consigned to the realm of mere trivia if it were not for the fact that they fit into a mosaic of what it was like in those days, and thus, they have earned their way into this Chronicle.

Take Fridays, for instance. It seemed that just about every cat in town could read the calendar and would be waiting on a corner for "John" to deposit his bamboo pole with its two baskets of fish, and then trot off to sell his wares. "John", of course, was the Chinese fish peddlar and his name probably wasn't John at all, but that didn't make any difference: all Chinese were called "John". At Christmas he would leave a small parcel of ginger with his customers, and at Easter the housewife would look forward to a lily bulb, and as for the cats, "John" never failed to have a supply of fish heads for his feline friends. Then there was another "John", the vegetable peddlar who drove a truck so antiquated that it must have been one of the first trucks to come off the Ford assembly line. No one could tell this always-smiling little man that his prices were way out of order, as for example, radishes were five cents a bunch or three for a quarter. Then there were the men who toted whetstones to sharpen household knives; tall, turbanned Sikhs selling cordwood, the milkman on his daily rounds, as well as the baker, the laundryman and the iceman. Every so often a gypsy fortune teller or tinker would arrive in town and age-old stories about them would be dusted off and told to the children, and who can ever forget the heavy acrid smell of carbide lamps as skiers, down from Hollyburn or Westlake ski camps, boarded the Upper Levels bus on Sunday evenings? All these, and many more little vignettes, form part of West Vancouver's passing parade of things past and of things that will never be seen again.

Across the span of years since planning and dreaming for a First Narrows bridge began, much has been forgotten or, at best, tucked away in files that have yellowed with age, but thanks to a West Vancouver man, Frank DeWest, a complete history of the bridge was preserved in a souvenir booklet he issued in 1938 upon completion of the span. Mr. DeWest, a Maltese by birth, was an ebullient figure in West Vancouver during the 1930s. During the Second World War, as a photographer for the National Film Board of Canada, he gained fame by being parachuted into Yugoslavia to photograph the partisan leader, Marshal Josep Tito, in a mountain hideway. He is said to have obtained the photos of the almost unknown guerilla chief by challenging him to a game of chess. If DeWest won, then the photographs would be taken if however, Tito won, then photographer DeWest would go away empty-handed. Tito lost through what chess players recognize as a three or four move sucker play, and the world got its first look at the man who was defying the German military machine. Whether that story is true or not, it can be said that Frank DeWest told it with a twinkle in his eye, but then, that twinkle was always there. As far as the company was concerned, his story of the building of the Lions Gate Bridge was "authorized", and this is spelled out on the cover of his twenty-five-cent souvenir booklet.

Mr. DeWest gives credit to James Ollason, the municipal clerk for West Vancouver, as doing "the most to get the bridge started."

"In 1926, Mr. James Ollafson (sic), the municipal clerk of West Vancouver, impressed with the large amount of property which had reverted to the municipality for non-payment of taxes (subsequent to the real estate boom and the Great War) endeavoured to persuade eastern interests to take some two millions of dollars of tax sale lands in return for the construction of a bridge. Mr. David Morgan, then reeve of West Vancouver, took the idea to Mayor L.D. Taylor, the Mayor of the City of Vancouver, endeavouring to gain his support for the idea. In course of time the idea came to the notice of Mr. A.J.T. Taylor...."

Now for Mr. DeWest's full story of the building of the Lions Gate Bridge, one of the major stepping stones in making West Vancouver a place of excellence.

"For some four years or more, Messrs. Monsarrat & Pratley, of Montreal, had been engaged on the construction of a suspen-

186

sion bridge over the St. Lawrence River, between the North Shore and the Island of Orleans, some five miles below Quebec. This firm was therefore invited to submit a practical scheme for the bridging of the First Narrows. The requirements of the Orleans bridge demanded an unobstructed fairway of at least 600 feet, with minimum headroom of 106 feet at high tide. The bridge, 20 feet wide with two five-foot sidewalks, is the first long span suspension bridge to be entirely designed, fabricated and erected in the Dominion of Canada. It was opened to traffic on July 6th, 1935. Tentative plans for a practical scheme to bridge the First Narrows, consisting of a proposed 1,500 foot span with a 29-foot roadway designed to carry three lanes of traffic were speedily submitted to the authorities concerned. On October 27th, 1933, the joint Vancouver City Council and Parks Board Committee gave the project its initial approval. Publication of these plans in the daily newspapers was the signal for a storm of criticism. 'The Bridge was not wide enough.' 'There was insufficient clearance between high water and the bottom of the bridge.' 'The span should be widened to 1,800 feet,' etc. On November 9th, 1933, Vancouver City Council was the scene of a bitter debate in which the chief point of contention was that the city should not give its approval to any structure unless it was shown beyond all possible doubt that there would be no hindrance or limitation to free passage of shipping in and out of Port. Other Aldermen observed that the Federal Authorities were just as anxious as City Administrators to preserve the Port and that they would not do anything to hinder the entrance, pointing out that in the final analysis, final approval of dimensions rested with Ottawa.

"On November 10th, 1933, a plebiscite was ordered by the Vancouver City Council, the Council ratifying the Bridge Agreement by ten votes to two. Opposition from the Board of Trade came in the form of a report, on November 16th, 1933, stating that it was considered desirable that the bridge be an 1,800-foot span. The memorandum of Agreement between the Bridge Company and the Local Administrative authorities was published on December 1st, 1933, while on December 5th one of the City's Aldermen said that there was no necessity of a Bridge at the present time, it being detrimental to the City's interests, and so the controversy raged. Practically every issue of the newspapers at that time, carried protests of one sort or another against the

187

Bridge. The Citizens of Vancouver had their say at the polling booths on December 14th, 1933. A practically unanimous shout of approval, from every section of the City, gave a majority of 17,806 in favor of the Bridge, a total of 7,615 voters voting against the project.

"Approval of the Agreement on behalf of the Citizens of the North Shore quickly followed and the project was then submitted to the Dominion Government in Ottawa for their approval. The proposition still continued to meet with the most violent opposition on the part of certain interests, chiefly on the possible effect on navigation of the First Narrows, due to pier foundations, etc., causing obstructions to be formed in the channel. Ottawa moved slowly and on June 6th, 1934, ordered a tidal survey of the Narrows which was immediately undertaken. As a result, the Dominion Authorities at Ottawa intimated on August 23rd, 1934, that they would approve the scheme if the span was lengthened. On August 30, 1934, the Bridge Company issued a statement that they would not lengthen the Bridge. On September 29th, 1933, one of the newspapers published a table showing the tonnage and height of funnels and masts of ships with a mast height exceeding 180 feet. Of these the **Majestic** proved to be the tallest with a mast height of 228 feet. The published statement quoted Mr. Edward Beatty's suggestion of 220 feet as suitable clearance and Sir Alexander Gibb was said to consider a height of 170 feet as the minimum. Attention was drawn to the fact the United States War Department had set the clearance for the San Francisco Bridge at 214 feet. The mast of the **Empress of Britain** was said to be 208 feet.

"Controversy continued in intermittent bursts for the following two and a half years or so, until April 30th, 1936, when the design was approved by order of the Governor-General-in-Council. On July 6th, 1936, Messrs. Boyles Bros. of Vancouver, having received a contract for the boring of test holes, commenced work on the Stanley Park side to determine the suitability of the substratum for the foundations of the Anchor Pier. Four holes were also bored in the bed of the Narrows to test the foundations for the south channel pier. On August 13th, 1936, a civic banquet was held in the auditorium of the Inglewood High School in West Vancouver at which Mr. A.J.T. Taylor...informed the citizens that if all went well, the bridge would be open to traffic two years from that day, and on August 27, 1936, Messrs. Stuart

Cameron, of Vancouver, were awarded a contract for the construction of the bridge piers and roads, etc., through Stanley Park.

"On September 25th, 1936, the last of the legal difficulties faced by the bridge company was eliminated by the passing by the Vancouver Parks Board commissioners of a number of resolutions to meet the technicalities required by the British interests who were constructing the bridge. These had already been passed by the other authorities concerned. On September 29th an order was passed by the Governor-General-in-Council permitting the bridge company to extend the length of the span fifty feet northwards in place of the 1,500 foot span called for in the original plans. It is worthy of mention that this is the only major alteration in the bridge plan, as originally proposed in 1933, which speaks volumes for the thorough manner in which the original plans were drawn up by the designing and supervising engineers, Messrs. Monsarrat & Pratley of Montreal, and Major W.G. Swan of Vancouver who acted as associate.

"The contract for the building of the steel superstructure was signed in Montreal on January 22nd, 1937. This contract, which provided for the supply of 10,000 tons of steel, was shared by the Dominion Bridge Company and the Hamilton Bridge Company of Hamilton. The total cost of the bridge was estimated at $6,000,000, which sum was to be furnished by the bridge company in return for the privilege of collecting tolls over a fifty year period. At the expiration of which time, local authorities would be permitted to purchase the structure if they so desired. July 7th, 1936, marked the turning of the first sod. Actual work of clearing the right-of-way through Stanley park commenced on March 31st, 1937 when a gang of men commenced clearing a 60-foot wide right-of-way. In all, the work called for the clearing of a total of 10 acres of forest, care being taken to preserve as much of the larger and finer timber as possible. . . . On April 15th, 1937, Mr. W.F. Way, field superintendent for the Stuart Cameron Company, had some thirty men and a floating derrick engaged in the work of driving piles for cribwork, etc., of the south pier. Controversy had not yet ceased, however, for on May 22nd, 1937 the First Narrows Bridge Company asked the Vancouver City Council to consent to a minor change in specifications. The company wished to save money by not facing the piers of the bridge with granite, the reason being that in the comparatively mild climate of Vancouver ice in any quantity was practically unknown, and the granite protection could, therefore, be dispensed with. The company offered to expend the money thus saved on various improvements of the original design and, in addition, to give Vancouver Parks Board the sum of $25,000 for the improvement of roads in Stanley Park. A further storm of protest on the part of interested parties caused this offer to be withdrawn, but on June 2nd, having in mind the assistance given by the citizens as a whole of West Vancouver and Vancouver city, the bridge company offered to construct a plaza gratuitously.

"On June 24th, 1937 a slight jar and a few bubbles on the water was all that marked the explosion of six charges of dynamite on the floor of the Narrows. These charges were exploded to level off the floor preparatory to the setting of the caissons. July 9th, 1937 marked the delivery of the first steel to be used on the bridge project, when a steel cutting edge for the caisson was delivered on the North Shore. Work proceeded under ideal conditions, 196 men being engaged on July 23rd, 1937, when Messrs. Stuart Cameron commenced the pouring of concrete in the caissons of the north pier. Meanwhile, the caissons for the south main pier were being set in 40 feet of water and on September 29th the work of sealing these caissons, preparatory to pumping out the water, was commenced. The bridge contractors were exceptionally fortunate. Many hungry "sand hogs" were watching the work with gradually diminishing hopes, as it was found that the work on both piers could be completed without the use of compression chambers, air locks and compressors, usually indispensable from a work of this nature. Instead, the caissons were sealed, pumped dry the foundations proved to be solid and the piers constructed in excellent time, without an accident or hitch of any description. Indeed, the only fatal accident on the foundation work of the bridge was due to a cave-in on the south anchor pier when a mucker, by name Lester Thorstad, was crushed by falling debris in the anchor pit. . . . The first unit for the steel work of the north viaduct was erected on November 26th, 1937.

"Under the supervision of Mr. James Robertson, chief engineer, and Mr. E.E. Davis, erection superintendent, erection of steelwork for the south main pier commenced on February 2nd, 1938, when workmen of the Dominion Bridge Company placed the all-welded tower shoes in position. These present a notable departure from the usual type of cast steel pedestals in that they are built up entirely of steel slabs welded together. Each pedestal rests on a double layer of heavily painted ten and a half ounce canvass and is anchored to the pier by twenty-eight bolts. Workers and engineers are said to have placed all their small change, amounting to 35 cents, below the foot of the first steel. (Publishers Note: This about sums up the position of the rest of us.). There it will remain until the bridge is dismantled. Mr. J.W. Roland was the resident engineer and Mr. R.S. Banks, engineer for the superstructure.

"By the middle of April, 1938, steel work on both towers was finished, and preparations were under way for the stringing of the catwalk cables. For the first time in the recorded history of the Narrows, traffic was held up on Monday morning, May 2nd, 1938, for one hour only, while a heavily laden scow paid out the cables across the Narrows. The cables were hoisted to the top of each of the towers, and anchored at both ends in such a manner as to be three feet below the main cables of the span. The **Loyal Chinook,** a fish packer, with a launch in tow, were the first craft to pass below the cables. The work of stringing the catwalk cables was completed on the morning of May 3rd. Each cable weighed eight tons, with four cables to each catwalk. The catwalk of clear British Columbia spruce was rapidly slid, section by section, into position on the cables, and the first man was reported to have walked across the Narrows on Tuesday, May 11th, 1938. With the completion of the catwalk, no time was lost in the stringing of 122 strands, built up to form the main suspension cables of the bridge, which commenced on June 1st.

"Before continuing with the description of the remainder of the structure, it may be of interest to describe the pre-stressing of the cables. In a structure of this description, the various component parts must be up to pre-determined strength to do the work which is expected of them. The main cables are each of sixty-one prefabricated strands of forty-seven wires each, of sizes appropriate. The strands are one and seven-sixteenths of an inch in diameter and 3,391 feet long, the longest prefabricated strands ever made, the wire being supplied by Messrs. John A. Roebling's Sons & Company Limited. Prestressing of the 122 ropes used in the two main cables was carried out in the plant of the Dominion Bridge Company, Montreal, the only plant of its kind in the Dominion of Canada. It is interesting to note that it was first used for the pre-stressing of the counterweight ropes of the recently reconstructed Second Narrows Bridge. Each rope is finished to a length in excess of the final length of the strand in place. One end is then fixed to an anchor block at the end of a long table, the other end being fixed to a hydraulic ram which exerts a pull on the rope of at least one-half of the specified ultimate strength of the rope. The rope is then measured and the necessary reference points established on the rope for use by the engineers during erection. Pre-stressing was also carried out on the suspender ropes. In all, no less than 11,500 separate tests were made to ensure that the cables were flawless and capable of carrying the designated weight.

"On each side of the bridge, two carefully calibrated guide strands measured with more than ordinary care during the pre-stressing process, were laid and then checked by a force of thirteen instrument men. Five transits, a level and specially made level rods were employed for two hours in the early morning to check the levels of the cables with the previously prepared charts. After the necessary small adjustments were made, the survey was repeated, as a check, the following morning. Vancouver's ideal climate enabled the work to be completed in two days. It may be of interest to state here that there is an error of three eighths of an inch in the 1,550 foot length of the main span. Once the guide strands had been set, adjustment of the other strands was simple. The erection of these cables is believed to constitute one more world record, on a job where record-breaking seems to have been part of the ordinary day's work. As weight was hung from the completed cables, the cables sagged. To compensate, adjustment of catwalk cables therefore became necessary to keep them lower than the main cables. The next process was the assembly of cable bands and suspender ropes, followed by the erection of the Warren-type stiffening truss from scows in the Narrows without interruption to traffic of any description. This truss is used to give rigidity to the suspended structures. Sway is prevented by the use of lateral X-type sway bracing beneath the road bed.

"Longitudinal steel stringers, carried on lateral floor beams, four feet deep, carry the road deck. Here another interesting departure is made from conventional practice. Following its employment on the Island of Orleans bridge, the engineers determined on the use of what is known as the "teegrid" slab of composite steel and concrete construction, in which welded connections are used throughout, resulting in a saving in weight of approximately thirty pounds per square foot of road section, and a consequent saving in weight of towers, cables and trusses and a corresponding relief of the anchorage pull. The usual type of expansion detail when provision has to be made for temperature movements of long spans, is by the use of expansion fingers, somewhat like the teeth of a comb, one such comb being attached to either side of the joint with the teeth meshing between each other, thus providing a continuous surface regardless of the temperature, except for narrow longitudinal slits. This type is used on the Lions Gate Bridge, with the improvement that the fingers are slightly tapered to prevent their becoming clogged with snow or debris.

"The cables are anchored to large blocks of concrete. The North anchor pier, founded on gravel, is of the gravity type built to withstand a maximum cable pull of about 6,300 tons, the weight of the pier being in the neighborhood of 19,000 tons. The southern anchor pier is wedgeshaped, sunk forty feet deep in hard boulder clay, and weighs approximately 15,000 tons. This clay is so solid that no revetment work was necesary during construction. The total length of the span is 1,550 feet between the towers and for the central 200 feet there is a clearance of 200 feet above the water, under all conditions of tide, temperature and loading. The side spans are 614 feet long. On the North Shore approach there is a viaduct of 2,196 feet, carried on twenty-five deck plate girder spans ranging in length from eighty-one feet six inches to 123 feet. Four rigid frame towers render longitudinal stability, and on these the spans are shorter being of 42 feet and fifty-five feet six inches respectively. The contract for lighting was awarded to the C.H.E. Williams Company of Vancouver. This was to be of the sodium vapor type, as installed on the Pattullo Bridge in New Westminster. Mercury lamps are installed on the approach roadways.

"Erection of the First Narrows Bridge has obscured the view of the signal station on Prospect Point. It was, accordingly, made mandatory on the bridge company to provide a new signal station and a house for the signalman. The new signal station is constructed across, and in the centre of the bridge. To conform with international aircraft regulations the cables and suspenders have been painted International Orange, the steelwork being an an attractive olive green.

"Access to the north approach of the bridge from Marine Drive is gained by means of a modified 'clover-leaf' grade separation, the only one of its kind in western Canada. By its use traffic in either direction is enabled to gain access to, or from, the bridge without obstructing the normal flow of traffic. Tollbooths for vehicles and pedestrians are erected on south (sic) end of the bridge. The attractive woven wire fencing of the bridge was manufactured in Vancouver by the B.C. Anchor Fence Company Limited.

"The Stanley Park driveway, following a wide, sweeping curve through the forest to the west of Beaver Lake, is landscaped by the Anglo-Construction Co. Ltd., to blend with the natural beauty. Against the mountains of the North Shore rise the twin cable towers, with Charles Marega's couchant lions at the base of massive pylons, set in a vista of green lawns and dwarf shrubs, the whole forming a grand approach to the south end of the bridge."

On the morning of Saturday, November 11, 1938, crowds gathered at each end of the new bridge to see who would be the first to cross, and the honor fell to R.F. Hearns, of Caulfeild, who made the first north to south crossing. Now all that remained to be done was to have it officially opened by Their Majesties King George VI and Queen Elizabeth.

West Vancouver was in a high state of expectancy in May, 1939, with the prospect the Royal couple would drive through the municipality, but at the last moment, that leg of the trip was cancelled. Instead, every one milled around the Marine Drive approach as the King and Queen came down from tea at the guest house on the British Pacific Properties and slowly drove by as the Scouts, Cubs, Guides and Brownies, and the host of others who lined the bridge approaches cheered wildly.

At the south end of the bridge, a ceremonial ribbon was cut and a plaque unveiled. The long-sought First Narrows Bridge was now a reality.

The bridge had cost precisely $5,873,837.17 to build, and more vast sums of money were being poured into such things as land clearing, road building, and the eighteen-hole championship golf course which was being laid out on the old Hadden Hall site. All this meant jobs for hundreds of men who had almost forgotten what a pay cheque looked like. The bad times appeared, at long last, to be over.

In September, 1938, the man with the vision, A.J.T. Taylor, resigned from the company and the project he had helped to bring to fruition. He now built a fine home for himself and his family at Kew Beach and prepared to tackle new fields.

The West Vancouver Schools Band in 1930. In 1933 Arthur Delamont, leader of the world famous Kitsilano School Band, became conductor of the local band. Subsequently, over the years, several members graduated to and toured with the "Kits" Band.
Back Row L to R: Ted Elfstrom, Bill Parker, Tom Timbrell, Jack Masterman, Tom Back.
2nd Row L to R: Frank Beamish, Wilbert Phillips, Walter Parker, John Parker, Ken Vernon, John Wright, Bob Kinloch.
3rd Row L to R: Ken McMillan, Garnet (Nick) Williamson, Hugh Montgomery, Edith White, Jack Howdle, Bob McCartney, Doug Denniston, Joan Matthews.
4th Row L to R: Bill Harker, Jim Turner, Albert McLeod, Bill McMillan, Dick Lester, Marjorie Rivers, Marjorie Crawford, Jack Watson.
Front Row L to R: Mr. J.E. Condon (Band Organizer), Rupert Harrison, Jack Mercer, Doug Lycett, Tom Hicklenton, Ross Minions, Jim McDonald, Dorothy Dickinson, Joyce Dickinson, Mr. Jordan (Band Master). (WVMA)

Long since gone from the scene is the old Dundarave School. The site is now occupied by Altamont Private Hospital. (WVML)

West Vancouver was excited when the brick Hollyburn post office was opened in 1936. It has been replaced by another on the site of the old Hollyburn Pavilion (WVMA), and a new building occupied by the Royal Bank will open in January 1987.

Dan Sewell, the man who made Horseshoe Bay famous. (PP)

Horseshoe Bay Hotel and docks, about 1936. (VPL)

Signing the agreement leading to the construction of the Lions Gate Bridge. At a council meeting on May 4, 1934 were left to right, James Duncan, municipal engineer; Councillor Lance Garthorne, Councillor William Dickinson; John Anderson, secretary treasurer of First Narrows Bridge Co. Ltd.; Reeve J.B. Leyland; William Herrin, municipal clerk; Councillor Robert Fiddes; Councillor Gerald D. Elgar. Standing, R.P. Stockton, solicitor for the Bridge company, and R. Gordon Robson, municipal solicitor. (WVMA)

A.J.T. Taylor, the genius behind the British Pacific Properties. (BPP)

Lord Southborough made the British Pacific Properties become a reality. (BPP)

*A.J.T. Taylor's palatial Kew House at Kew Beach, a far cry from the spot where "Holy Joe" built his ill-fated boat **Holy Terror**. (VPL)*

Building the north approach to the Lions Gate Bridge. (NS)

West Vancouver ferry passengers got this view of construction of the south foundation of the Lions Gate Bridge. (NS)

201

Smiling Queen Elizabeth and King George VI as they pass over the Lions Gate Bridge for official opening ceremonies in May, 1939. (NS)

Eagle Harbor. Charlie Smith's coffee shop, rowboats rental and swimming/diving float. (DM)

Chapter Eight

A STEP TOWARDS EXCELLENCE

In the Year of Our Lord 1889 a certain Douglas Sladen visited the very young Vancouver and six years later he published a book describing a "pilgrimage along the Queen's Highway to the East from Halifax in Nova Scotia to Victoria in Vancouver's Island". It is a highly improbable account, and one almost feels he must have met the Holy Terror of Kew Beach during one of his notable pub crawls. We enter this item into the Chronicle, because Mr. Sladen's remarks are included in a brochure issued by Capilano Estates, the official name of the British Pacific Properties development.

"I fancy that I can see Vancouver where her hour has come. . . ." he wrote. "Many of the wealthy prefer to have villas. . .on the foothills of the grand mountains which line the north side of Burrard Inlet—the north side made beautiful. . .and planted with beautiful maples whose carmine leaves in the fall show up gloriously against the dark spruce and cedar of the original forests. . ."

The **Canadian Pacific Railway** would have been the last to agree with Mr Sladen's prediction as they were jealously guarding their Shaughnessy Heights residential area. It was where the wealthy were going to have their villas, and nowhere else. This argument was one that was used, ever so softly, mind you, but just the same *forcefully*, by the railway company in opposing the building of the Lions Gate Bridge. If that bridge were built, the C.P.R. argued, it would open the way for a rival prestigious residential area, and the plans drawn up by Olmstead Brothers of Brooklynn, Massachusetts, with its golf course, polo field and large lots, indeed, provided such a threat. By 1937 lots in the Capilano Estates were on sale, with prices averaging $5,600 for each lot. This compared with the $4,000 price tag on the property in the University of British Columbia Endowment Lands and $1,000 being asked for "view property" in West Vancouver.

Robert W. Keyserlingk, who was manager of the Estates, and later general manager of British United Press, allowed his pen to run free and honeyed as he turned out sales promotion brochures. (The writer used to work for BUP, and if a story like the one that follows was sent over **his** newswire there would have been a memo from "RWK " and goodbye to the $25 a week job).

"Today those far-sighted men who planned and worked to open up for human habitation what five years ago was still virgin forest are ready to let a community arise, where natural beauty and healthful climate are coupled with all the practical advantages of proximity to a large city. 'Other residential communities have grown haphazardly, as the need developed,' writes one newspaper. 'This one was built for the future, with meticulous care and with not one single detail of future requirement overlooked. It stands in the midst of a forest in an area where the rumble of machinery in factories and their smoking stacks **are forever banned**.' Not until all preparations were completed, all roads built, avenues planted, lawns laid and shrubs set out was any house to be erected. The years of preparation required to create this ideal location for homes were contributions to a future community. Here the hand of man, the art of the builder, will not mar but mingle with, the beauties with which Nature has so richly endowed this spot. It would have been impossible to assure this if building had started before the whole land was landscaped and the locations made ready.

"Today among the tall timbers left standing on each plot the founder of a home can create his own garden, retaining as much or as little of the virgin growth as will fit in best with his plans and ideas, without disturbing the whole appearance. Gently rising from sea level the land stretches up the southern slopes of the mountains facing Vancouver to an elevation of 1,500 feet. Wide roads reach every plot and their careful grading makes it possible to drive to the highest point on the Estates without ever changing gear. Behind the Estates, like a natural background, rise the steeper slopes of the Coast Range— those beautiful hilltops which have become landmarks of Burrard Inlet, the Lions, Hollyburn and Grouse. The view on the other three sides roams over stretches of water to varying but equally entrancing views.

"Over the waters of Burrard Inlet, the first rays of the morning sun emerge on our East, lightening up the Harbour of Vancouver and awakening the busy port to the activity of its world-wide trade. As the riches of the West pour into this port, ships from every land come to take the wealth of Canada to the markets of the world. As one gazes from the slopes of the Capilano Estates the still pale rays of the morning sun dissipate the morning mist. The whole panorama of a world port, the romance of those who go down to the sea in ships, the vastness of man's enterprise and hopes, the planning for the future and the security inherent in the gift of Providence—natural advantages—greet one. The sun travels on brightening up the southern slope on which the Capilano Estates is situated. To the south of us we look over the Lions Gate where the majestic span of the largest suspension bridge in the British Empire rises to link the Estates with the city. We let our gaze roam further over acres of natural beauty, the tall virgin timber of Stanley Park. Through them a wide avenue leads up to the bridge and into the heart of the City of Vancouver. We can see across the tops of the trees of Stanley Park, over English Bay to the high peninsula of Point Grey where the white buildings of the University stand out against the blue sky. If we go to the higher points of the Estates we can see even beyond to where the mighty Fraser River pours its waters into the Gulf of Georgia.

"Let us follow the sun as it tinges the sky with varying shades of red in its descent into the waters of the Gulf of Georgia. The western view across the waters of the Gulf opens up a vista of incomparable beauty. We see the Islands of the Gulf stand out in dark contrast against the evening sky. Beyond we see the outlines of Vancouver Island rising in the distance. As the sun disappears in the exuberance of color, mountains, sea and islands are obscured and the evening breeze gently whispers through the tall trees around us. It is here that one can now build and establish for one's family the home which in such surroundings becomes a safe anchorage close to Nature's bounty."

Another brochure informs us: "One of the notable attractions, specially from the point of building and protection of view, is that no two lots on the Capilano Estates are similar. Due to the sloping contour of the land the lots have been designed in such

207

a way as to take full advantage of the views by placing each building site sufficiently above the one below. Besides, adjoining lots are also laid out in such a way as to have slightly different shape and size and thus avoid that uniformity and monotony which checker-board planning would offer. The lots range anywhere from a little below an acre to anywhere up to seven acres—the average being around one acre.''

Would-be purchasers were also told about certain restrictions the company had placed on the property, ones which today would be called scandalous. One read ''. . . to ensure a permanent high class residential area throughout the development. . . . No person of Asiatic or African descent (other than servants) may reside on the Estates.'' Another note stated that a first-class Chinese cook, living in, would want $45 to $60 a month, and an experienced maid, living in, can demand $25 to $40 a month, while additional help would cost approximately $15 a month, plus board.

To reach this ''masterpiece of planning'' and the world-famous Capilano golf course, a broad, stately avenue, lined with Japanese cherry trees, was built straight up from Marine Drive, and it was named after A.J.T. Taylor, president of the company. It reached Mount Moyne Square, the nerve centre for the intricate network of roads which serve the area. At Mount Moyne Square, Lord Southborough erected a fountain of Carrera marble depicting a woman and four children. It is now located in the Park Royal Shopping Centre.

All the honeyed words R.W. Keyserlingk could pour out in those late 1930s could not offset the screamings of Adolf Hitler from the Sportzplatz in Berlin and the diplomatic engineering of a one-time wine salesman in Vancouver by the name of Joachim von Ribbentrop, his foreign minister. As Austria and Czechoslovakia fell, Memel on the Baltic was seized, and Poland was being threatened, would-be purchasers of homes in the British Pacific Properties became jittery. Sales were not up to expectation. For the second time since incorporation, the dreams and resources of those seeking a place of excellence were being swallowed up by the threat of war.

Fifteen days before the outbreak of the war in September, 1939, Ottawa ordered the mobilization of three Vancouver militia units, including the 15th Coast Brigade, and a few days later six men from that Brigade were sent to ''occupy'' a position on the north side of the First Narrows, right under the Lions Gate Bridge. Construction soon began of a three-storey cement gun emplacement, while two 12-pounder guns were placed on a gravel spit at the mouth of the Capilano River. By October 6, West Vancouver's mini-fort was completed, and just in time. Two weeks after the guns were mounted, heavy rains flooded the original gun emplacement. At Ambleside Park, eight manually-controlled 18-inch reflector searchlights, said to have come from Niagara Falls, were installed and barracks were erected on "stilts" to prevent tidal flooding. The lights served other purposes than the defence of West Vancouver and surrounding areas from enemy attack. Late at night the soldiers stationed beside the beach would aim their lights at a lovers lane at Prospect Point and then, through binoculars, watch the mad scramble around the parked cars. They also served to confuse the captain of a West Vancouver ferry, who in the late evening fog, mistook the lights of the barracks for the lights of Ambleside pier and drove his ship aground.

Narrows North fort was part of an intricate system of military establishments in the Vancouver area. These included guns at Stanley Park's Ferguson Point, Point Grey and Steveston, and a searchlight and check point at Point Atkinson. Their purpose was detailed by Peter Moogk in his book, **Vancouver Defended**:

"Early in September, 1939, the port of Vancouver had come under the authority of the Royal Canadian Navy and Public Traffic Regulations were issued to control vessels entering or leaving the harbor. On Point Atkinson the navy maintained the Port War Signal Station that received advance warning by radio of major warships and a lookout that identified all inbound naval vessels. From Point Atkinson lighthouse to the tip of Point Grey ran the imaginary "Examination Line" which marked off the harbor area where no unauthorized movement of ships was permitted. A half mile or more to the west of this line were two naval launches known as X-Vics, or examination vessels. A third X-Vic lay a mile off Ferguson Point. These vessels flew a distinctive flag of white and red horizontal bars with a blue border. Incoming merchant ships were required to cut speed when approaching the examination line and to identify themselves to the X-Vics with signal pennants. No private radio transmissions were allowed within the controlled area. Shipowners and shipping agents were expected to inform the naval authorities in advance of expected arrivals and give them the particulars of each vessel. Suspect and unheralded ships were escorted to the examination anchorage situated under the guns of Stanley Park for detailed inspection. When a vessel was cleared for admission into the inner harbor it was informed of the signal of the day and the gun batteries were notified to let it pass. Simpler rules applied to small craft of less than 120-tons displacement. Tugs, fishing boats and pleasure craft that regularly used the port had a recognition number painted on their sides and they were to identify themselves to the Point Atkinson signal station in passing. They then proceeded to a patrol boat in English Bay to obtain clearance to pass the First Narrows.''

There were other signs, too, that the nation was at war. For several years, ferry passengers had seen the **Canadian National Railway's** sleek passenger liner **Prince Robert** tied up beside the West Vancouver ferry dock in Vancouver. Now she was the fully-armed **H.M.C.S. Prince Robert** and due for action on many fronts, including the liberation of Greece and Hong Kong. The great white **Empress** liners were now painted a dull grey with black camouflage stripes painted along their graceful lines, and even familiar coastal ships that plied between Vancouver, Victoria, Nanaimo and up-coast ports, donned a grey mantle. Incoming freighters often displayed guns placed on their sterns, ready for action in case of U-Boat attack.

Even with these visible signs of war, it all seemed to be so very far removed from the peace and quiet of West Vancouver. There were a few inconveniences such as having to go to the post office and fill out National Registration cards, and in a society which was not yet prepared to be regimented, many thought this was an invasion of privacy.

For the first eight months the war was fought at sea and in the air. On land it was called the ''phoney war'' with the Allies sitting behind the impregnable Maginot Line facing the equally impregnable German Seigfreid Line along the Franco-German border. Suddenly, with lightning and frightening fury, the German army smashed through Belgium and Holland, outflanked the Maginot Line and headed straight for Paris which soon echoed to the sounds of German jackboots. France, under the aged 'Hero of Verdun,'' Marshal Philippe Petain, surrendered, leaving the British army trapped at the English Channel port of Dunkirk. In the evacuation of the badly-mauled, but not demoralized, British Army by thousands of small boats, a West Vancouver man became a hero and was awarded the Distinguished Service

Cross for his bravery. Sub-Lieutenant Robert Timbrell, son of Mrs. E.H. Jupp, who lived at 20th and Inglewood, had joined the peacetime Royal Navy serving on the tall training ship **H.M.S. Conway**. He later transferred to the Royal Canadian Navy and in the post-war years was Admiral Timbrell, NATO commander in the North Atlantic. With a practically useless compass, out of date charts and no tide table, he had taken a 100-foot yacht out of Ramsgate and crossed the Channel to the "hell on the beaches." Although he was on shore for five hours due to the yacht's cable being broken by a bomb burst, Sub.-Lieut. Timbrell made three trips across the Channel carrying 350 soldiers to safety and also salvaging at the same time two more yachts before returning to Portsmouth. In November he came home to a hero's welcome and a civic dinner which embarrassed and bewildered him. In those days, following the fall of France, we needed a hero. In the ensuing months that turned into agonizing years, there was very little good news in the newspapers as the Nazi war machine rumbled over almost the entire continent of Europe. During the Battle of Britain more West Vancouver heroes were created and some of them have their names enscribed on the memorial opposite the Memorial Library.

On the homefront, "Win the War" organizations sprung into action to fill a variety of roles. The Red Cross set up headquarters in Dr. Fred Stainsby's old residence across from the War Memorial and this became the hub for many "Bundles for Britain" efforts, as well as the "Comforts for the Boys" drives. Mrs. Mary Seiburth was "Head Mary" for the Vancouver area, which drew all the ladies with the name "Mary" into the "Marys of Canada Spitfire Club" which bought several Spitfire fighter planes for the Royal Canadian Air Force. Mrs. Seiburth was a remarkable woman, a gentle lady, who contributed much to the appreciation of British Columbia's native and ethnic handicrafts, and her home on Argyle, between 21st and 22nd, reflected her wide interests which ranged through many areas from hiking, knitting to natural history.

A reflection of something very sinister followed the German invasion of Denmark and Norway and it came about as the result of the betrayal of Norway by Vidkun Quisling to the Germans; two terms of utter contempt emerged and the name "Quisling" and "Fifth Column" became as much a phrase of warning as "The Enemy is Listening" signs which were posted on the ferry

211

dock. The shock of Quisling's betrayal shook what was left of the "free world" and steps were taken in Canada to see that such an undermining of the faith of freedom was not repeated here. West Vancouver responded with the formation of the West Vancouver Volunteer Defence Corps, out of which grew the A.R.P., (Air Raid Precautions) organization, of which more will be recorded as the Chronicle continues. Early in the war, the 84th Nursing Division of the St. John Ambulance Association was formed in West Vancouver and Miss Lucy Smith, one of the ambulance's drivers, recalls some of the events associated with that dedicated group of volunteers:

"There were no ambulances in West Vancouver then so we acquired a Fargo truck which was converted into an ambulance. At that time, we were the only nursing division anywhere with an ambulance. We had to have special instruction as it was necessary to double-clutch on the hills, then we had to drive a policeman around to prove we could handle it. From then on it was very busy, busy, busy, taking turns to drive out to Horseshoe Bay, and wouldn't you know it, I had the most inexperienced companion in the whole brigade with me that day! A five-year old boy had climbed into a boat, turned the key, and shot across the bay, slicing a rowboat in two and almost disemboweling a 12-year-old boy from California who was out fishing with his father. I did what little I could for him and then drove him and his father to St. Paul's Hospital. He was hospitalized for a long time both here and in California, but did recover. I was all right until I returned to Horseshoe Bay to tidy up our room there, and as I got out of the van I was greeted by newspaper reporters. I started to shake from head to foot. Fortunately, a good friend, who happened to be picknicking there that day, elbowed her way through the crowd and said, "You're not going to ask her any questions until she's had a cup of tea."

"Other times, in the winter," Miss Smith recalls, "we would be on call for transporting injured skiers from Hollyburn Ridge to St. Paul's. This was before they had a chairlift, but there was a road of sorts. One day I had a call from the mountain and asked them to be sure that no half-track, used for transportation, would be coming down, and was assured that there would be none. At the top of an S-curve I came face to face with a descending half-track. Stalemate! The driver said, "Well, I can't back up, so you'll have to." After I had safely negotiated it and had found a place where I could pull far enough off for him to pass, Oscar Britton, who had been riding with me in the van, wiped his brow, and my companion riding in the back, either Barbara Gamage or Moira McLeod, said she had never been so scared in her life. At one point, apparently, one of my double back wheels was right on the very edge of an overhang.''

As the war progressed, evacuees from bomb-battered British cities began to arrive to stay with relatives or friends in West Vancouver. There were shortages of such staples as meat, sugar, butter and gasoline and the Wartime Prices and Trade Board in Ottawa instituted rationing. Even sliced bread vanished from the stores and bananas were unobtainable. To get them, one had to go to the United States, but that presented another complication, as you couldn't take any currency across the border.

It was a cheerless Sunday morning, that seventh day of December, 1941, when all regular programming on the radio was pre-empted by a flow of news bulletins after news bulletins as Japanese aircraft swooped down on the United States naval base at Pearl Harbor. Despite the devastating damage done by the carrier-based bombers — the full extent of the damage was not made public until a year later — there was a sort of sense of relief that Britain was no longer standing alone against the foe. A hatred for the Japanese erupted immediately, but that was, really, nothing new. For years, such organizations as the Asiatic Exclusion League had been sowing seeds that were about to bear fruit, and one must cite the sheer courage of the Japanese-Canadian kids from the cannery at Sherman, Dundarave and Ambleside, who turned up for school the next day. Most, if not all, had been born in Canada, and, like everybody else in the community, had invested in War Savings Bonds. Now they were classified as enemies and they lived in fear.

The immediate effect of the Pearl Harbor attack was the need for precaution. ''The Enemy is Listening!'' . . . ''Careless Talk Costs Lives!'' . . . ''Nip the Nips!'', all these poster slogans now had a sense of reality about them. Neon signs were shut-off, car headlights were painted blue, or were covered with tape leaving only a narrow strip of light to pass through; blackout curtains were hung in homes; street lights were dimmed and every householder kept a bucket of sand handy in case of an incendiary air attack. Air Raid Precaution (A.R.P.) wardens swung into action and a general blackout was ordered. The *West Van.*

213

News reported that the Ladies Auxiliary to the Legion was asking for a mass meeting to be called for the "purpose of inducing the government to take immediate steps to remove all Japanese, male and female, and other enemy aliens from the coastal area." The West Vancouver ladies were by no means alone in this feeling; the cry also came from the pulpits, from councils throughout the Lower Mainland, and from nearly all segments of the community. There were stories in the newspapers, particularly in *The Vancouver News-Herald,* about the secret "Black Dragon Society" run by Japanese naval officers who dominated the lives of the Japanese in Vancouver's "Little Tokyo," at Steveston and at Sherman. The fact that all the stories were pure fiction made no difference in the orgy of hate that engulfed the Lower Mainland. In April, 1942, the sad procession of Japanese, who by now had suffered the confiscation of everything they owned, began to go to relocation camps in the interior of the province.

Skiers on Hollyburn Ridge were put on the alert in March, 1942 when the Hollyburn Rangers No. 2 Company, Coast Defence Guards was formed as a "guerilla" unit to deal with any "Fifth Column" activity. The war came perilously close in June, 1942, when the Japanese invaded the Aleutian Islands in Alaska; on June 7 an American freighter was torpedoed in Cape Flattery at the entrance to the Strait of Juan de Fuca; on June 20 a Japanese submarine shelled the Estevan lighthouse on the west coast of Vancouver Island, and on the afternoon of September 13, the guns of Narrows North roared.

A fish packer passing Point Atkinson failed to identify itself and word was sent to Narrows North to fire a warning shot across her bow. The packer stopped all right, but the shell, instead of kicking up a splash and sinking, hit a wave and ricochetted across the water to smack into the No. 3 hold of a brand-new freighter, coming out just below the waterline on the other side. The ship, *Fort Rae* was undergoing speed trials and was hastily beached just inside the First Narrows. To say that everybody was happy with the day's work would be exaggerating the truth. The incident was supposed to have been wrapped in wartime secrecy, but it was poorly kept. It was not the first time that the Narrows North guns had been "in action," and it was with a great deal of embarrassment the gunners had to admit that one of their guns accidently went off and darn near took out the Point Atkinson lighthouse! That, too, was supposed to be a secret. While not disputing the seriousness of these incidents, they were, for the civilians, if not for the military, morale boosters and provided a badly-needed good laugh.

On another occasion, the West Vancouver School Board came in for a round of guffaws. When the huge liner *RMS Queen Elizabeth* was anchored off Jericho Beach, opposite West Vancouver, the high school was nearly deserted as the kids went down to the waterfront to gawk at the grey monster. Many overstayed their lunch hour and the board, or somebody, ordered them to make up classtime on Saturday. It was then discovered that the *School Act* did not allow such a "sentence", but one teacher ordered his hookey-playing students to write "lines" or do "square roots." Funny thing about that visit of the *Queen Elizabeth*: nobody was supposed to know anything about it.

Gradually, ever so gradually, the fortunes of war began to turn in favor of the Allies. In 1943, Canadian, British and American forces landed on the coast of Sicily and fought their way across that Italian island and onto the "heel" of Italy. Men from West Vancouver were there. In 1944 West Vancouver men took part in the storming of beaches of Normandy and the subsequent battles for the Falaise Gap and Caen. In Italy they stood before the mighty fortress-monastery of Monte Cassino.

Finally, with France, Holland and Belgium liberated, and the Soviet forces in Berlin, the war in Europe came to an end in May, 1945, and in August, after the surrender of Japan, *HMCS Prince Robert* steamed into Hong Kong to liberate the Canadian contingent which had been held prisoner of war since Christmas Day, 1941.

The "boys" now came home. They were veterans, but unlike their fathers or their grandfathers who returned after the First World War, there was hope for the future in the air. The terrible years of the 1930s had vanished, even though some bitter scars remained. General Victor W. Odlum, of the Rockcliff estate, who had led the Second Canadian Division overseas, returned to his book-lined home after serving as Canadian ambassador to China and Turkey. In an interview with Dan Illingworth of *The Province*, the general summed up what surely must be a major stepping-stone in man's search for a place of excellence:

"One starts out life in wanting to get things and places, but ends up not worrying very much about either. Instead, a man turns to his friends. If he could only learn that lesson earlier he would make his life much richer. It's strange, that at the beginning, when a man has energy, strength and acute senses, he has very little wisdom. Later, through mistakes, wisdom comes, yet he has lost energy and some of that quickness of perception. Friendship is a permanent asset without liabilities and disadvantages. I wouldn't want to change the world at all, because with all its bad features, it still has so many good ones that you have freedom of choice. It is that freedom of choice, often misused but sometimes widely used, that makes life so rich."

Landing clearing in the British Pacific Properties at the junction of Elveden and Eyremount. (WVMA)

When the cherry blossoms are in bloom, on Taylor Way, leading to the British Pacific Properties, the effect is eye-catching. (WVML)

The gift of Lord Southborough this fine piece of sculpture originally stood at the top of Taylor Way but now has a place of honor in the Park Royal shopping plaza. (BPP)

218

The Capilano Golf and Country Club in the British Pacific Properties rates as one of the world's finest, and many famous players have gathered in the charming Club House pictured above. (BPP)

Members of the West Vancouver Women's Auxiliary Air Corps parade to Christ Church Cathedral in Vancouver in 1940. (WVMA)

If this little fish boat didn't give the right signal, the guns of Narrows North, under the main tower of the Lions Gate Bridge would open fire. (WVMA)

Chapter Nine

THE FERRY QUEENS

There was something enchanting, something unforgettably great, about riding the West Vancouver ferries through the riptide swells of the First Narrows, bobbing up and down, rolling sideways from port to starboard and trying to dodge the fare-collecting mate by keeping just a bit ahead of him, or a bit behind him, as the occasion arose. For a nickel a kid could let his or her imagination run wild. There you were, rounding Cape Horn when wind and tide combined in an improper way, or, in the evening being on a moonlight cruise through some enchanted waterway.

In the real world, however, they were utilitarian in every sense of the word, carrying passengers and freight back and forth to Vancouver before the Lions Gate Bridge made them redunant. In the fact they were owned and operated by the municipality made them unique. In the fact they sailed the treacherous waters of the First Narrows with only one fatal mishap is nothing less than a miracle.

Nobody would ever call them beautiful, or graceful, but they were seaworthy, and they did inspire one of Canada's foremost poets, Earle Birney. Here is the first verse of his poem **West Vancouver Ferry**, written in 1940:

Down below the crazy piles
Fetchingly the ferry toots
And down the gangway shedding smiles
Wiggles a cutie, avoiding the boots
Of the knock-kneed hiker ahead.
Women with bags and babies follow,

221

Four loud boys and a lady in red,
Yankees in slacks, a squaw and a hollow-
Cheeked Chinese. She toots again,
A leathery virgin achieves the deck,
And at last, and unbreathing, complete
    with cane,
An Englishman.

(West Vancouver Ferry is from "David and Other Poems,"
Ryerson Press, Toronto, 1942).

An Englishman! Remember the immaculately-dressed gentleman, cane in one hand, briefcase in the other, who, at the very last moment, would come charging down the dock and make a flying leap aboard just as the ferry was pulling out? And then the lady (Was she the 'leathery virgin' of Earle Birney's poem?) who rushed down the wharf thinking the ferry was pulling out and walked right off the end of the dock!? Actually, the ferry was just coming in to tie up. In order to fish the lady out of the briny the captain stopped short of the wharf end. The engineer thought they were docked and stepped out of the cabin and into the salt-chuck. What about the "knock-kneed hikers"? Substitute "hikers" for "skiers" and you have this tale. Once a ticket collector, by accident, knocked over a monstrous skier's pack, a flap opened, and out popped a dancing girl! Believe it or not, but oldtimer John Broderick says its true!

At one time or another there were eight boats in the fleet: the **West Vancouver, Sea Foam, Doncella, Sonrisa, West Vancouver No. 5, West Vancouver No. 6, Bonabelle** and **Hollyburn** and each bore its own stamp of character.

On the **Bonabelle** and **Hollyburn**, for instance, the forward salon was either officially or unofficially the gentleman's preserve. No woman would ever think of entering that hallowed salon, not that she would not have been welcomed, but the dense clouds of cigarette and cigar smoke was a bit overwhelming. Here, in this dense fog, all the world's problems would be solved in the matter of half an hour.

Down from the forward salon was the "listening gallery" where one could listen to the chug-chug-chug of the engines or watch the engineer at work. The captain would signal down to the engineer the required speed over the "engine room telegraph"

222

and he expected a quick and accurate response. One day, engineer Harry Thompson, of **West Vancouver No. 6,** stormed up to the bridge in a magnificent rage, and at the same time, Captain Darius Smith was on his way down to the engine room in an equally magnificient rage. They met half way. Mothers clapped their hands over their children's ears, grown men paled, and Poseidon, the god of the sea and earthquakes, skedaddled away as the confrontation was not one for even the god of the sea and earthquakes to interfere in. Engineer Thompson opened the verbal battle against the ruddy-cheeked, pipe-smoking captain by charging the signals were coming in too fast. Captain Smith counterattacked by reciting some alleged genealogical background and suggesting that the engineer was lazy and incompetent. That did it. As all the witnesses to this encounter had their ears covered by now, it is not known what Mr. Thompson's exact reply was. The scene lasted only a few minutes, and when the air was cleared and both went back to their appointed tasks, Poseidon returned and all was well once more.

The engine rooms were models of cleanliness. The spotless enamelled bulkheads and beams, the natural steel deck, stairs and railing, and the green, pulsating engines with their highly polished brassworks would make the most fastidious housekeeper green with envy, but that was not enough for Harold Massey of the **Bonabelle.** His engine room was truly a work of art. In addition to the standard green engine, he painted the bolt caps and pipe joint a brilliant red; the decks were metallic silver, the stairways and upper deck grids were of metallic gold, the air compressors and electric light generators were a bright yellow and and the bulkhead beams were black against stark white walls. Where applicable, he used pastels and to cap it all off, the usual engine room sign was replaced with "Rainbow Room,"

From the semi-open stern section one could listen to the churning of the propellors, but it appears that was not the main reason this part of the boat was popular. Late at night young couples would gather there to watch the lights of the city fade away. The only problem was that the ticket collectors wore soft leather shoes which could be a little disconcerting.

The upper deck was favored in the summertime, but seldom during the winter. No matter what time of the year this deck might beckon a passenger, there were dive-bombing seagulls and hair-ruffling winds to reckon with. Up there was the bridge where, for a few thrilling moments, a youngster could stand beside the captain as he fingered the great mahogany wheel and, perhaps, help him pull the whistle lanyard or listen to wonderful tales of the sea. The skippers and mates who served on these little ships were all men of the sea, salty and confident men who knew all the tricks of their trade and were often called on to use most of them. There were men like Captain A.A. Findlay, the first to join the fleet, G.B. Warren, Darius Smith, John Watson, D.O. Lunn, Henry Skeet, Peter Johnson, Walter Johnson, Roy Barry, Arthur Edwards, Harry Vince, Walter Partington, Dan Macdonald, Roy Holland, James Brayshaw, Ronald Jackson, Gerry Lancaster, Bill Rae, George Hayes, L.R.W. Beavis, Charles Nichol.

Captain Beavis, master of tall ships, was the only West Vancouver skipper to leave any form of memoir, and these were published in 1986 in Seattle under the title **Passage**. In the 1920s he was captain-mate of the **Sonrisa** and he tells us what it was like to be captain of one of these ferries:

"These little ferries were run on a nine-hour shift which was not arduous except in foggy weather. Then it was decidedly harrassing, criminal, if you like. Running full speed with numerous courses and more often than not, we had a very hot tide. The captain steered. It was a case of looking at the compass, looking ahead, blowing the whistle, looking at his watch and **listening** all the time. The courses were all run on time. (This is also known as the echo system). It was really wonderful how well they maintained the schedule and how free from accidents we were. The mate had to keep a look out as soon as he collected the fares which were taken on board. Hardly any of the passengers realized the risk they ran or the nerve-wracking the skipper was going through. The ferries were owned by the municipality and the council did not care about operations. They were not sea-minded people and knew very little about it."

An example of the seamanship required to operate through the then much narrower and stormy First Narrows appeared in a story in the **West Vancouver Leader** for October 25, 1934:

"Sunday was a rough day along the Coast. The wind blew steadily and in gusts of squalls 50-60-70 miles an hour and the rain beat down in torrents. . . West Vancouver suffered practically no damage, fortunately, though across the Inlet in Stanley Park 2500 trees were uprooted and in the city store windows were crushed and overhead signs torn from their fastenings. The storm was a spectacle locally and crowds watched the tossing ocean from Ambleside Beach and from the ferry dock.

"The worst storm I have ever seen here," said Captain Vince, superintendent of West Van. ferries.

"True to the best tradition of the sea, the sturdy little ships that make up the ferry service kept well on schedule and the hardy mariners who make up their crews, the captains and the mates and the deckhands, stood staunchly at their posts. 'Carry on' was the watchword and carry on they did. Waves were mountains high and the troughs were valleys deep. From the shore there were times when the ships were hidden from sight, and sightseers held their breath. But with the decks awash and spray smothering the wheel houses, the gallant little vessels proved that West Vancouver has a navy to be proud of. At 5:00, however, Capt. Vince decided that enough was enough. He gave the order to tie up and ride out the storm.

"The gale, which had been blowing south-east had suddenly lulled and for ten minutes there was practically no wind, then it came in massed fury directly from the south-west. Imagine the result! Waves that had been running before the wind now found themselves thrown back on their heels and into a churning tumult of chaotic water! 'Gosh,' said an old beach-comber, 'look at them waves.' At 8:30 the **Sonrisa** ventured forth. She got half way between Battery Park and Prospect Point. Then she hit the chaos. Tossed onto high crests and sliding down into deep holes, it was a voyage like unto a trip on a roller coaster, only much worse. The captain was hanging onto his wheel while the crew hung to rails and stanchions and things. 'We can't make it, we're going about,' and waiting his chance the skipper caught her on the crest of a vicious wave and swung her like a top. Back to the city and safe harbor she ran and the crew breathed normally once more. At 10 o'clock the service was permanently resumed. All in all it was a gallant effort and as we said before, West Vancouver can be proud of her navy."

It was under like conditions that an elderly lady, obviously on her first crossing of the First Narrows, got down on her knees and began to sing the **Mariner's Hymn**:

O hear us when we cry to thee
For those in peril on the sea.

225

On Monday, February 4, 1935, at 8:47 a.m. the worst fears became stark reality: **West Vancouver 5** was rammed and sunk by the CPR's **Princess Alice**.

"It is alleged," said the **West Van. News** on February 7, "the ferry was on her right course and going slowly. She was struck on the port side of the large cabin aft, the sharp bow of the **Alice** striking at an acute angle and bringing up at the bulkhead on the port side of the stairway. This allowed those in the cabin to escape up the stairway, but an elderly lady, believed to be Mrs. William E. Burritt, mother of Mrs. A.P. Croker, of 2869 Bellevue Avenue, was trapped between the bow of the **Alice** and the side of the cabin. Captain [Darius] Smith risked his life, as did Mate [George] Hayes and Lookout Arnold Garthorne, who came to his assistance, in a gallant attempt to save her, the captain receiving a bad cut in the head, but the ferry sank before she could be extricated. The surviving passengers, Malcolm Reid, 1373 Gordon Avenue, Harry Sundbacken, 2611 Bellevue Avenue, and Miles Bell, teller of the Royal Bank here, Frank Worster, Jean Wong and Ching Woo, all of Vancouver, also Engineer W.F. Merrick, were taken on the **Alice** to the city, while the remainder of the crew were rescued by the **Sonrisa**. It should be remarked that W.F. Merrick did not leave his engine room until ordered to do so by Captain Smith by which time the water was up to his knees.... Both Captain Smith and all his crew upheld the best traditions of the British Mercantile Marine and those who saw the accident and the subsequent sinking pay eloquent testimony to their conduct in the crisis."

Mr. Merrick's action in shutting off the **No. 5's** valves saved the engines, but the hull was deemed beyond repair. Before making a decision on what course to take in replacing the sunken ship, council looked at the **M.V. Norsal**, owned by the Powell River Company.

"The **Norsal**," stated the **Leader**, "is 135 feet long and possesses luxurious appointments. At present it is used to convey directors of the Powell River Company to and from the paper town. Before it could be used as a ferry considerable reconstruction would be necessary. If converted, however, it would be the biggest and fastest of the municipal fleet."

In the long run, council felt, it would be cheaper to build a new hull, powering her with the engines from the **West Vancouver No. 5** and thus it came to be that the Bonabelle joined the fleet.

A Court of Enquiry into the tragedy was held under Mr. Justice Lucas in March and after four days of deliberations the tribunal reported, "We are happy to express the highest praise for the bravery of Captain Smith in trying to prevent loss of life, and for the skill of Captain Palmer [of the **Princess Alice**]. The actions of both officers were well in keeping with the international traditions of the sea." To the direct question, "Was the collision the result of any wrongful act of either master?" the answer of the board was "No."

It had already been recognized that another ferry would be required and a contract was let late in 1935 for what would be the last of the ferry boats, the **Hollyburn**. She was launched in May, 1936, at the North Vancouver Ship Repairs yards at the foot of Lonsdale. "A humorous feature of the launching," reported the **West Van. News**, "was the sudden descent of the champagne onto the hat of one of the dock employees who was standing by the bow beneath the launching platform. A careful handling of the hat and he might have had most of the champagne. As it was his hasty removal of himself and hat resulted in the liquid being wasted "down his back."

As the "junior kid" in the fleet, **Hollyburn** was the inheritor of a tradition that began when John Lawson and his friends purchased the 34-passenger launch **West Vancouver** back in 1910 to help them sell real estate. The next year they added a larger boat, the 40-passenger **Sea Foam**, sometimes called the "sturdiest of all the ferries." These two vessels were the ones acquired by the municipality shortly after incorporation and were soon disposed of. The fate of the **West Vancouver** is not known, but the **Sea Foam** was sold to the Defiance Cannery at Sherman and blew up in the mid-1930s.

To replace **West Vancouver and Sea Foam**, council went down to Tacoma, Washington, in 1912, to purchase the 80-passenger **Doncella**, a trim little ship if there ever was one. Joining her the following year was **Sonrisa**, destined to become, for many, the "darling of the fleet." **Sonrisa**, like the radio show of the 1930s, **Amos 'n' Andy**, was a "fresh air taxi" with outside seats or rather, benches. By the time she came to the rescue during the **West Vancouver No. 5** disaster, **Sonrisa** was showing her years and was just about ready for the boneyard. **No. 5** came along in 1914, and on July 25, 1925, a new ferry, with a majestic, but well-remembered name, **West Vancouver No. 6** came into service.

Necessity called for the ferries to have a feeder system to get passengers from the Ambleside wharf to their homes, and in the early days, it must be remembered, there were no such luxuries as sidewalks or paved roads for most of the length and breadth of West Vancouver. There was mud in the spring, dust in the summer, a combination of both in the fall, and mud and slush in the winter. The municipality, then only three years old and faced with wartime problems, launched, in 1915, a scheme that would be hailed as the first public passenger bus operation in Western Canada.

By today's standards the first of the "Blue Buses" were as awkward-looking as the **West Vancouver** and the **Sea Foam**, but in those days, a seven-passenger Pierce-Arrow touring car was "the cat's meow." It ran between Ambleside and Dundarave, but the winter of 1915 brought up the old tale that the motor car would never give way to the horse. That winter it snowed so hard the fledgling bus service had to be suspended and John Lawson came to the rescue with a team of horses and a sleigh.

In 1917 a 1909 Thomas touring car was purchased and then underwent extensive automotive surgery by having the original body removed, the chassis extended and a new wooden body built to accommodate 25 passengers.

It was also a "fresh air taxi" and on its sides were boldly lettered "West Vancouver Municipal Ferries." After the First World War came the "old toast rack," a magnificient Model T Ford with seats full across the width of the truck. Entrance was gained through four slots on the left hand side, with canvass curtains hung to "protect the 1919 lady of fashion from the inclement weather."

During 1920, 1921 and 1922 a new bus was added to the fleet each year because of the steadily growing population. These could each handle 40 passengers, and at the time, buses of such a size were unheard of in North America and could not be purchased anywhere in the United States or Canada. They were rebuilt in the North Vancouver shipyard shops by Harry L. Thompson, using Pierce-Arrow passenger cars. In 1926, the first factory-built bus was purchased from General Motors. It was a 25-passenger "Yellow Coach" and, when repainted blue, and nicknamed the "Mountain Goat", saw service for many years on the Upper Levels run. That purchase marked the beginning of a "keep-up-to-date" attitude by council, albeit economic and wartime conditions often frustrated the effort.

The Blue Buses, like the ferries, except for the **No. 5** tragedy, had a marvelous safety record, and one can compare the competence of the drivers to the captains and mates. In the early days of the transportation system, everybody who piled on the buses knew the drivers by their first—and last—names: Percy Hawtin, Frank Ellis, Bill Green, Ed Rathje, Harry Nesbitt, Charlie and Art Ridley, Robbie Robinson, Bert Gisby, Bert Thompson, Fred Murray, Met Chapman.

There are many stories told about the old buses and their drivers.

"The first bus that I recollect," former municipal solicitor Gordon Robson recalled, "was a Pierce-Arrow car and the driver was [Bill] Murphy who later became chief of the fire department in North Vancouver. I then lived out at Altamont and would walk down to Dundarave. The bus would be sitting outside Murphy's home. He would run out in his shirt sleeves and off we would go to the ferry, arriving about two minutes later." It may have been to Bill Murphy that the minute of council of November 20, 1916 referred:

"A letter was read from the Secretary of the Vancouver Automobile Club re over speed by the Driver of the Municipal Buses and his lack of a chauffeur's badge. The clerk was instructed to reply thanking the writer for calling attention to the excess speed of the motor bus and to see that necessary steps would be taken to regulate same. The Clerk was further instructed to write the Ferry Manager on the subject, intimating the desire of the Council that more time should be taken to cover the distance between 25th Street and Ambleside and more care taken to see that passengers at intermediate streets were not left behind."

Mrs. Dulcie Nesbitt, whose late husband, Harry, was one of the early drivers, was interviewed by municipal archivist Rupert Harrison:

"When they got bus No. 3 they needed another driver, and so they put my brother, Ken Robinson, on, and as Bill Murphy had left, Percy Hawtin was hired. My brother didn't do a darn thing from the time he came back from overseas at the end of 1918 until mid-1920 when he started to drive. He was unemployed because he'd never done any work at all until he went into the army and in the army he was a motorcycle driver, so that was what he was good for. Anyway, Ken and Percy drove, and then in 1926 Ken decided to go in with Ed Black down at Dundarave and build a garage and he became the mechanic. At the same time Percy went into the mechanics end of the bus system. They now needed two new bus drivers and the man that was running the buses then was a man named [H.H.] Peggler. I suppose he had watched Harry drive milk around for Fullager's Dairy in North Vancouver, and he asked Harry if he would try out on the buses. He went to work in February, 1926. Frank Ellis was, I think, about six weeks behind him, and they had reservations about Frank Ellis. All he was good for was flying airplanes for the Royal Flying Corps. Anyway he turned into quite a decent driver, although he did fly low a few times.''

Frank Ellis's head, it is true, was often in the skies, for he was one of Canada's pioneer aviators, having built and flown planes before the First World War, and had the distinction of not only being the first man in Canada to make a parachute jump, but through his book, **Canada's Flying Heritage,** he is the chronicler of this country's aerial history. He was not the only Canadian aviation pioneer to live in West Vancouver. The **West Van. = Guard**, on September 15, 1922 noted that Captain Hoy "is a permanent resident of West Vancouver." Early in August, 1919, Captain Ernest C. Hoy, DFC, made the first flight across the Rocky Mountains between Vancouver and Lethbridge, Alberta.

Nigel Snelgrove, who before the Second World War worked as a parts washer at the bus garage, tells a good story about Frank Ellis: "Bus tickets were sold in strips for varying prices depending upon the number of tickets in the strip. Seated at the wheel of a bus on a warm summer afternoon waiting for the ferry to arrive with another load of passengers, dozing and day-dreaming, he was startled and alarmed when a large woman loomed up, thrust 25 cents at him and said, 'Strip, please!'''

"The next bus driver," Mrs. Nesbitt continued, "was Ed. Rathje, who was also a veteran, and Bill Green had come here with his wife. I think he'd been gassed in the war and came here on a stretcher. They all thought he'd only have a month or two, three to six months to live and the only chance he had was to get out of England and get him where there was some sunshine. His wife took a chance. She was a trained nurse and knew she'd get a job. She brought her son Stan with her and landed in West Vancouver as close to the sea as they could get. About a year

230

later he was wandering around the buses, and they tried him on as an extra."

Harry Nesbitt had a reputation for courtesy. He would help mothers collapse baby buggies before placing them in the outside side racks of the bus and Mrs. Nesbitt recalled "he used to look up and down the street when he came to a crossing to see whether people were running for the bus. Once Harry saw somebody running for the bus and figured it would be quicker to back the bus up to meet the person rather than wait for him." His daughter, Dolly Cartwright, had another story about the early morning run: "Once he got past 25th Street he'd "pop" the air horn at each corner so people would have time to get up, have a bit of breakfast and be ready for the return run from West Bay. One used to rush for the bus, one pant leg on and one pant leg off. There was another who rushed for the bus, what he was like when he got the bus I don't know, but when he got on the boat he'd tie up his shoe laces, get out his tie, do up two or three buttons and tuck in his shirt so he'd be perfectly presentable when he reached Vancouver."

In 1923, a private company, North and West Vancouver Stages, founded by Messrs. Soday and O'Hara, began operating between North and West Vancouver, and in June, 1926, they announced, "On the opening of the new road we have made arrangements to supply an adequate service between Whytecliffe and North Vancouver... Two new parlor cars have recently been added to the fleet, and no care or expense has been spared to make them modern and up-to-date in every particular. They are equipped with powerful and smoothy running motors. The interior fittings are equal to any on the Coast. A commodious smoking apartment is provided in the rear of the car.. The centre seats are upholstered in plush and reserved for ladies and non-smokers. Roof ventilators and adjustable glass windows give a cool and airy car in summer, with an open view. In winter every compartment is heated by a new process, and the cars are warm and cosy, and last but not least, the fares and rates on this line are, we confidently claim, lower than any other stage operating in British Columbia today." This service was ultimately incorporated into Pacific Stage Lines.

With the opening of the Lions Gate Bridge in 1938 a new vista opened for the Blue Buses, and ferry traffic dropped sharply, but as the war progressed and gas rationing came into effect, the

the bus service to the Howe and Dunsmuir Street depot was forced to cease, except for an early-morning and late-at-night run. For nearly two years after the end of the war the municipality tried to keep the ferry fleet "afloat", but it proved futile, and on February 8, 1947, the service came to an end.

"'Goodbye' is the saddest word in the English language," stated an editorial in the **West Van. News.**"Although we live in a world of change and know that nothing lasts forever, including ourselves, the act of saying 'goodbye' remains a matter we like to put off as long as possible."

Harry Thompson, who had been with the ferries since the service began, was engineer on that final run, and it must have been with a sense of sadness that he saw the remaining vessels of the fleet being put up for sale. The **Bonabelle** was sold for $18,000 to Charles E. Wilson; the **Hollyburn** had previously entered the service of Harbour Navigation and is still in service, and the **West Vancouver No. 6** was sold to the Barkley Sound Transportation Company Ltd. of Port Alberni and renamed **Uchuk II**. In 1965 she was transferred to the Nootka Sound Service Ltd. and the following year was purchased by the British Columbia Ministry of Highways, renamed **Sointula Queen** and was used to carry schoolchildren from several off-shore islands to Alert Bay. In 1974 the vessel was sold to Joseph Thorsteinson, of Ucluelet on the West Coast of Vancouver Island, and soon after she passed into the hands of a Mr. Vinnish who moored her at Mission City on the Fraser River and converted her into a floating residence.

As familiar as the West Vancouver ferries was the lighthouse at the mouth of the Capilano River. Built in 1915, its flashing light and groaning fog horn guided ships through the First Narrow's fogs until 1969 when it was replaced by a concrete, unmanned beacon.

No history of ferry service in West Vancouver would be complete without bringing into the picture the Sannie Transportation Company and Union Steamships, which operated out of Horseshoe Bay and Whytecliffe.

In 1920, an Australian by the name of J. Hilton Brown acquired a launch which he named **Sannie**, after a racehorse that had brought him luck, and began a service between Horseshoe Bay and Snug Cove on Bowen Island. Mr. Brown sold out to his partner, Thomas D. White, the following year but remained on as manager. On May 16, 1921, it was announced **Sannie I,**

II and **III** would be ferrying holiday-makers over to Bowen Island.

During the summer of 1924, Union Steamships of Vancouver placed in service the 54-foot long motor vessel **Comox** between Bowen Island and a float at Whytecliffe. This service lasted for only two years and was not restored until 1939 when the company acquired the Whytecliffe property, disposed of the residential lands, but kept the Cliff House open for business. Again, the little **Comox** was back churning up the waters between Whytecliffe and Bowen Island, and in 1941 she was joined by the MV **Bowen**. This service lasted until Labor Day, 1950, when the vessels were merged with the Sannie Transportation operations which Union had purchased in 1944.

John Muir Sinclair (left) and Robert Macpherson (right) who, with John Lawson and W.C. Thompson, established the West Vancouver Transportation Company in 1909. Below is a stock certificate issued by that company.

234

West Vancouver, the first of a fleet of proud little ships. (WVMA)

Seafoam. (WVMA)

Doncella, the third in West Vancouver's ferry fleet. (WVMA)

Doncella docked at the Hollyburn wharf, 17th Street, in 1913. (WVMA)

Sonrisa. (WVMA)

*Excursionists aboard **Sonrisa**. (WVMA)*

West Vancouver No. 5. (WVMA)

West Vancouver No. 5 in drydock following February, 1935 collision. (WVMA)

West Vancouver No. 6. (WVMA)

MV Bonabelle. (WVMA)

MV Hollyburn (WVMA)

Stormy Weather. (WVMA)

Engineer Harry L. Thompson, the first engineer who remained with the fleet until the end, 1947. (WVMA)

Captain A.A. Findlay, first captain of the fleet, 1909. (WVMA)

Capilano Lighthouse, with Baby Mountain, now Sentinel Hill in the background. (VPL)

241

Captain Darius Smith, here of the No. 5 mishap. (WVMA)

A Pierce Arrow automobile purchased by the municipality for conversion of chassis and engine to a bus. Man standing at front is William M. Thompson. Driver is Harry L. Thompson and standing at rear with a dog is Const. George Shepherd. Circa 1923 .(WVMA)

First West Vancouver bus converted from Thomas Flyer motor car, circa 1916-1917. Note the chain drive to the rear wheels and driver seated on right-hand side of the vehicle. (WVMA)

The same Thomas Flyer but at a slightly later date. Driver is Harry L. Thompson who supervised the conversion. Man standing is Mr. Fox who was manager of the municipal transportation system. (WVMA)

The "Toast Rack", named because of the slots in which the passengers rode. A 1919 Model "T" Ford chassis on which the body was built in the municipal garage. Man standing is James D. Thompson, whose first job on returning from overseas was driving buses. He later became an engineer on the ferries. (WVMA)

*A converted Pierce Arrow bus, circa 1921. Driver is James D. Thompson.
(WVMA)*

*Second Upper Levels bus, manufactured by the Yellow Coach Co. in 1927.
(WVMA)*

The "Princess Elizabeth," so named by its original owners, the Blue Funnel Bus Line of Vancouver who used it as a sight-seeing bus. Body and chassis built by Hayes Anderson of Vancouver. Affectionately called the 'Lizzie" by local residents. Picture circa 1934. (WVMA)

Cab over engine Ford Bus, the first with a rear exit door. Circa 1938. (WVMA)

A "formal portrait" of three of West Vancouver's popular buses. (WVMA)

Ford bus with engine in rear, circa 1941. Note municipal crest top and front. (WVMA)

Modern G.M.C. transit bus. (WVMA)

Among the popular early days bus drivers were Harry Nesbitt, top left, Percy Hawtin, Fred Murray, lower left, and Bert Thompson. (NS, WVMA)

Chapter Ten

TO BE OR NOT TO BE

The lack of planning in West Vancouver's early days had created what best can be described as an unholy mess. Lots were of uneven size, streets were not properly graded or laid out, houses could be built without even a building permit and, even at that, many were little more than summer cottages plunked down on a lot in a helter-skelter manner.

The first small step toward remedying this situation came on January 27, 1926, when then-councillor J.B. Leyland requested municipal solicitor Gordon Robson to draft a by-law to create the West Vancouver Town Planning Commission. It was this action that set West Vancouver on its road to excellence. The way would sometimes be wearisome and often very frustrating for those involved, as depression and all-out war set up obstacles that threatened to keep the community reduced to being nothing more than a summer resort.

By 1930, the Town Planning Commission had placed before council a set of zoning by-laws that banned the further building of "temporary" homes or summer cottages, except in the Horseshoe Bay area, and another fundamental restriction was laid down: all lots sold in the western part of the municipality would have a 75-foot minimum frontage while those in the eastern section would have a 50-foot frontage. In all cases, houses were to stand 30-feet back from the front property line. The following year the commission completed a survey of the municipality's parks and beaches and prepared a plan for their gradual development.

Despite the depression and the ensuing war, councils in those tumultuous years kept much-needed public works projects in their minds, but all too often they were frustrated by manpower shortages, wartime freezes on materials and, of course, shortages of immediate money. Everything was based on the hope that better days were about to come.

In his 1943 inaugural address Reeve Patrick Field had this to say: "We face a most interesting year. There is undoubtedly a possibility of the war coming to a successful conclusion during 1943. No one can tell, of course, but the hope is growing daily, which means we have a dual duty to perform in every department, namely, ordinary operation and post-war planning." Reeve Field was over-optimistic about the possibilities of peace, but in that year his council took a stride forward that, in some ways, was to make West Vancouver a place of excellence. On September 13, 1943, a Board of Park Commissioners was established by council and at the November municipal election, Claire S. Downing was elected a commissioner for a three-year term, Leonard E. Kyle for two years and Victor W. Griffiths for a one-year term. Mr. Downing was later named chairman of the commission.

Although the bloodiest days for the Canadian armed forces overseas were yet to come, the reeve had another kind of plan in his mind and he gave a hint of it in his 1943 address to council:

"I know," he said, "that it is in the mind of the Federal Government to request every municipality to take its share of post-war rehabilitation work. That is undoubtedly the logical method of handling a large portion of this problem from a national point of view, and I feel sure that our citizens will expect us to be ready to accept our share of the responsibility. Our municipality offers marvelous opportunities for such development work from one end to the other." That idea became a reality the following year when he and councillor William Dickinson headed a rehabilitation committee of council and, in naming that committee, the Reeve continued the theme that planning for the future must continue.

Victory in Europe was clearly ahead when William Dickinson was sworn in at the statutory initial meeting in 1945, a "year," he said, "which may be a very important one in the history of West Vancouver." Up until this time the municipality was on the septic tank system and in his maiden speech the reeve urged a start on a planned sewage system, at the same time saying he was prepared to tackle another major problem, that being an expanded water system. "This," he said, "will cost a large sum of money, and in this connection we should complete and forward to the provincial government, without further delay, our statement of intended post-war work." When council the previous year had presented a "pay-as-you-go" plan of levying for capital expenditures for water mains and roads, the voters turned it down and now councillors were forced to find other means to finance the projects.

Reeve Dickinson and his council were not the only ones planning for the future in this, the first year of peace. Boaters were getting together to form a yacht club and by the following winter they had formed the West Vancouver Yacht Club. The first sail past was held in May, 1946, at Sandy Cove and by 1947, with a membership of 84, the search began for a proper yacht basin and club house site. This goal was achieved in 1950 when a group of members bought property at Fishermans Cove and offered it to the club in return for basic privileges for the syndicate members. It is interesting to jump ahead to 1964 when 200 yachts sailed out from Fishermans Cove for the annual sail past.

The directors of the British Pacific Properties, too, were leaning over their drawing boards plotting a new course for the prestigious development on Hollyburn Ridge. They were quick to realize the war had brought about a great social change. Class distinctions were crumbling and now the "ordinary" people were clammering for a taste of gracious living. In 1945, a Vancouver consultant in planning and subdivisions, Alexander Walker, and Hugh Russell, of Seattle, were engaged to prepare a study covering the whole field of planning and sales for the Properties. Acting independently, they came up with three major points, all of which were acted on. The first was to resurvey the large lots which had been offered before the war, to provide smaller holdings; widespread clearing to open up the view and let the sun in, and finally, the acquisition of property at Taylor Way and Marine Drive for future development as a shopping centre and business district.

At the same time as the British Pacific Properties were being revitalized, a Vancouver restaurateur, Henri Aubeneau and his daughter, Younette were promoting sales in their development on what, for years, had been known as Baby Mountain, but was now called Sentinel Hill.

There was, however, a shadow hanging over the municipality

253

and there was every good reason to fear that a ghost from the past would appear to haunt it. There were reports coming out of Victoria that the **Pacific Great Eastern Railway** was going to return. "Rise in your wrath!" cried Reeve Dickinson on January 22, 1946. "If the railway returns it will destroy the whole district!"

Not everybody realized that when the railway stopped service in 1928 it had not abandoned the right-of-way through West Vancouver and some had even encroached on the track allowance to extend their gardens. It would be a subject of debate for several years to come.

There were so many plans in the wind, such as water supplies, a sewage system, and a hospital that Reeve Thomas J. Brown had to admit his 1947 council had "inherited many problems and projects that for one reason or another have not yet been carried through to a satisfactory completion. We frankly admit that it will not be possible to please everybody but so long as our approach and thinking are realistic and progressive and our action is positive, we should go far toward the accomplishment of our ideals."

West Vancouver, then, was having agonizing growing pains. While the **Pacific Great Eastern Railway** was looked upon with disfavor, the same cannot be said for a proposal launched by the provincial government to build an upper levels highway to Horseshoe Bay. This was part of a grand scheme launched by Premier John Hart to link Vancouver with the central interior by rail and by highway. Council hoped the new highway would go a long way to relieve the existing congestion along Marine Drive. New subdivisions close to the proposed highway were being opened up and two years later, when the preliminary survey had been located, Reeve Brown urged that a "special appropriation of funds" be made to complete the survey of contour roads leading to this area.

"During the past twelve months," the reeve said at the first meeting of his 1950 council, "our growth continued at an unabated pace. Our building department reported the issuance of more than three million dollars in building permits. This growth, while most gratifying and being indicative of the desirability of our municipality as a place in which to live, has nevertheless, taxed our capabilities to provide essential services such as roads, water works and school accommodation, etc. I feel that the council has been so pre-occupied with the provision of these services and in dealing with the normal day-to-day demands that insufficient time or thought is being devoted to future planning." To solve the problem of future planning, Reeve Brown then called for the formation of a Community Planning Association to help draw up a master plan for the municipality.

"It is significant," he said, "that all municipalities are woefully lacking in dealing with public relations and especially in the field of community planning. Too few of our people understand it as they have not had the opportunity to participate in it. The mode of operation which I am suggesting tonight would enable a larger number of people to actually participate in this planning and might serve as a step in the right direction in this all-important field of public relations. It must at all times be remembered that the process of planning must be continuous, recognizing the changes of growth and decay.

The need for a hospital in West Vancouver had long been on the mind of councils, but in 1950 the matter came to a head with the city of North Vancouver threatening to bar West Vancouver residents from being admitted into the North Vancouver General Hospital. Late that year, Mrs. T.A. Spencer offered her home and grounds on Mathers Avenue as a temporary 30-bed hospital, pending the preparation of specifications for a new one, a hospital by-law and other necessary details. With the understanding that West Vancouver would build its own hospital, Mayor Frank Goldsworthy of North Vancouver said he would postpone the previously announced ban.

As 1949 drew to a close, a violent rainstorm turned the Capilano River into a maelstrom of fury, sweeping away the approaches to the highway span and carving out a new channel for itself. It struck at noon on November 26. In no time at all, a 20-foot chasm separated the bridge from the rest of Marine Drive and hour by hour it ate away at the river-bank. Hundreds of cars were caught on either side of the bridge. Ambleside and Dundarave were flooded and McDonald Creek joined in the fury by rushing across Inglewood Avenue. That night, Vancouver **Sun** reporter Jim Hazelwood visited the scene and wrote: "The normally pint-sized Capilano River seemd to go berserk as it tore up trees, pushed over its bank and scooped out the hard-packed gravel of the single highway artery to West Vancouver. Hundreds of stranded people stood in three inches of mud on Dundarave pier during the first hours of the spasmodic ferry service which was the first link between the municipality and Vancouver. Their expressions were a mixture of worry and bewilderment as they watched the first tiny ferries bouncing against the pier in choppy seas. Many stood apart from the crowd anxiously scanning the incoming passengers for a glimpse of relatives who had been missing as long as six hours in the confusion of the municipality's isolation. Their worries were increased by swift-running rumors of West Vancouver residents attempting to cross the dangerous foot bridges further up the river and the knowledge that the raging stream had snatched a 24-year old man, Gordon Fullerton, to his death..." Army engineers swiftly went into action to build a Bailey bridge across the gap which had now widened to 138-feet, but this, too, was swept away. For ten days West Vancouver was isolated and as the river continued roaring, the roar of politicians and residents was just as furious as they clamoured for a second crossing of the Capilano to replace the condemned "footbridge" on Keith Road whose rickety condition made it completely useless—and dangerous even at the best of times.

"Proposed construction of a highway from Squamish to Vancouver may be a factor in the deciding if a larger bridge eventually replace the shattered Marine Drive crossing," said the **Sun**. "Another political problem stands in the way of a new bridge at Keith Road. It would not be on an arterial highway and for this reason the provincial government might disclaim any responsibility in the matter. Another possibility mentioned by Reeve Brown was the proposal once made by the Greater Vancouver Water District for a dam across the Capilano. This dam could be equipped with a roadway across the top. Fears that traffic would be further blocked by construction work at the washed-out eastern approach to the bridge were soon set aside when it was announced that a second bridge, alongside the old one would be put in place."

At the same time, British Pacific Properties Ltd. were putting the final touches to a project that would revolutionize shopping patterns, not only in West Vancouver but across the nation. Along with the pioneer Vancouver department store, Woodward's, the Guinness-backed company developing Park Royal, where Taylor Way joins Marine Drive, was completing construction of the Park Royal Shopping Centre. It covered some 130,000 square feet and when it opened in September, 1950, with 20 additional shops, it was hailed as the first regional shopping centre in Canada. From then on, Park Royal's growth was phenomenal with "expansion" being the key word used by the company over the next three decades. This expansion was to take in both sides of Marine Drive, moving onto Indian reserve land with the South Mall incorporating the Hudson's Bay Company and a highrise office tower.

One of the first things J. Howard Fletcher urged when he was elected reeve in the 1950 election was the formation of a hospital society to proceed with planning for a West Vancouver hospital, and at the same time he noted, "if the voters were satisfied to supply without question a considerable sum per annum to maintain a free library service, they, the voters will not fuss too much if we, or when we, call upon them for similar sums for other very worth while services."

It did not take Reeve Fletcher long to find himself in what he called a "tug-of-war" between the oldtimers and the new arrivals. "We are practically equally divided," he told his new council in January, 1952, "therefore all we appear to be doing is marking time. The cause or reason for this apparent inaction has been brought about because West Vancouver was originally peopled by those who were content with the simple life and desired to live alone in a country atmosphere. The coming of the Lions Gate Bridge, however, brought a new group who wanted to make West Vancouver an exclusive residential area—an expensive place in which to live. These two groups today constitute a giant tug-of-war with neither side able to make any headway, but progess cannot be denied. Those who co-operate prosper. Those who oppose find themselves beset with great difficulties. Because of the failure to recognize our responsibilities we are all, both sides, facing expenditures for services which will be most difficult to meet unless we recognize, immediately, that a secondary source of income must be developed."

If that secondary source of income were not found, then, he hinted, there would be disaster for West Vancouver. "The importance of this secondary source has been apparent for at least ten years," he said, "but even those who were sure were not positive enough to be able to come right out and advocate the obvious. So today, with no relief for the single family dwelling owner in sight, we are facing sharply increased assessments and even an increased mill rate. This is forcing the very thing that so many have fought against—multiple dwellings in an undesirable manner—basement and attic suites. This proves that we cannot avoid our responsibilities. We must either meet them in a courageous and business-like manner or they will overwhelm us to our discredit. I can see, unless a secondary source of income is found, that eventually, and before long, that the bulk of single family dwellings in West Vancouver will be converted into undesirable apartment blocks.''

It was during Reeve Fletcher's term of office that great changes to the waterfront—and to the lifestyle of residents of Horseshoe Bay came about. The Peabody Brothers of Seattle had sold their Black Ball Ferries to the State of Washington, but retained the name and a couple of their ships, and now were seeking to establish new routes. They approached West Vancouver council about the possibility of leasing property in Horseshoe Bay and it soon became a matter of controversy.

Fishermen were alarmed, fearing their sport would be ruined by the comings and goings of the ferries, but in 1951, the company put into service the **M.V. Machigonne**, which only carried passengers, and the **M.V. Quillyute** on a run over to Gibsons Landing, and in 1953 the **Kahloke** initiated a Horseshoe Bay-Nanaimo service.

When Hugo Ray took over the reins of office in 1953, he gave one of the longest and most philosophic of any inaugural address heard in West Vancouver's council chambers, and it sent out a strong warning:

"...we should continue the conservative practices that have built up our credit, maintained our values and many of the enviable characteristics of our municipality,'' he stated, "but we must face the fact that we are no longer a small municipality or an isolated one. We must adapt ourselves so that we can share the responsibilities and problems that we cannot escape as an important neighbor to a great city. The threatened return of the P.G.E., the construction of an arterial highway on the upper levels and a direct link by ferry to Vancouver Island are possibilities for which we must become prepared. Our by-laws will require revision to include regulations hitherto thought unnecessary and planning, especially along metropolitan lines, will grow in importance. To quote from a well-known textbook, 'At least in metropolitan centres, local town planning, zoning and housing must give way to regional planning, zoning and housing. The city or town (or municipality) can no longer be independent in these respects. The economic area is usually made up of the mother municipality and a number of other municipalities surrounding it. Movement of population, development of business centres and trends in values pay no attention to municipal boundaries. The economic area is the logical unit for planning, zoning and housing control.''

"It is, of course, essential, if we are to maintain our solvency, which in turns means our independence," Reeve Ray continued, "that our fiscal policy will need scrupulous attention, and this should include financial planning for capital expenditures to keep up with future developments as recommended by our Town Planning Commission. And this should include planning ahead to permit the orderly growth of the municipality and to avoid as far as possible the pitfalls and surprises of spot zoning unless it is quite certain that surrounding property values and amenities will not be adversely affected thereby. Your town planners will, no doubt, try to avoid ribbon development in connection with the new Upper Levels Highway and will also try and arrest such short-sighted development where it has already started. No doubt planning in connection with the proposed new Upper Levels Highway will visualize sub-divisions employing the contour plan rather than the checkerboard or grid-iron plan in connection with side roads. When you consider the rugged nature and length of our District, it will be no mean accomplishment to approximate the complete services one expects in a city particularly when we are a residential suburb without industrial revenue in the usual sense of the term. However, our merchants in the established shopping centres and in those planned for the future, will no doubt gear their merchandising with a view to selling more and more to visitors from neighboring municipalities and to tourists. If we are to maintain our position and keep up to our standards, we must guard against widespread development throughout the length of the Upper Levels Highway.''

Even as Reeve Ray was speaking there were signs that the cottage, or traditional way of life in West Vancouver was fast drawing to a close and that a giant step forward was in the offing. Its course would take many directions, and there was no stopping the juggernaut towards excellence. The council was faced with situations never before encountered. The greatest pressure was the question of highrise apartments, but there were equally momentous problems arising: harbor developments for Horseshoe

Bay due to the Black Ball Ferry's advent, the necessity of entering into a joint sewerage system with neighboring municipalities, a senior citizens' housing development; an agreement had been reached with the city and district of North Vancouver toward the building of the Lions Gate Hospital, and, the **Pacific Great Eastern Railway** was "an acute problem once again."

There was, as Reeve John Richardson pointed out the following year, "a deep-rooted pride" in the community. Showing also was a determination to say good-bye to the past, while at the same time appreciating the stepping stones on the path to excellence which had been laid down over the past years.

Construction of the Upper Levels Highway and the **Pacific Great Eastern** were well underway during 1955 and on August 27, 1956, a train with coaches borrowed from hither and yon left the terminal in North Vancouver and headed westward through West Vancouver to Horseshoe Bay.

A non-scheduled event in the great British Columbia Centennial celebrations set the municipality off with a new problem. The series of events began on May 17 when employees of the Canadian Pacific Steamships went on strike, leaving Vancouver Island dependent upon the Nanaimo-Horseshoe Bay service provided by the Black Ball Ferries, and on June 21, employees of that company served 72 hours strike notice.

"Premier [W.A.C.] Bennett acted quickly," notes Captain H.L. Cadieux and Garth Griffiths in their book, **Dogwood Fleet**. "To him it was unthinkable that labor strife should isolate the island. On 23 June, 1958, B.C.'s cabinet invoked the Civil Defence Act and authorized the government to take possession and use of the property and undertakings of the Black Ball Ferries Limited for such periods as might appear to be necessary. The staff of the Black Ball thus lost the right to strike: the service, inadequate as it was when overtaxed, appeared to be assured. The unions agreed to man the ships under government jurisdiction. . . . In June and early July the government conducted a survey of the whole problem of surface transportation to and from Vancouver Island. The two major companies, Canadian Pacific and Black Ball, were asked if they were interested in meeting the expanding needs. They were not. Would they be interested if the Province built the necessary wharves and approaches? No. Hence the government was ready for the climax which came on 18 July, 1958. Negotiations having failed, Black Ball was struck in defiance of the Civil

Defence Act. Back to work orders were ignored and a court injunction was defied. Premier Bennett chose that day to announce that the government would establish its own ferry service between the Saanich peninsula and the Lower Mainland and that work on the vast project of building docks and access routes would be undertaken immediately.''

Black Ball continued to operate its run between Horseshoe Bay and Nanaimo, as well as across Howe Sound to Langdale on the Sunshine Coast, until late 1961 when the provincial government purchased the system and put its own ferries into service. With that improvement, traffic naturally increased along the Upper Levels Highway and the bottleneck at Taylor Way and Marine Drive, not to mention that on the Lions Gate Bridge, became an even more vexing problem.

At the same time, growth problems were facing the members of the Gleneagles Golf and Country Club. They were considering extending the greens to include 18 holes, but the surrounding subdivision closed them in. The solution reached was to sell off the existing course and develop a new one in Richmond. An appraisal of the land was made by a prominent real estate firm and soon afterwards negotiations began between the owners and the council of Reeve Russell Richards to acquire the property. The price set for the land and the five-year-old club house was $350,000. The municipality countered with an offer of $275,000. In the meantime, the club had received a firm offer from another source of $350,000 and it was expected the membership would accept that offer. Faced with that ultimatum, and with an indication that the club would prefer to see the course under municipal ownership, council accepted the club's figure subject to it being approved by the ratepayers through a money by-law. The by-law passed with an overwhelming majority. In fact, Rupert Harrison, then the municipal clerk, said the 90.75 affirmative vote was the highest majority ever given a money by-law in West Vancouver's history.

A glimpse of the old and the present. The venerable Hollyburn School is in the foregound, with the Sentinel Hill residential development in the background. (WVMA)

Nick Kogas' Parthenon between Kew Beach and Eagle Harbour. Many of the Greek art replicas now grace the West Vancouver Municipal Hall. (WVML)

West Vancouver's huge Park Royal Shopping Centre as it appears today. (BPP)

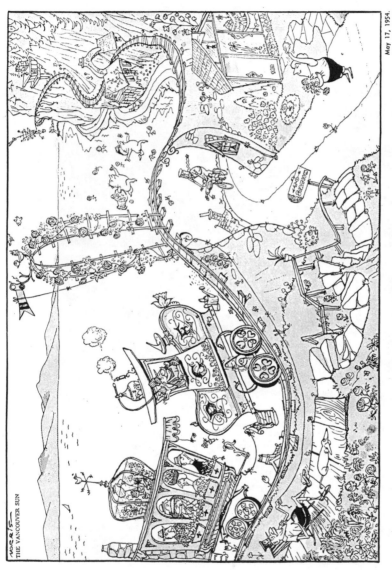

May 17, 1954.

Resolved, by the West Van Beautification and Adoration Society . . . that if the PGE is inevitable, it
be made to conform to the local surroundings . . .

*Popular Vancouver Sun cartoonist Len Norris pokes fun at West Vancouver's concerns over the Pacific
Great Eastern Railway return.*

NORRIS
THE VANCOUVER SUN

July 20, 1955

"Nothing, of course, will ever convince Rodney that they'll go through with their ridiculous plans to build the railway . . ."

Len Norris' "Rodney", like many other residents, found the Pacific Great Eastern Railway cutting through their gardens.

The fury of nature swept away the approaches to the Capilano Bridge in 1949. (WVMHS)

West Vancouver Yacht Club at Fishermans Cove. (WVMA)

B.C. Ferries docking facilities at Horseshoe Bay. (WVMA)

The Upper Levels Highway at Caulfeild. (WVMA)

Gleneagles Golf Course Clubhouse. (WVMA)

John Lawson Park, "where West Vancouver began". (WVMA)

Lawn bowling at Memorial Park has been a popular sport in West Vancouver for years. (WVMA)

*The **Royal Hudson**, which in 1939 brought Their Majesties King George VI and Queen Elizabeth to Vancouver takes excursionists through West Vancouver and up Howe Sound to Squamish. (WVMA)*

Chapter Eleven

MARTINUS VERSUS MARTINI

Premier Bennett had acted swiftly in establishing his British Columbia Ferry Corporation, but on another matter, the much-needed second crossing of the First Narrows, he was dragging his feet. It seemed that the Second Coming would come before the Second Crossing.

Reeve Stanley Collier, who took on the responsibility of being chief magistrate, or reeve, of West Vancouver at 8 p.m., January 5, 1959, was a car dealer and his customers knew, if anybody did, the horrendous problems drivers encountered after leaving home in the morning as fresh as a daisy, then battling the traffic to the entrance to the bridge, lining up at the toll booth, slowly threading their way across the bridge, through Stanley Park and arriving in the office in somewhat wilted condition. In the evening, the funeral procession would leave the driver a nervous wreck by the time he got to the home hearth. It might be a libel to say this, but in earlier times they might have been content with martinus (Latin singular) but now they were having martini (plural).

When details of the Lions Gate design were first announced in the mid-1930s, "sidewalk superintendents" at the time argued that the three-lane bridge was too narrow, but the engineers stood by their calculations, never dreaming, of course, what the future held in store for not only West Vancouver but the whole of the North Shore. Promises of the type politicians make now and again, to wit, "something must be done about it", had been made on numerous occasions, but newly-elected reeve Stanley Collier was so upset about the dilly-dallying that in his inaugural address he tore a strip off the premier.

271

"The only thing that is disappointing and disheartening is the fact that to date just nothing has been done to guarantee another crossing of the First Narrows. This still is, and always has been, a responsibility of the provincial government. Their many promises have failed to materialize, while many large projects with less urgency than ours are being built and more new ones are being added to the list. The rather ridiculous television suggestion of the premier (he has never committed himself in any other way than by the airlanes), his offer to recommend the gift of the Lions Gate Bridge, which we the users have paid for over and over again, with the proviso that we build our own crossing, and which procedure he in the same breath said he did not recommend, I say his fantastic and ridiculous proposal just meant nothing. The so-called offer was his proposition, we did not solicit it—then he refused to discuss it with either the City of Vancouver or ourselves. We don't want more promises at the time of the forthcoming election because we don't have any reason to believe there will be any action then. Why the premier has a determination to isolate and penalize the people of the North Shore is beyond me. I have never taken any part in party politics and don't intend to, but in the former elections I have voted every time for Social Credit and I believe I speak for the majority of people in this area. Mr. Premier surely doesn't overlook the large overwhelming majority given his government which I would think was contributed to by North and West Shore people just as liberally as any other area. Why does he pick on us? Perhaps we should demand definite and positive action on a Second Crossing **before** election time, or, on the other hand 30,000 or 40,000 people affected by the existing conditions could join in a movement under the caption of 'No Crossing—No Vote.'"

Late in 1959 the economy took a severe slump and it was feared "tight money" would mean many public and private programs would go down the drain. One such project could have been the proposal put forward by Panorama Productions Ltd. for a television production centre north of the Upper Levels Highway between 22nd and 24th Streets. An earlier council, back in 1927, had received such a proposal from Lions Gate Cinema Studios, in which the Calgary meatking Senator Pat Burns had an interest. It proposed making "Canadian films for Canadians" in West Vancouver and Panorama's presentation had a similar ring to it, as, in the company's application to council for land, they

272

stated, "It appears that Canada has several advantages over other countries. . . as apparently films produced in this country qualify as British quota films for distribution in the United Kingdom. Such films would also qualify as Canadian quota films. A Canadian TV quota had been established by the Board of Broadcast Governors. American producers who produce their shows in Canada are thus assured of acceptance on the Commonwealth market." The plan called for large, sound-proof studios a Studio Club in which West Vancouver residents could become members. This Club would have 50 guest rooms, first-class dining facilities, a ball room, some indoor recreation facilities, and, possibly, a golf course, tennis courts and a swimming pool. But Hollywood in West Vancouver? "**Never!**" screamed a vocal opposition to the proposal. It would detract from the popular image of West Vancouver as an exclusive residential community and, "well, my dear, you **know** what actors are like!" (Forgetting, of course, that one of West Vancouver's own, Angus Young, now known as Alan, was one of them. He was raised at the corner of 21st and Marine and is probably best-known for his role in **Mr. Ed**, the story of a talking horse.). The presence of actors, actresses "and others" in West Vancouver, the opposition felt, would provide nothing but "cheap sensationalism," "low standards," and "extravagant living." West Vancouver's municipal planning officer, W.P. Paterson, made a wise recommendation to council, when, after careful study of the pros and cons, on February 12, 1960, he gave the green light, as far as he was concerned, for the project to go ahead. In the years that followed, West Vancouver became a "little Hollywood," with many feature films starring the big names of the industry being made here, but none of the fears expressed earlier ever came to pass.

Construction of the film studio got underway almost immediately. Steel began to rise, too, for an extension to Park Royal, the first million-dollar apartment block was rising and the British Columbia Teachers' Federation had filed a set of plans for another one with the municipality. A multi-million dollar sewage plant beside the Lions Gate Bridge was also under construction, and this led to the installing of sewer mains along West Vancouver's streets which, of course, left them in pretty poor condition for a while. "Such upheavals spell progress," Reeve Collier said.

In the December elections the voters gave strong support for a $430,000 waterworks construction by-law, which, with $300,000 held in reserve funds, allowed an immediate and urgent extension of the water system to begin. At the same time the voters approved a $680,000 sewer lateral by-law.

"I would say West Vancouver is the most active centre of progress in the whole Lower Mainland stepping into 1961," Reeve Collier boasted. "With the last minute approval of council of a scheme to replace every streetlight in West Vancouver with higher-powered illumination, our hopes for 1961 certainly take on a much brighter outlook." With that, Reeve Collier's council entered 1961.

This year was to be another banner one. The new sewage plant, "the most modern in British Columbia," was completed; a large Safeway store was under construction at Ambleside, and, biggest project of all, Park Royal Shopping Centre had crossed Marine Drive and steel was now rising "replacing the old Indian habitat of shacks and forest". The Hollyburn Country Club was also being built and much work was being done to improve Ambleside Park and other municipal recreation areas. There was, however, still no second bridge, and another round of Bennett-bashing began, this time during Reeve Alex Forst's first speech as reeve in 1962.

"A frustrating task that I set for myself six years ago, when I was first elected to council, was to enter the battle for another First Narrows is as overcrowded as it ever was. It is inadequate and unsafe, as it was never intended to handle the volume of traffic it is exposed to. The population of the North Shore is fast construction we were told that traffic would fall off on the First Narrow Bridge. Just as predicted by those who knew better, the First Narrows is as overcrowded as it ever was. It is inadequate and unsafe, as it was never intended to handle the volume or traffic it is exposed to. The population of the North Shore is fast approaching the 90,000 mark, plus all the traffic that now originates in the Sechelt Peninsula, Powell River, Vancouver Island and Howe Sound communities. We have had nothing but a number of fantastic proposals such as the so-called gift of the bridge with strings attached to it. Another crossing must be planned immediately or the growth of this great North Shore will grind to a standstill. If the present government continues to take this off-hand attitude, then we will have no alternative but to elect a government that will take action. This bridge or tunnel is definitely a provincial responsibility and not municipal as the premier would have us believe. The reeves and mayors of the Lower Mainland must stand together and force the government to get on with the job.''

Again, progress was unbounded during 1963. Single family dwellings were being built at a faster pace than had been seen for years, and, with more apartments going up, more commercial facilities coming on stream, and more money flowing into the municipal coffers, Reeve Forst predicted that taxes would go **down** for some home owners.

"Ever since I first became interested in municipal matters,'' he said, ''it has been my declared intention to work towards a more attractive and beautiful community. Now progress is not entirely a question of how far we have to go, but how far we have come. In this respect, we must agree, that West Vancouver has come further than any other municipality in the province.''

In 1964 there was, again, the matter of the bridge, but this time it wasn't all bad news. It was good news mixed with bad. The bad news being there was still no sign of a Second Crossing, although the premier *did* order another study.

"When the provincial government first indicated that tolls would be taken off interior bridges,'' Reeve Forst told the 1964 council, ''it was pointed out by representatives of this area that this was grossly unfair. The government might have removed the tolls off the Burrard Inlet crossing on their own, but they did not do so before a **joint** protest was made. The savings to West Vancouver residents in toll charges total well over $500,000.'' The tolls were actually removed in 1960.

Major developments in 1964 included a $750,000 addition to the sewage treatment plant, the cost being shared by the three North Shore municipalities, the opening of the Inglewood Private Hospital on Taylor Way, the expansion of the Hollyburn Club, the sight of nine new high-rise apartment blocks going up, and on November 20, the lieutenant-governor of British Columbia, Major General George Pearkes, V.C., arrived to officially open the new municipal hall.

When Reeve Forst went before the inaugural meeting on January 3, 1966, he was able to look back at 1965 with a great deal of satisfaction. "Never before has there been so much construction for municipal purposes,'' he said. School construction was valued at $1.5 million; a skating rink and additional parking for the community centre was being put in. There were improvements to Ambleside Park, with an 18-hole pitch-and-putt course being laid out, and other public works projects included road paving, sidewalks and more water works construction.

"It has been suggested," he stated, "that we discourage further development until another First Narrows crossing is built. With respect, the impracticability of this proposal must be apparent as a logical approach to the problem. It would seem grossly unfair to freeze property on which the owners have been and will continue to pay taxes. It must be noted that there was a greater investment last year in single family than apartment houses. The only answer, of course, is another crossing. In this respect the highways minister promised that a start would be made in 1966. Premier W.A.C. Bennett repudiated this promise. It would seem reasonable that the responsibilities of highways and bridges would be that of the minister holding that portfolio. Mr. Gaglardi should have his way and get on with the job. If the provincial government feels this problem is too complex for their administration to tackle, perhaps it might consider the formation of a separate authority to bring about a plan for a new crossing and approaches."

The changes sweeping West Vancouver also involved the Millerd family's Great Northern Cannery, at Sherman, although it was more of a status change than anything else. Instead of becoming a forest of apartment dwellings, the Fisheries Research Board of Canada purchased the site for $340,000 and converted the old plant into one of the most modern fisheries research stations on the continent.

It is said that growth brings problems that must be dealt with before further growth can take place and it is that combination that faced Reeve Forst as he entered another term of office. "In view of the municipality's continued growth 1967 should be a year when priority will be given for municipal works toward services in the interest of safety," he said. He pledged a new firehall would be built at Fulton and 16th, the public safety building would be expanded to fill the space to be vacated by the firemen, and more court room space would be provided as well as an improved training program for the volunteer fire department.

The bridge:

"If something is not done now to relieve the traffic bottleneck at Taylor Way and Marine Drive the Lions Gate Bridge, will indeed, become nothing more than the world's longest parking lot due to the eventual backing up of traffic...the patience of residents of the North Shore is wearing thin."

There will be those who remember "the slough" just east of Ambleside Park, which in some times past had possibly served as an exit for waters of the unpredictable Capilano River. What beach parties were held down there on the spit which divided the First Narrows from the sluggish waters of the slough! The bonfires! The raft trips up its unchartered waters! Perhaps more than anything else, the memories of the solitude, the quacking of ducks and the squawking of marine birds stand out the most. It was like going into the heart of the woodland where one could find peace and contentment, and a place to stay for a while. And what did council do? They made it into a bird sanctuary and created a thing of beauty which will be a joy forever...a place of excellence.

There is only one jarring feature to offset the peace and serenity of the bird sanctuary and that is the noise created by the unceasing traffic on the Lions Gate Bridge only a few hundred yards to the east. Once again, Reeve Forst had to mention "the timeworn subject" in his 1969 inaugural address in which he said he and Mayor Tom Campbell of Vancouver had called upon Prime Minister Lester B. Pearson in Ottawa to discuss the possibility of the federal government becoming involved in the building of the second crossing.

"During our talks," Reeve Forst said, "we were given to understand that the federal government would build a toll facility if the provincial government would share the cost to the amount of $27,000,000. Provincial Prime Minister Bennett has since agreed to share to the above amount. The designated federal authority appointed was the National Harbours Board. During the fall of 1967 the Hon. Paul Hellyer was made the new minister of transport. He has since appointed government engineers to assess the many designs and proposals that have been produced for the crossing. They were in Vancouver for discussions just before Christmas and we have now been assured that a decision will be made public by February of this year. It would appear that definite progress has been made."

The result of the engineers' meeting was the appointment of Swan & Wooster, well known Vancouver engineers, to design a new crossing with Welch Street in North Vancouver being the

277

connecting link with West Vancouver. It was said the design would be completed within a year and the long-awaited Second Crossing would become a reality by 1973. When the plan was finally announced it called for a crossing between Brockton Point and North Vancouver, designed to accommodate rapid transit through either a bridge or a tunnel. The cost of the project was staggering and soon the design was consigned to the pigeon holes of the archives of Dreamland.

Alex Forst entered his last term of office in 1970 in the midst of a bitter controversy over the private development of what came to be known as the Cypress Bowl. It was a bitter argument, fought not only round the West Vancouver municipal council table, but in the halls of the Legislative Assembly in Victoria and in the courts. He summed it up, he said "with some reluctance," in his 1970 inaugural address:

"I want to say...that Council acted throughout the entire period of development in the public interest and in good faith on the basis of information available to it. If the provincial government withheld information which affected the changes in ownership of the company [Benquet Consolidated], then the turn of events was their responsibility. If the company did likewise despite their undertaking to keep council informed and guaranteed by bond, then they must shoulder the responsibility. If Mr. Ken Farquharson, as the chairman of the Cypress Bowl Advisory Committee, withheld information that should have been made available to his committee and council, then some of the responsibility of the confusion that developed must rest with him. It was Mr. Farquharson who personally approved the appointment by council of Mr. Mel Borgersen of Seattle as consultant on the planning of the bowl. When Mr. Farquharson ran for council in 1968, he stated publicly that the Cypress Bowl was no longer an issue. In November, 1969, Mr. Farquharson could have called a meeting of his committee at any time. To my knowledge, when he had secured secret information in respect to the Bowl that was not known to council, he did not do so. I do not wish to indulge in recrimination. Mr. Farquharson probably acted as his conscience guided him."

The mayor then quoted from an article Mr. Farquharson wrote for the **Lions Gate Times** on January 30, 1969: "That as our local ski slopes are overcrowded, that Cypress Bowl be developed quickly and to ensure that the area be developed for the best possible development for both winter and summer use." To that the mayor added, "This view supports the actions of council during 1969. Council has always taken the position that it was in the public interest to permit Cypress Bowl to be opened up to serve the people of Greater Vancouver and zoned the area for recreational use only and nothing else, with the added protection that no construction of any kind was to take place without coming back to council. . . . If other municipalities in this area agree with us that Cypress Bowl, and yes, Hollyburn Ridge as well, would become a much needed recreational facility, and for the common good, we would welcome their interest and support. There are literally thousands of acres available for a summer and winter playground. Much has been said of this great controversy. For my part, I believe that many of the statements would have been better left unsaid. Now I would ask that all of us close ranks and work towards a common goal in the interests of all of the citizens."

This unsettling state of affairs came to a well-accepted conclusion in 1975 when Cypress Bowl became the 2,100 hectare Cypress Provincial Park, the entrance to which provides one of the finest views obtainable of the entrance to Vancouver's harbor, and, of course, of that place of excellence, West Vancouver.

At the start of his term of office in 1971, Mayor Arthur E. Langley called on West Vancouver citizens to rededicate themselves to work for a better country, province and municipality, to work "in co-operation with one another, not working as oppositionists, not as obstructionists, not as individuals thinking of ones-self first, but as one dedicated to that which is best for all mankind."

Although much had been accomplished during Mayor Langley's 4 years in office including a new firehall in British Pacific Properties, a seniors only apartment at 15th Street and Esquimalt Avenue, near completion of the rebuilding of the Upper Levels Highway and the start of the Capilano River regional park, he closed his term, as he had started, recognizing the need to work for each other. . . . . . "I know that working together we will deal with every challenge for the good of all".

The problems facing West Vancouver now were matters that reached into every household across the land, —inflation and the ever-increasing proportion of every dollar earned that goes into taxation in one form or another. Mayor C.P. Jones put it this way: "Today, every worker who starts work at 9:00 in the morning and works an eight-hour day works all of his morning and part of his afternoon to pay taxes. Only when he's finished that does he earn money that he can spend himself. Something like 45 per cent of all goods and services produced in Canada go to taxes. Several years ago, this council decided it was time to stop this and although West Vancouver council cannot change the course of society, we have stuck with the philosophy over two years. In 1976 the increase in taxes in West Vancouver was less than the rate of inflation. That is, the proportion of your wealth that we took to run the municipality decreased. In 1977, this past year, when inflation was running at six per cent, our mill rate rose 5.1 per cent and we carried our philosophies through."

While new apartments continued to push their way skyward, and new subdivisions were appearing, amenities for the senior citizens and recreational facilities were, within the framework of the tax system, becoming the major concerns of council.

"The transformation of West Vancouver from the Martini Capital of Canada has been accompanied by those grins of happiness that you see on the faces of all the joggers, usually after they stop jogging," Mayor Jones remarked.

THE VANCOUVER SUN

June 18, 1955

"... and what's more, we'd thank the First Narrows First Do-It-Yourself Society to stay out of this controversy ..."

The residence of pioneer resident John Sinclair in the 1800- Block Bellevue falls to the demolitionist's hammer to make way for the Mona Loa Apartment block. (EP)

The Mona Loa Apartment block which was built by developer Ed. Prescesky on the old Sinclair property. (WVMA)

The stylish West Vancouver Municipal Hall, opened November 20, 1964. (WVMA)

Oldtimers will remember paddling their canoes in what was called the slough (VPL). Today it is a parklike bird sanctuary. (WVMA)

The West Vancouver Memorial Library. (WVMA)

Apartments in the Place of Excellence. (WVMA)

Beautiful homes on the Caulfeild Plateau. (WVMA)

Gracious living in the Kew Beach area. (WVMA)

Waterfront homes on Eagle Island. (WVMA)

Glenmore Park playscope. (WVMA)

Pergola at Whytecliffe Park on site of original Cliff House restaurant.

*Dundarave pier and the Japanese training ship **Nippon Maru**, 1967. (WVMA)*

West Vancouver Aquatic Centre on site of original St. Stephen's Church. (WVMA)

Plaza outside West Vancouver Senior's Recreation Centre. (WVMA)

West Vancouver's heritage building, the old ferry office at the foot of 14th Street. (WVMA)

Young and old find their place in West Vancouver's renowned recreation areas. (WVMA)

Chapter Twelve

ALL SYSTEMS GO

A new era dawned in West Vancouver in 1975 during the term of office of Mayor C. Peter Jones, and its outward and visible sign was purely and simply this: it saved money for the taxpayers. The secret of "it" was electronic wizardry which, in a fraction of a second, could perform mathematical and other miracles. "It" had a memory better than the proverbial elephant, although its size gave no indication as to its capabilities. It solved problems that would have taken hours, perhaps longer, to work out by the old methods using pencil and paper. It could store in a few cubic feet of space records that previously took up more valuable storage space. With its arrival, new sets of procedures were laid down, all of which were geared to provide greater efficiency. And the word "streamlined" came to the fore, a word that was introduced into the West Vancouver lingo in the mid-thirties when Pacific Stages, which ran between North Vancouver and Horseshoe Bay put "streamlined" buses into service. Now it had a new meaning. In the thirties, when the old municipal hall was the nerve centre of the municipality, clanking hand-jerked adding machines, and noisy Remington typewriters were the office machines of the day. And it was said in those days, which seem today as being in the Dark Ages, that an office was most efficient when it **sounded** busy. But now, the reverse is true and it is silence that is the test to efficiency. All this came about with the introduction of the computer in 1975 and many thought this new gadget would eliminate jobs. But this has not been the case, in fact the opposite is true. Technology and its rapid acceleration has opened the door to new worlds in planning, accounting, engineering and other services and well might the shades of

293

municipal employees of the olden days, who witnessed the introduction of electric light and telephones, have said to themselves "What has God wrought?." The computer technology is ever changing, and West Vancouver which has never balked at progress, has responded to the challenge of the new "hi-tech" in the same way it has always responded to change. But the computer does have its limits. There are some who will say, and with good reason, too, that computers are impersonal and cannot deal with human problems, and that includes Victoria, the capital city of British Columbia.

In the summer of 1975, at the dawn of the computer era, the Justice Development Commission in Victoria began to probe the possibility of taking away from the West Vancouver courts the more serious cases on the docket and having those proceedings in Vancouver with all other cases, with the exception of Family Court, being heard in North Vancouver. The proposal was not well received. The West Vancouver Municipal Police objected on the grounds such a move would be a strain on manpower if several members from one shift were called in to give their testimony. Time and money were involved here. But the Crown prosecutor, Lorne Topham, had a more philosophical approach when he made his objections known to the proposed move.

"Someone has assumed," he wrote to the Regional Crown Counsel in Vancouver," that because Court only sits three days per week, it does not handle a sufficient number of cases to warrant keeping it operating as an independent Court." And then he went on to explain "that an independent full-time West Vancouver Court will not only be necessary in the near future, but will be essential to maintain the present quality of justice in the Community."

"Most important, in my opinion, it is absolutely essential that West Vancouver have its own Court in its own Community. It is a unique and compact Community with its own Police Force and its own special problems and needs. It has a character of its own and is very different in all respects from North Vancouver. The majority of the cases heard in its Court involve the citizens of West Vancouver and the cases often reflect the special problems in the Community which are dealt with appropriately by a Judge and Prosecutor who are fully cognizant of these problems, as they both live and work in the Community. It is this aspect which makes it essential for the Community to have its own Court where its citizens are held to account in their own Court in their own Community. To consider moving the West Vancouver Court and its cases into the North Vancouver Court would be detrimental to both Courts and would cearly be an impossible burden on an already busy Court facility in North Vancouver. In addition, such a move would severely limit the constant communication that is always necessary between police and court staff in order to run an efficient Court system. Costs of Police Court time and overtime would increase substantially due to the distance and time spent by Police in North Vancouver, attending interviews, consultations and as witnesses in trials. Finally, and exceedingly important, the inconvenience to the citizens of West Vancouver in having to deal with their Court problems in North Vancouver instead if their own Community is unwarranted from every standpoint. From simply paying a parking fine to attending Court as a witness or complainant, it is not an acceptable alternative to the present Court system. Anyone who will take the time to examine the facts will agree that West Vancouver has the case volume to warrant its own Court within the Community and because of its unique character to have its own Court.''

As they said in the stories of the "olden days", once upon a time the courts were held in the West Vancouver municipal hall, and down below, in the basement, were the offices of the municipal police force with its iron-barred cell. The writer remembers being in that cell, not for any breach of the law, but rather in **support** of His Majesty the King. It was during the Second World War when Air Raid Precaution (ARP) tests were given there. There are many stories told, some true and some not quite so true, about those cells but that was a true one. As the municipality expanded, the police department expanded as well, and there was need for an enlarged police station. As a result, in 1954, the Public Safety Building, with facilities for both police and for 13 years, fire protection, was erected at the corner of 13th and Marine, opposite Ambleside Park. But at the very dawn of the computer age, 1975, the West Vancouver Police Commission was recommending to Council that the police building be extended, not only for their own use, but to include an expanded court facility.

Council was told by a court official that such a facility "would provide a larger work area which we desperately need for additional help, office furniture and equipment. Crown Counsel had no office which means there is no place in which to interview Crown witnesses, other Counsel, or to keep prosecution files and records. We have no Barristers Room, as this has been taken over by the Provincial Deputy Sheriff. We do not have an office or any office space for the use of the Court Reporter."

A great many meetings were held with various concerned groups, all of whom expressed the same feeling as that of the Crown Prosecutor, that being, that the courts must remain in West Vancouver. It became a highly contentious issue and years were to pass before it was finally resolved. During this time there were many semantic arguments between the Municipality and the Attorney-General's Department in Victoria particularly over the interpretation of "Family Court." Victoria insisted it included those cases laid under the Young Offender's Act and should be heard in the North Vancouver Court.

Victoria's response was that "it would be ludicrous to have a juvenile court in West Vancouver when a new facility with Judges specializing in Family and Juvenile Law is situated only a couple of miles away."

"There are also distinct advantages to your municipality in that more court sitting time will be available for the adult court and the presiding Judge will be dealing only with adults," an official of the Attorney-General's Department wrote. "The Family Court Judge will quickly get to know the West Vancouver juveniles who are 'repeaters' and your Municipality will, in effect, have the services of two Judges rather than one."

In the meantime, while waiting for Victoria to make up its mind about the use of the Public Safety Building, which would include court room facilities, costs had soared and new budgetary projections had to be made. Finally an agreement was entered into and a five year lease was signed for the court space and renovations to the building began. On November 23, 1981 the Attorney-General, Alan Williams, who was West Vancouver's Member of the Legislative Assembly, officially opened the expanded facility at the corner of Thirteenth and Marine Drive.

Mayor C. Peter Jones, like his recent predecessors had, in addition to Victoria, other forces to contend with, and one of the major issues facing his council was the need for storm sewers, a fact which had been brought home with floods during the Christmas season of 1972. Alderman Don Lanskail sought financial assistance under the Canada Water Act and seemed to be getting the run-around. It was inevitable, some said, that the higher up the slopes of Hollyburn Ridge development went there would be flooding on the lower levels. It was also inevitable that the senior levels of government would try to pass the buck. The federal minister of the environment, Jack Davis, wrote that it "is possible that Ottawa could participate with the provincial government in the construction of remedial and other works," but, the minister added, "your first hurdle, of course, is the Province." After more than a year of trying to get together with officials in Victoria, a meeting was finally arranged, the results of which were set forth in a memorandum to council from Terry Lester, the municipal manager.

"To the probable delight of the Provincial taxpayer, we came away from this meeting with no commitment for provincial assistance and, indeed, the minister [Bob Williams] stated that their concern was for flood protection and dyking along the low-lying areas adjoining major rivers..."

Deficiencies had been noted in several culverts installed under the Upper Levels Highway by the Ministry of Highways and steps were taken to remedy this situation, but no major steps were taken until 1975 when Mayor Jones was informed that the National Housing Act had been amended to provide for loans for storm sewer construction works and grants equal to one sixth of the costs, but several major problems were cited.

"Council cannot," Mr. Lester wrote, "with any sense of fiscal responsibility, proceed with work of this magnitude as, even with CMHC assistance, it would mean an additional $120 per year taxation on each of the 10,000 single family homes over a 20-year period. Our debt load would increase to approximately $28 million dollars for a per capita debt of $700. This is so clearly excessive that even if the electorate were to approve such a scheme, it is doubtful the Provincial government would allow a Municipality to acquire a debt of this magnitude."

In Mr. Lester's opinion two avenues were open, first to make further attempts to obtain joint provincial and federal sharing costs, and secondly, to proceed with limited work.

Meanwhile, a by-law was drawn up designed to prevent the building of structures along creek banks and to prevent the disturbance of natural grown cover on such banks.

Fast flowing, destructive water was not the only water problem council had to face, and there was no magic formula available to solve it. Most of West Vancouver's water supply was purchased from the Greater Vancouver Water Board from the reservoir behind the Cleveland Dam on the Capilano River. But residents of the western part of the municipality drew their supplies from either Cypress or Nelson Creeks, the latter from an intake behind a small timber dam at the outlet of Eagle Lake. This source had the potential for greater development, and it was to Eagle Lake that council turned its attention.

The rapid expansion of West Vancouver from its original core at Ambleside, Hollyburn and Dundarave which was, for all practical purposes, the foreshore area to the "foot" of Hollyburn Ridge, brought with it many challenges, and good old Mother Nature was, in a large part responsible. The further west the development went, the rockier the land became and this brought into sharp focus the skills of the engineer and the architect and nightmare visions to the treasurer. Homes were designed and built to blend in with the rugged, almost soilless terrain, and following in the footsteps of Mr. Caulfeild, the engineers followed the natural contours in building the roads. Often enough it was a case of major sculpturing to get the job done. This brought about a very worrisome problem to the men of the West Vancouver Fire Department as it was soon found that some of the lovely cliff-hanging houses with their winding and sometimes steep driveways, made it virtually impossible to reach in case of emergency. Here again, another skill was brought to bear and the firefighters began a study of every property with a potential access problem, and, working with the owners of the land, a master emergency plan was drawn up.

At the same time, council realized that an expanded water and sewer system was vital in all areas of the municipality. Between 1973 and 1977 a full-scale sewer project was undertaken in the western end of the municipality, tied in with another costly undertaking, that being the tapping of Eagle Lake as a major water supply source.

Wherever one looked in West Vancouver there was growth. Subdivisions were being opened up above the Upper Levels Highway, the British Pacific Properties were being filled up, and added to the westward expansion, the older sections of the community were also undergoing growing pains with new apartment blocks and towers rising everywhere. In acknowledging that this development was an orderly one, one must appreciate the fact that for many years the municipality had carried out a far sighted town planning program and now it had paid off.

All this put a severe strain on the public works department, as well as the park's department. The main depot was in the Park Royal area, a far from satisfactory location, being at the extreme eastern part part of the municipality. And this depot, just kept on growing, just like topsy, with offices and equipment being scattered throughout the municipality. The Parks Branch, for instance, had their equipment stationed at Ambleside Park, the cemetery, Gleneagles Golf Course, the nursery and at Lighthouse Park. Council, in 1976, took steps to centralize this operation and a site for a new facility was selected close to the centre of the far-flung municipality. The property on the highway leading up to the Cypress Bowl recreation area was deemed to be the best location and would allow for future expansion as the need arose. Aside from the convenience, there was another benefit to the new location and Mayor Jones spelled it out in a letter to a taxpayer in September, 1978: "The total cost of the new Works Yard, including land, is anticipated to be less than the value of the land that is now tied up at its present location."

On September 20, 1979, at 4 p.m., Mayor Derrick Humphreys officially opened what now became known as the Municipal Parks & Public Works Yard.

Mayor Humphreys brought into the paneled council chamber a theme, a vision if you like, of what West Vancouver should be, and in his inaugural address of December 7, 1981 he spelled it out:

"It has been shown that West Vancouver is one of the four or five prestigious and attractive suburbs in Canada. I believe there has to be places in this world for some excellence. I believe West Vancouver is such a place, and it is the duty, not only of the Council but of all its residents to maintain a standard of quality and style for the place we have chosen to live. Each of us can play our part in improving both the private and public property of our area. These things can be done by an active concerned participation in what goes on and what should not go on in West Vancouver. Our recreational areas of all types should be used and conserved. Personal property should be protected and improved. Nothing will stay the same without our individual and collective effort. The Municipal forces, public works, parks, police, recreation and fire departments are ready and able to be of service for the good order and enjoyment of the people of West Vancouver, but they cannot do it alone without the support of all of us.''

''A place of excellence'' became his byword, and perhaps it reached its high point when in 1981 the West Vancouver Seniors' Activity Centre was awarded the Canadian Architects' Award of Excellence. This was followed in 1985 when the Canadian Parks and Recreation Association, meeting in Edmonton, gave the Centre its 1985 Facility Excellence Award.

The citation for the Architects' Awards made West Vancouver feel proud:

''This Activity Centre is much more than an aesthetic structure, it portrays the ultimate in the blend of function and beauty. It is a focal point for seniors in the community. An important factor that broadened the dimension of planning for the Centre was the involvement of lay seniors, professional people in the community, and senior service related professionals besides the two main senior citizen organizations. The Centre was designed as an addition to an existing recreational complex and is linked by the creation of a landscaped plaza. Construction is post and beam and clerestories provide natural northern light. An internal 'meeting place' concept is stressed by way of transparencies and free-flowing spaces which make activities visible from within the lobby area. Major activity rooms and workshops for visual arts, fabric arts, music and recreation are a backdrop to the social areas which form the 'heart' of the Centre. An internal courtyard and winter garden provide an alternative to the exterior spaces and generate gardening activities year-round. The sophisticated use of cedar left in its natural state, the introduction of numerous skylights, and the use of rich warm colours and texture create an intimate and home-like atmosphere. The design has won the Canadian Architect Award of Excellence.''

While the building was new, a bit of the days of yore were kept. Oak trees planted beside what was then Fulton Avenue by the late Fred Burgess during the mid-1930s were kept. And the holly trees which graced the front of St. Stephens Anglican Church and Rectory were left in place, and the old cherry tree, on which the writer and his friends used to play is still there.

The Eagle Harbour Community Centre was another step on the road to excellence. In 1984, the Eagle Harbour Community

School closed and the School Board proposed it be leased to the Municipality for a recreation centre, and things began to happen quickly. Saturday, September 22, 1984 was a gala day for Eagle Harbour. There were hot air balloon rides, sky diving demonstration, performances by knights in armour and other events as Mayor Humphreys opened the new community centre.

Horseshoe Bay was not to be left behind. In September 1985 the Horseshoe Bay Business and Professional Association requested the bay area be declared a Downtown Revitalization Area, and from that initiative a plan was drawn up, which was summarized as follows: "In Horseshoe Bay a number of factors coalesce: a unique village atmosphere; a business community with enthusiasm, energy, organization and leadership; a spectacular natural setting proving built-in drawing power; . . . . Downtown Revitilization now will be the foundation for a strong, healthy business community far into the future. This is an exceptional opportunity not to be missed." The opportunity was not missed.

Another major development was at Caulfeild, where, on "the Plateau", just below the Upper Levels Highway, some 280 acres of raw, undeveloped land, came under development.

A magnificient concept, with the charming name "Ambleside-by-the-Sea" was also underway, and this called for the redevelopment of all the waterfront along Argyle Avenue between 13th and 18th Streets into a park-like setting and truly would enhance the already beautiful entrance to the entrance to Vancouver's harbour. It was not a new theme, as each mayor since the days of Charles Nelson had the same idea, but they expressed it in different terms. This time, however, the hard times which had beset the municipality for generations had vanished, and West Vancouver was by now affluent. Ever since the early 1950s councils had been taking the idea seriously and had begun the acquisition of land for what was to be a long-term project which would make Ambleside "a showpiece community."

Big projects, however, are not the only things that go into the making of a place of excellence. There are seemingly little things that add to the quality of life, like the work of the service clubs, the multitude of organizations associated with the cultural life of the community, some of which are known only by a few. The Memorial Library and the Museum and Historical Society add richness to the community, and its sports activities are known beyond the borders of the community. As West Vancouver prepared its 75th Anniversary celebration, it was announced that the Women's World Tennis Championship would be held at the Hollyburn Country Club between July 26 and August 2. Top tennis stars from many nations will be on hand, and television viewers from around the world will have West Vancouver in their living rooms.

There are other amenities, too, of which West Vancouver can be justly proud. There are private hospitals, a professional community second to none, backed by the North Shore Union Board of Health, whose West Vancouver office opposite the Library was the home of Captain Vince, a man who, as manager of the West Vancouver ferry system, played no small part in this Chronicle. And, we must not forget the work of the West Vancouver branch of the Society for the Prevention of Cruelty to Animals.

The Blue Buses still run, carrying some three million passengers each year, but they are no longer based at the foot of 14th Street. Under a regional transit operating agreement, signed on April 1, 1985, the buses are now based in North Vancouver and are owned by B.C. Transit, a Crown corporation but operated by West Vancouver.

This Chronicle began with the Indian people who dwelt at the mouth of the Capilano River and who witnessed the arrival of the first white men to see what is now West Vancouver, and we shall bring our story to an end with them, a people who have always played a role in the community. Any who lived in the muncipality in the 1930s can never forget Chief Joe Mathias, son of Joe Capilano, dressed in resplendent regalia, leading the May Day parade to the beat of his tom-tom. Chief Mathias is gone now and is resting beside his illustrious father, the man who took Indian rights to the throne of King Edward VII. The Squamish Band of Indian Reservation No. 5 have prospered tremendously since the days of Joe Capilano, but it has not been easy for them to reach the position they now occupy. There are still problems to be solved and there does not appear to be any easy solution. An outline of progress and problems is not out of place here. In 1983 the Provincial Government prepared a background paper for Council which traces the confusing path of Indian land history and the often heavy hand of the senior governments in trying to resolve the problems.

Louise Spratley, editor of the Municipal News, wrote in the June 1986 issue:

"Twenty-six acres of West Vancouver parkland on the west bank of the Capilano, and the site of a sewage treatment plant are innocent pawns in a century-long drama played out between senior governments and the Indian people of British Columbia."

"And the unwilling victims in our area are not only the District of West Vancouver, which has spent more than half a million dollars to create a pitch-and-putt golf course, duck pond and seawalk in Ambleside Park, but the Squamish Indian Band. Their members saw 131 acres taken from the Capilano Indian Reserve No. 5 without their consent. And the term 'cut-off lands' was born."

"Historically, reserves themselves came into being during the colonial period of the province's history. It was Sir James Douglas who felt a system of 'reserves' should be established as a means of protecting some of the traditional land uses of the Indian people against the pressures of non-Indian settlement. Generally speaking, the reserves were established in localities where the Indians tended to reside, or in areas which were specifically used for hunting and fishing. In 1877 the Reserve Allotment Commission created for the Squamish Indian Band, Mission I.R. No. 1, Seymour Creek, I.R. No. 2 and Capilano I.R. No. 5."

"If a villain has to be named, it would be B.C. Premier Richard McBride who set up the McKenna-McBride Royal Commission in 1913. This followed years of federal-provincial controversy respecting not only who had jurisdiction over Indian Reserves, but creation and size of the reserves themselves. The Commission had these terms of reference: (a) To identify reserves which were too small and those to which land should be added; (b) to identify additional reserve areas, and (c) to identify reserves too large and which should be decreased in size. When the Royal Commission completed its report, land totalling approximately 83,000 acres were identified to be added to existing reserves; the need to establish some new reserves was identified; lands totalling approximately 33,500 acres were recommended to be removed from existing reserves. The terms of reference of the Royal Commission provided a requirement for the consent of the Indian Bands and Tribes in any reserve acreage reduction. This was made known during the course of the Commission's work. There is no record of consent being obtained from any Indian band.''

"British Columbia adopted the report and brought in legislation to give it full effect. At the same time it sought advice from the Federal Government as to the manner in which the question of 'consent' could be dealt with. In 1920 the Federal Government, apparently despairing of gaining Indian consent for Reserve reduction, introduced legislation extinguishing the need for such consent. It is from this Act that the dispute with the 22 Indian Bands concerning the cut-off lands emanates."

"In 1975 the government of British Columbia entered into an understanding with the representatives of the 22 Indian Bands whereby the Province of British Columbia acknowledged the 'impropriety of the manner in which each of the Reserves was reduced in acreage.' In March 1977 the Federal Minister of Native Affairs and Northern Development acknowledged the 'impropriety of the manner in which the Reserves had been reduced by ignoring the consent requirement in the McKenna-McBride agreement."

"Principles of settlement, including return of the cut-off lands to the Indians, were drawn up and submitted to the Indian Bands. There was no requirement for the Bands to give back lands by which their Reserves were increased in 1913. While representatives of the 22 Indian Bands were generally in agreement with the principles of settlement, there was a major disagreement with the Federal Government on the formula of compensation. Negotiations between the Squamish Band relating to Capilano I.R. No. 5 cut-off lands and the Federal Government have resolved the matter of financial compensation plus an outstanding dispute relating to the southerly boundary of those lands. On the Provincial side, the elements of settlement touching upon compensation have been identified. The only remaining issue is the return of lands presently in the name of Crown Provincial to the Federal Government in trust for the Squamish Indian Band. These lands include the parcels utilized by the Ministry of Transportation and Highways as a worksyard, the sewage treatment facilities and 26 acres of parkland lying west of the Capilano River."

"The next step is for the Federal Government to issue an Order-in-Council accepting the Provincial Order-in-Council returning the land to the Federal Government in trust for the Band. When it is done, the cut-off lands will be legally returned to the Squamish Indian Band."

"While negotiations between federal and provincial governments and the Squamish Indian Band revolved around financial issues and jurisdiction over the land, West Vancouver Council found other issues surfaced in their quest for a lease of the 26 acres of developed parkland."

"This," (the following chronology) reported the **Municipal News,** "is a synopsis of the lease negotiations and the last Municipal proposal presently before the Band for their consideration:"

"October 1984: The Band agreed to negotiate a lease. The Band stipulated the lease was subject to the Municipality's agreement to provide municipal services, such as water, roads, police and fire protection, to one additional development in the Park Royal Shopping area. West Vancouver agreed to this precondition, subject to traffic, building by-laws, etc., concerns being jointly addressed by the Band and Council."

"March 15, 1985: The Municipality proposed a rent of $20,000 a year, taking into account these facts: (a) $500,000 spent to fill in former swampland and build sea-walk to stabilize shoreline. (b) There would be a net cost of more than $100,000 per year to maintain the proposed lease area. (c) Land exists as a result of reclamation by the Municipality."

"October 11, 1985: Band proposed $50,000 per year for two years only for the parkland, retroactive to November 1, 1984 and therefore finishing on October 31, 1986. A draft 'servicing agreement' was given to the Municipality at this time for the proposed Kapilano 200 development in the Park Royal Shopping Centre area. The issue of legality of the Indian Band entering into formal agreements was questioned by the federal and municipal solicitors."

"February 28, 1986: The Band dropped its precondition for servicing the Kapilano 200 building before entering into parkland lease negotiations. The Squamish Band repeated its proposal for $50,00 per year rent and requested a 'yes' or 'no' answer."

"March 6, 1986: The Municipality responded by offering $50,000 for each two year term commencing February 1, 1986, with a two-year cancellation clause."

There is where the matter stands at present, although, talks continued into 1987.

Thus far we have presented a Chronicle from the beginning up to the present. Many, many people have been involved to make

West Vancouver the place of excellence it is today. Some of them have left no record of their achievements and some are too modest to "toot their own horn." But in the annals, the names of the reeves and mayors who led the way, are remembered as the representatives of all. They are:

1912	Charles Nelson	1945-1946	William Dickinson
1913-1914	John Lawson	1947-1950	Thomas J. Brown
1915-1917	Geo. Hay	1951-1952	J. Howard Fletcher
1918-1920	V.V. Vinson	1953-1954	A. Hugo Ray
1921	D. Morgan	1955-1956	John Richardson
1922	V.V. Vinson	1957-1958	Russell J.G. Richards
1923	R.C. Proctor	1959-1962	Stanley G. Collier
1924-1925	S. Gibsy	1963-1970	Alex Forst
1926	D. Morgan	1971-1974	A.E. Langley
1927-1929	V.V. Vinson	1975-1978	C. Peter Jones
1930-1940	J.B. Leyland	1979-1986	Derrick Humphreys
1941-1942	J. Edward Sears	1987-	D.A.S. Lanskail
1943-1944	Patrick W. Field		

Sanitary sewer pipe laying crew — Wellington St. — 1976. (WVMA)

West Vancouver Public Safety Building. (WVMA)

Seniors' Activity Centre. (WVMA)

North Shore Union Board of Health. (WVMA)

Aerial view Parks & Public Works Yard, Cyrpess Bowl Road. (WVMA)

Eagle Lake. (WVMA)

Cypress Creek in flood, October 1985. (WVMA)

Chapter Thirteen

A WALK WITH HISTORY

The Chronicle of more than seventy-five years of colorful history of West Vancouver is now completed, but before affixing the journalist's -30- to this tale, we should, perhaps, take to our feet and follow the pathway of history through a walking tour of the older parts of the municipality. The routes were designed by Bernard G. Holt, of the West Vancouver Museum and Historical Society, in consultation with Municipal Archivist Rupert Harrison and in conjunction with a Diamond Jubilee promotion of the Ambleside and Dundarave Ratepayers' Association.

This guide proposes several walking routes which pass through the communities of Dundarave, Ambleside, Park Royal and Cedardale. Only the most dedicated hiker would wish to traverse the entire encompassing route in one day's walk. For that reason we have made the walk divisible into shorter segments. It is suggested that interested pedestrians begin a walk along part of the Principal Walk "A", indicated on the map by the solid line. People not wishing to extend their walks beyond a certain point can divert onto a cut-off or secondary route that allows them to return to their starting point without necessarily going over the route already traversed.

The entire encompassing or principal route is designated as Route A and roughly takes three and a half hours to walk without stopping. All important junctions or stations are referred to in the text by the abbreviation "Stn." The number of each station on Route "A" is given a prefix "A" before its sequential number. The secondary route "B" along Braeside Street and through Leyland Park cuts off the Cedardale area. The route "C" is strictly not part of this guide, but is available to those interested, (see note under Stn. A8). Only highlights of this walk are referred to in this text for information and completeness. Route "D" is an exclusively Dundarave walk, which follows along a large portion of the principal route "A", west of 22nd Street.

For visitors to West Vancouver, the walks present an extraordinarily diverse urban environment. While they do not take the walker to the very spectacular larger homes of the British Properties, they do provide a far more varied number of attractions. Those who take these walks will see exceptionally fine public buildings, such as the Memorial Library, Community Health Centre, Recreation Centre and Seniors' Centre. You will pass through several mini-parks, from those of a formal nature to those displaying wilderness and forest environments. You will see streams, tiny brooks and rushing rivers, vistas of mountains and high-rise apartments, charming older and newer homes, schools, a superlative shopping mall and waterfront villages each with their own commercial areas. You will enjoy the special beauty and spectacle of Ambleside Park at the entrance to Burrard Inlet. An interconnecting sea-walk promenade joins the two village communities of Ambleside and Dundarave. Dundarave Village has its own mini-waterfront access, which will be discussed later.

All the circumventing routes are taken in clockwise direction. We believe this is the preferable way to do these walks. For all those going in the opposite direction, it should be remembered that indications in this guide to turn left or right should be opposite from those read.

Principal Walk: "Route A":

For purposes of this guide book, we shall begin this walk at West Vancouver's Memorial Library. There are a number of car parking facilities in this area north of Marine Drive. One will find these at the foot of 20th Street and in the Community Recreation Centre at the 2100 block of Fulton Avenue.

Memorial Library and Memorial Gardens: Stn. A1:

(It is 50 minutes walk from Stn. "A1" to Jefferson Avenue and Braeside Street Stn. "A5".)

Across Marine Drive from the Memorial Library is West Vancouver's War Memorial Archway, which leads to the Memorial Gardens behind. Pass through the arch into the garden behind and afterwards explore the beautiful park to the north and on either side of McDonald Creek. Cross the footbridge to the east side of this creek, and follow the pathway uphill to where

312

the trail exits onto 19th Street intersection with Esquimalt Avenue. Continue up 19th Street, which leads onto a footpath and bridge over McDonald Creek to Fulton Avenue, and turn right (east).

A few paces east along Fulton Avenue brings the walker to the south end of Sinclair Street. Follow this street northwards until meeting Inglewood Avenue. Turn left (westwards) along Inglewood Avenue and walk half a block until reaching the centre of a mini-park on the north side of Inglewood Avenue.

Hay Park: Stn. A2:

This is the south entrance to Hay Park. Take the trail which follows along the eastern side of the creek. This is a delightful small wilderness park following along McDonald Creek and having a variety of native trees. A leisurely stroll in this park with a naturalist's keen eye for detail will prove to be most rewarding! Pass through this park to its northern end, where you meet with an east-west trail running into Kings Avenue at both ends. Turn right to exit by way of Hay Park's north-east access onto a section of Kings Avenue. Cross over Sinclair Street and continue eastwards over a footbridge crossing over Lawson Creek. The path then rises up onto a school playground. The route continues eastwards along a cut grass embankment with the continuation of Kings Avenue immediately to the east.

West Van. Secondary High School & Inglewood Centre: Stn. A3:

A pause here is worth making for a number of reasons, apart from the vantage point of watching the kids participate in active sport. To the north, across the athletic track and playground, can be seen West Vancouver's Secondary High School, which was opened in 1950. It is interesting to note how all levels of government assisted in funding the large workshop complex on the south side of the main school building. In the 1960s the federal government was anxious for the nation to have more skilled trades people. Thus, when the West Vancouver School Board applied for a grant for the $500,000 complex, the federal government paid 90 per cent, or $450,000 of the amount. The provincial government shared on a 50:50 basis the $50,000 balance!

On the south will be seen the old Inglewood Junior Secondary School, which was opened in 1927. The premises are now used as a Y.M.C.A. recreation centre. To the west of this building one will see a lower single-storey structure which is the Jewish Community centre, Kehilat Har-El. Originally, these were Canadian Army huts located in Ambleside Park during the war. Immediately west of this centre is a wooded area which obscures Lawson Creek. This was the site of one of West Vancouver's early saw mills. Robt. Shields built a mill spanning the creek sometime around 1918. There is now very little evidence that a mill was ever here.

In proceeding across the playing fields, you are advised to walk beside the low wire fence adjacent the cinder track at the top of the grass embankment. At the eastern end of the school's playing fields, pass onto Kings Avenue. Continue eastwards on the sidewalk, and cross over both 15th and 14th Streets.

Chatwin Park: Stn. A4:

Before reaching 13th Street and Kings Avenue, turn right into Chatwin mini-park. Take the trail which follows a south-easterly direction, and emerge from this park at the intersection of 13th Street and Jefferson Avenue. This is a semi-wilderness park with particularly fine specimens of Douglas Firs and Western Red Cedar. A small brook runs through this park, which is bridged for convenience. Part of this park has cut grass and is suitable for picnicking.

Continue eastwards along Jefferson Avenue, crossing 12th and 11th Streets. A further block East of 11th Street we come to Braeside Avenue, our first official 'cut-off' route, which is to turn right down Braeside Street for those who wish to leave out the Cedardale section of the principal walk.

Jefferson Avenue and Braeside Street: Stn. A5 for details of the Cut-Off Route "B":

(It is a 30-minute walk from Stn. A5 to the lower Capilano River trail: Stn. A8).

To continue on the Route "A", keep going eastwards along Jefferson Avenue, keeping the Sentinel Hill summit on your right. Good views of both Grouse Mountain, elevation 3,974 ft. with its gondola chair lift and with Goat Mountain behind, elevation 4,587 ft. can be seen to the north from the eastern end of Jefferson Avenue. The British Properties are also seen to good advantage before reaching the end of Jefferson Avenue.

Jefferson Avenue and Younette Drive: Stn. A6:

Jefferson Avenue continues eastwards as a cul-de-sac. Both the properties 805 Jefferson Avenue and 802 Younette Drive have driveways leading off this small section of road. At the bottom far end of this cul-de-sac, look for the signpost directing you onto a footpath which leads south onto Inglewood Avenue.

Turn eastwards again and follow Inglewood Avenue down to its intersection with Taylor Way. At the north-west corner of Taylor Way and Inglewood Avenue is the Inglewood Lodge and private hospital for senior citizens. Cross over Taylor Way at the traffic lights, and continue down Inglewood Avenue to where it ends. On your right, looking south across the playing fields of Cedardale private kindergarten school, you can catch a glimpse of downtown Vancouver. Cedardale Elementary School was originally opened in 1934. However, it was closed down as a public school in 1984 owing to insufficient number of students.

At the end of Inglewood Avenue pass onto a footpath which leads down to a concrete footbridge which spans Brothers Creek. Continue up along this pathway to re-emerge onto Inglewood Avenue.

Two rather interesting homes on the north side of Inglewood Avenue should be noted. The first one is 490 Inglewood Avenue, named "Holdfast". This is a lovely old log cabin residence with an unusual stone annex and large chimney. Next to it is another large property, 315 Inglewood Avenue. Its boundary is skirted with a series of brick pedestals forming a front fence. On top of each are statues which include Snow White and the Seven Dwarfs and miscellaneous figurines. The western part of this garden has been made into a mini-world of landscaped mountains and figurines, complete with a stream and dwarf plantings.

At Inglewood Avenue and 3rd Street, turn right (south) onto 3rd Street, and continue on this street until meeting with Keith Road.

Keith Road and 3rd Street: Stn. A7:

(It is a 4-minute walk from Stn. A7 to the Capilano River Trail, Stn. A8).

Keith Road was the original cross-town road on the North Shore.

At this junction, you have a choice to save about 12 minutes of walking time to reach Stn. A8 on the Capilano River bank. If you decide to do this, then merely take the sign-posted footpath immediately opposite the southern end of 3rd Street to the Capilano River Trail. On the way to the river, the trail passes beneath a canopy of young fir, maple and alder trees. Glimpses of Woodcroft Park high-rise apartments are noted on either side of this trail. It is only a short walk down to the bank of the spec-

315

tacular Capilano River.

Extended Route A to Klee Wyck House and Park:

(It is a 16-minute walk to Stn. A8 on this extension walk).

The pedestrian who wishes to visit Klee Wyck House and gardens, together with the opportunity to view the original Keith Road bridge crossing of the Capilano River, should turn left and proceed up Keith Road.

Continue along Keith Road to its end, passing the entrance to Klee Wyck House on your right. Here, under the present Upper Levels Highway crossing of the Capilano River, was also the location of the original land crossing from North Vancouver. The four concrete footings of the old Keith Road central bridge span are still able to be seen.

After viewing this, return to the entrance to Klee Wyck House at 200 Keith Road. Enjoy a stroll through this lovely park and take a short rest. This land was originally assembled in 1911 by Ed Mahon. He sold it to Clarence F. Fernside in 1925, who then had the present house built on the property. By 1942 this property belonged to Kenneth T. Fernside, who sold it to a C.V. Winch. Eventually, a Dr. (Mrs.) Trapp acquired the property and subsequently bequeathed it all to the Municipality. The house now serves as the headquarters of the West Vancouver Arts Council. Part of the grounds are given over for use as a nursery which the Parks Board uses to supply trees, shrubs and plants to put around various locations within the municipality.

Across Keith Road is another house, known as Spuraway. This dwelling, with an architectural style peculiar to the Orient, was built by Japanese carpenters for a Mr. Dillon of North Vancouver in 1911. In 1912 the property was bought by Edward Mahon and in 1923 sold to George Hermann. Mr. Hermann was a keen horseman and had some stables on the property, which was given the name Spuraway. Later the house and property were bought by the timber industrialist, Gordon Gibson, Sr.

After leaving this park, retrace your steps down Keith Road until reaching the corner of the park and nursery. A trail runs south from Keith Road beside the western boundary of this park. On the other side of the steel wire mesh fence that the trail follows, can be seen the municipal nursery. Take this footpath to the river bank, and continue following this trail until reaching Stn. A8, which is at the junction of the next trail marked as a hiking trail to your right.

Lower Capilano River: Stn. A8 (Access to Route C):

The trail going upstream is referred to in this guide as Route C. It is beyond the scope of this chapter to give a detailed account of this impressive walk. However, highlights include the spectacular gorge through which the river passes; the federal government fish hatchery; the suspension bridge; the gondola skyrides to Grouse Mountain and views across Capilano Lake to the twin 5,000-foot peaks of the Lions. The pathway going upstream from Stn. A8 can be negotiated over the rocks by agile hikers. For those who would prefer not to do this, it is recommended to pass up the trail to Stn. A7 on Keith Road and Third Street. Turn right up Keith Road and pass Klee Wyck House on your right. Continue on the road which passes under the Upper Levels Highway bridge. This road ends at a gate, which is the beginning of the trail proper leading into the Capilano Gorge.

Lower Capilano River to Park Royal: Stn. A8:

(It is a 20-minutes walk to Park Royal south trail, which leads to Ambleside Park, Stn. A10).

We continue Route "A" by turning right downstream. The river-bed is usually seen with an abundance of worn boulders and hard smooth outcrops of granite sub-strata. During times of heavy rainfull, the river can rise dramatically and cover most of the boulders and rocks. A few minutes' walk south from Stn. A8 brings one to a seniors' home known as Beacon Hill Lodge. Follow the signs on the service road which crosses Brothers Creek, and on to Clyde Avenue.

Clyde Avenue and Park Royal North: Stn. A9:

From this location you may wish to pass along Clyde Avenue westwards to reach Woodward's department store and food floor, together with the rest of North Park Royal Mall. The trail, however, continues along the river's bank behind the tudor styled Park Royal hotel, where you can stop for a meal or other refreshment. As you continue a little further, the trail passes under the two road bridges of Marine Drive. Immediately, the pedestrian is confronted by a fourteen-storey black office tower. The Burrard Inlet Harbor Masters' offices are located here on the top floor, and so also are the British Pacific Properties Ltd. offices. The latter are the owners and developers of both North and South Park Royal shopping areas. Together, both the north and south malls are madeup of about 170 retail shops and service businesses. This shopping centre was the first one to be built in Canada, the earliest part of which goes back to 1950.

Park Royal South:

After passing the black office tower, you may wish to visit the south shopping mall. Both The Bay and Eatons department stores are located here, together with many other retail shops and offices. There are a number of eating establishments in both the north and south malls.

Whether you are following along the river bank trail or passing through the south shopping mall, a slight diversion to a position south of the glazed-over Winter Gardens, adjacent to the Super-Valu's food floor, should be made. In the centre of a pond will be seen a very lovely marble statue by the French sculptor Sylvain Salliere. It depicts a muse seated upon a rock playing a stringed instrument with four cherubims around the base. It must be among the most valuable statues of its kind in the province.

Park Royal South Trail to Ambleside Park: Stn. A10:

(It is a 30-minute walk to the Ambleside and Dundarave Centennial Sea-Walk, Stn. A12).

You return to the river bank trail on a sign-posted pathway to the south of Super-Valu's food floor. After passing through a wooded area, the path continues under the British Columbia Rail bridge. Here you enter the beautiful Ambleside Park at the eastern end of which the Capilano River meets the sea.

Ambleside Park:

Views of Vancouver's inner and outer harbours with all manner of water-borne craft from ocean cruise liners to sail-surfing boards can be seen. The spectacular view of the First Narrows, Stanley Park, University of British Columbia and Point Grey and Vancouver Island on the horizon is seen to good advantage from the Sea Walk. On a clear day Mt. Baker elevation of 10,778 ft. can be seen framed by the Lions Gate bridge.

The eastern portion of Ambleside Park is on lease from the Squamish Indian Band. This part contains a 'keep-fit' area, dog exercise area, pitch and putt golf course and waterfowl pond. Further facilities and attractions at Ambleside Park are: a refreshment and snack bar open throughout most of the year; picnicking areas on the grass or beach; children's play area; playing fields and tennis courts; sand beaches to swim and play on; fishing from the breakwater; the western parking lot and limited parking spaces along the road systems; Hollyburn Sailing Club at the extreme

318

end of the park.

Before leaving the park at the western end, you should inspect two monuments. The first consists of a fourteen-foot post on a stone base which commemorates a coast-to-coast walk by Clyde McRae. He finished the 96-day walk across Canada on August 4, 1973. The second monument commemorates Piloto Don Jose Maria Narvaez, who was the first European to see mainland western Canada. The inscription on the commemorative plaque gives the date on which Narvaez left "Puerto de Bodega y Quadra", now Port Discovery. This is located on the Olympic peninsula in the bay to the southwest of Port Townsend, near the entrance to Puget Sound. He began this twenty-two day voyage of discovery by leaving this haven on July 1, 1791. He would have seen present-day West Vancouver from a distance sometime between the 10th and 16th of July.

Ambleside Village: Stn. A11:

As you leave Ambleside Park's Centennial Sea Walk, you enter Ambleside Village area. In 1985 there were 245 businesses operating in this commercial zone. Turn left (west) down Argyle Avenue, which is immediately north of the Hollyburn Sailing Club. On reaching 14th Street, it should be appreciated that the area to the south will become known as Heritage Square. It is the site of the 1914 Ambleside pier and ferry terminal. The building with the clock was erected in 1913 as a ferry ticket office. After this area became the West Vancouver 'Blue Bus' maintenance depot, this building became the Bus Management office. The whole area is due for redevelopment once the approved relocation into North Vancouver of this bus depot becomes a reality. At a later date, the waterfront properties in the 1400 and 1500 blocks are scheduled also to be redeveloped, hopefully as a parkland for public enjoyment.

Just before reaching a waterfront mini-park, we come to 16th Street. A photograph known to have been taken in 1908, shows that this street marks the approximate location of a small pier connected with a Dudley Walking Railway which ran in a straight line to the present Eyremont area in the British Properties. It dealt in timber which the Dudley hauled down to the waterfront. It can be presumed to have been built sometime around 1900 to 1905, and was the only one of its kind ever to be built in B.C. It is thought to have ceased operations around 1911 after the cable snapped and the Dudley engine went into the sea.

319

John Lawson Park and 1700-Block Argyle Avenue:

After crossing over 16th Street, the walker enters the delightful mini-park known as John Lawson Park. It is named after the pioneer who bequeathed part of his waterfront land to the municipality. At the western end, one will notice in the kiddie play area an old holly tree. Mr. Lawson, who was of Scottish ancestry, had a fondness for this tree. It is also to be noted that a creek, which became known as Lawson Creek, passed through his property to the sea. The Scottish name for creek is 'burn', and thus it became an obvious choice for Mr. Lawson to name his house Hollyburn. He worked for the Canadian Pacific Railway, and noticed on his way through Agassiz that holly bushes grew there. Eventually, he collected some of these trees and planted them around his house. It is presumed that Navvy Jack's original house, into which Mr. Lawson settled his own family, was located about sixty-five paces west of the western side of 17th Street, and in line with the present 1700-block homes of Argyle Avenue. Mr. Lawson was the first postmaster and his home was the first post office in West Vancouver. Four more post offices were to be built in Ambleside, culminating in the present 1956 Post Office on 17th Street and Bellevue Avenue. Between where the present railway track runs and Bellevue Avenue, on the west side of 17th Street is the site of Mr. Lawson's real estate office. It also had two holly trees planted on either side of its entrance. The name Hollyburn became associated with this area, and the mountain above us retains this name. Mr. Lawson's 160 acres of property took in all the land from 16th to 18th Streets, and from the shoreline to Haywood Avenue. He also donated the land for the city hall, built originally in 1912.

As previously stated, the pier from John Lawson Park was the site of the first ferry operation in West Vancouver. The park itself is considered to be a "Family Park" for kiddies and for those who seek a break from the bustle of a busy commercial area. This is an ideal park for picnics and views of the outer Vancouver Harbor.

West Vancouver's Oldest House:

There is no certain date that can establish the building of West Vancouver's oldest home that still exists today, albeit in a much altered condition. We have been given to understand that in 1887, Navvy Jack had been living in West Vancouver the longest of six other people named. He had been located at Lawson Creek

320

at that time, and in 1889 actually obtained legal title to the land. It would not be unreasonable to conjecture that he built this house in the early to mid-1880s. As mentioned previously, Mr. John Lawson acquired this house in 1905, and ultimately named it Hollyburn House. Several other owners took possession of it sometime during which time it was moved to its present site. This is immediately to the west of Lawson Creek, at 1768 Argyle Avenue. It has over the years been greatly modified and looks quite different from its original appearance.

Before we pass on from the 1700-block of Argyle Avenue, observe the curious white wrought iron fences of 1734 Argyle Avenue. These come from an early courthouse which was situated in the vicinity of Main Street and Cordova Street in downtown Vancouver. This building was demolished more than 45 years ago. They were the balusters and railings from the stairs leading from the first-floor lobby to the second-floor court rooms. Note the dogwood emblem in the centre of the diagonal-shaped Union Jack basic pattern. In front of this property, between the railway tracks and Argyle Avenue, also stood an outsized "winter-hardy" apple tree. It was cut down sometime during 1956 by the Pacific Great Eastern (British Columbia Rail) authorities in preparation for the re-opening of the lines for trains. This was probably the last tree of Navvy Jack's and John Lawson's orchard, which originally occupied much of this area.

Horse Chestnut Trees on 17th Street:

Before leaving Ambleside area, a word should be made of the 17th Street's canopy of horse chestnut trees. Strictly speaking these are not on the walk itself, but can be seen when looking-up 17th Street from Argyle Avenue. These trees were planted on both sides between Clyde Avenue and Inglewood Avenue, on May 24, 1934, by the Second Troop of West Vancouver's Scout Movement. It is understood that the planting of these trees was to commemorate the visit in April 1934 of the founder of the Boy Scout Movement, Lord Baden-Powell. The project was made possible through a public subscription. Some of these trees have succumbed to disease and other damage. A survey taken in 1981 showed the overwhelming number of citizens canvassed appreciated both the beauty and the cooling shade these trees provide during the hot sunny days.

Ambleside and Dundarave Centennial Sea-Walk: Stn. A12:

(It is a 23-minute walk from Stn. A12 to the outer end of Dundarave pier, Stn. A14).

Continue along Argyle Avenue to 18th Street and turn left (south) to the continuation of the Centennial Sea-Walk. Continue westwards along this walkway for one block, which is the foot of 19th Street. Walkers may return to the beginning of this Route A, which is the Memorial Library and Gardens. Stn. A1. Merely walk up 19th Street to Marine Drive and turn left (west).

For those who wish to enter Dundarave area, carry on along the Sea-Walk.

Centennial Sea-Walk and 22nd Street: Stn. A13:

A little further on, you will notice another pathway coming across the railway tracks after passing through a mini-park area between high-rise apartments. This is the southern connection of the Dundarave Route D where it rejoins the Principal Route A on its final leg back to its starting point at the outer end of Dundarave pier.

The Sea-Walk continues to 24th Street. Eventually, it is hoped to extend this Centennial Walk right up to Dundarave pier, which is only one block west of the end of the present walkway.

Dundarave Village below Marine Drive:

Looking north from the end of the Sea-Walk, you will note the tall 'Sea Strand' apartment building on the right. It is hoped by the majority of residents that this will be the most westerly of waterfront multi-storied apartment blocks. The large house on your left was built in 1920. It used to be a boarding house which also was used for social events.

Walk up to Argyle Avenue behind the waterfront properties and turn left. All the waterfront properties in the 2400-block originally had buildings on them by 1920. It is hoped someday this whole area will become a waterfront park. North of the railway track and Bellevue Avenue will be seen new semi-commercial buildings with luxury apartment units built over.

Dundarave Park and Pier: Stn. A14:

(It is a 35-minute walk from the outer end of Dundarave Pier. Stn. A14 to the Memorial Library and Gardens, Stn. A1).

(This is the beginning of the Dundavare Route D).

Continuing the principal Route A, turn left when Argyle Avenue reaches 25th Street and proceed down onto Dundarave pier, continuing to the outer end. The view of the outer harbor,

Vancouver Island and the shoreline is better than it is at Ambleside Park. A panorama of the foreshore from Point Atkinson in Lighthouse Park to Navvy Jack Point can be appreciated against the backdrop of Hollyburn Mountain. It was from here that George B. Tocher, and a navigator, sailed on May 14, 1978 in a three-ton Haida-style hollowed-out log canoe. They arrived on Waikiki Beach, Oahu on July 17, 1978. This established the feasibility that the native Hawaiian people could have migrated from British Columbia. However, it must be stated that most experts believe the Hawaiian people came from the islands in the eastern Pacific Ocean.

The municipality first built this pier in 1914 for $40,000. It proved to be too exposed for its original purpose, that of a ferry slip. However, it became a tourist attraction and an on-shore fishing facility. A Mrs. Meek in more recent times enhanced the appearance of the pier with a $26,000 donation. It is thanks to her generosity that we have the nautical-style chain fence, soft ornamental lighting and the anchor at the entrance to the pier. During the 1920s a number of provincial swimming and diving regattas took place from Dundarave pier, which proved to be most popular.

On the east side of the pier can be seen a concrete culvert, which is the discharge point of Marr Creek. This creek takes its name from George Marr, who was probably Dundarave's first officially-registered white settler. He came to Dundarave around the turn of the century and established a lumber camp close to this creek, which flows underground from just north of Marine Drive to its exit into the sea.

The delightful Dundarave Park comprises at present of only six building lots. There is a children's play area, concession stand and a semi-sand and gravel beach.

The Clachan:

On the east side of 25th Street, a waterfront building in Dundarave Park is called Peppi's Restaurant. It was built by the Stevenson family in 1912, and was called originally The Clachan. The name is Gaelic for "meeting place". They operated it as a restaurant and hotel. Later it was converted to facilitate dancing. The municipality bought the property in the 1940s, and continued it as a restaurant known as The Breakers. Later, three other leaseholders continued the use of the premises under the name of St. Mawes. The present owners took the place over in 1966.

The Fortune Cup Inn:

Opposite Peppi's, on the west side of 25th Street, once stood the Fortune Cup Inn. It was built in the 1920s as a hotel and restaurant. The P.T.A. had their first meetings here, and in 1930 planned what was to become the annual May Day celebrations in this municipality. The building was finally demolished in 1971 to increase the park area.

The 2400-Block of Marine Drive: Stn. A15:

You are advised to move to 25th Street and Marine Drive, and then to turn right (east). You see what is the High Street of Dundarave commercial area. It is rapidly expanding onto Bellevue Avenue and Haywood Avenue. In 1985 there were 90 businesses currently in operation.

On the south-east corner of 25th Street and Marine Drive is a small parking lot. This may well be the site of Dundarave's first grocery shop. A photograph and other documents record its use for refreshments and provisions back in 1919. It had, of course, existed here for a number of years earlier than this.

The parking lot on the north-east corner of 25th Street and Marine Drive used to be the site of the western bus terminus when it first started up in 1916. The buses travelled between here and the 14th Street ferry terminus. During the 1920s the bus service was extended as far as 29th Street.

The Sagers Building:

The most famous building in Dundarave is Sager's. In 1913, W.J. Irwin built this structure which was rented to the Conservative Party, who named it Conservative Hall. From 1922 it was known as the Dundarave Hall, and continued in a variety of public uses such as a general public meeting hall, exhibition centre and a badminton court. For a time it contained a cabaret dine-and-dance place named The Palms, and was even used as a Presbyterian church. The eastern side was once a separate structure. In 1934, Miss Helen Hunter built beside the Dundarave Hall a smaller premises known as "The Old English Tearoom". Later, this part became an antique shop.

In 1956, Henry and Shirley Sager purchased the main building and, with the smaller antique shop structure, extensively remodelled the two complexes into one entity known as Sager's Maple Shop. In 1982 the local community was split on the issue of whether part of this building could not be converted into a neighbourhood pub. Eventually, it was decided not to proceed with this application. In 1985 the Maple Shop closed, and the premises extensively remodelled.

The Mulberry Tree:

Before leaving Marine Drive via 24th Street, you should look at what is presumed to be the oldest mulberry tree in the Lower Mainland. It is sited east of the last shop on the north side of Marine Drive, about 40 paces east of 24th Street. This gnarled old tree was planted in 1922 by the Sweetman family, but a builder in 1985 damaged what had been scheduled as a tree of special merit.

You should now proceed up 24th Street to Haywood Avenue which is Stn. A16. This is where the Dundarave Route D separates from the principal Route A, to go westwards up Haywood Avenue.

For those continuing on the principal Route A continue up 24th Street to Jefferson Avenue and turn right (east). The school on your left is Irwin Park Elementary School, established in 1955. Behind the school, along 24th Street is Irwin Park.

After heading into Jefferson Avenue, you walk eastwards through an area having small residential properties. On reaching 22nd Street, turn right (south).

Jefferson Avenue and 22nd Street: Stn. A17:

This is where the Dundarave Route D rejoins the principal Route A. As you proceed south along 22nd Street, another school building is seen on the left. This is Pauline Johnson Elementary School, established in 1922. This is one of the oldest schools in West Vancouver. It was closed, but in 1985 was re-opened as part of the district's French immersion program. The West Vancouver Arts Council, together with the West Vancouver Museum and Historical Society, use parts of the building, as does a day and play school.

Continuing down 22nd Street, you pass on your left the Kiwanis Centre for Seniors on Gordon Avenue.

Recreation Centre and Seniors' Centre: Stn. A18:

Continuing south along 22nd Street, you see on your right St. Stephen's Anglican Church. On your left between Gordon Avenue and Marine Drive is West Vancouver's Recreation Centre with Kiwanis Park on the south. The Recreation Centre was originally opened in 1958 with various additional facilities being subsequently added. Midway down this block a pedestrian way provides access for people going to the buildings and onto Fulton

325

Avenue. (It should be noted the Dundarave Route D leaves principal Route A at this Stn. A18. The Route D continues down 22nd Street.)

Continuing on the principal Route A, you should note while walking through the Recreation Centre the variety of facilities available here for the community. These include: an aquatic centre, ice rink, gymnasiums, meeting rooms and tennis courts.

On reaching 21st Street, turn right (south) until reaching Esquimalt Avenue. The building on your right with the wedged-shaped roofs is West Vancouver's Seniors' Centre, which is well worth a visit. This centre officially opened in 1981.

On the south-east side of 21st Street and Esquimalt Avenue there is the United Church of Canada.

You should then proceed one block eastwards along Esquimalt Avenue to 20th Street, and then turn right again (south). At the north-east corner of 20th Street and Esquimalt there is the Christian Science Church. Just before meeting Marine Drive, you should stop to look at West Vancouver's Lawn Bowling Club on the east side of the street.

Finally, at Marine Drive you turn left to the starting point in front of the War Memorial Archway.

Regional and "Cut-Off" Walks:

(There are two other shorter walks to be covered briefly by this guide).

Ambleside Walk (with Cut-Off Route B):

Timings: (This walk takes about one hour and 48 minutes with the use of the Cut-Off Route B via Park Royal and returning to the Memorial Archway via 18th or 19th Streets).

(The Cut-Off Route B itself takes 22 minutes to reach Park Royal south, Stn. A10).

Begin at the War Memorial Arch and follow the walking route as far as Stn. A6. This occurs at Jefferson Avenue and Braeside Street. Proceed south down Braeside Street to its extreme southern end. At this point the road bears sharply left (eastwards) and becomes Anderson Crescent.

You will find some steps leading down the road's south-west corner of the bend. This leads into Leyland Park. At the foot of these steps, the trail divides into two directions. Those who wish to return by the more gentle slopes of the roads are advised to take the right fork into Fulton Avenue, and continue along this road until reaching 13th Street, and then turn left (south).

Proceed across Marine Drive and the railway tracks to rejoin the principal Route A to Stn. A11, which is Argyle Avenue.

Alternatively, for those who do not mind a lot of steps and steeper slopes to walk on, turn left (south). Follow the trail for about 100 paces to reach a viewing spot. This is Stn. B1, which looks down upon both Ambleside and Dundarave villages. Trees somewhat obscure the full potential of a marvellous view, nevertheless it is still well worth the visit.

Continue south along the trail and descend a flight of steps to Esquimalt Avenue. Cross over this road and continue south on a downhill, sloping paved lane. After a short distance this lane makes a sharp bend left (east). From this stretch of lane, the very best view of downtown Vancouver, Burrard Inlet and Burnaby is possible. Continue along this lane until it meets with Keith Road.

Turn right (west) along Keith Road and walk about 120 paces until reaching some steps located between the properties 886 and 910 Keith Road. These steps and trail lead down to the end of Evelyn Drive and to Woodward's Food Store, Park Royal North. From the foot of this trail proceed across the parking lot in the general direction of Super-Valu Food Store. Note: you can avoid crossing Marine Drive itself by taking the footpath over the road bridge on the right.

Behind Super-Valu and the Winter Garden is the famous marble statue of Sylvain Salliere. You rejoin the principal Route A walk at Stn. A10.

The Dundarave Walk: 'Route D':

(This walk takes about one hour and five minutes).

This walk begins at Dundarave pier, Stn. A14. Most of this is part of the principal walk, Route A. Start off by proceeding up 25th Street to Stn. A15 and on to Stn. A16.

On reaching Haywood Avenue, Stn. A16, turn left (west) along this road. On the north side is Irwin Park Elementary School, opened in 1955, and enlarged in 1964. Few of the original homes on the south side of the 2400-block of Haywood Avenue remain. Two large developments were completed in 1985. They comprise the concept of having office or business accommodation at the lower levels, and apartment units above. The earliest house remaining on this block is 2495 Haywood Avenue, which was built in 1911.

Passing into the 2500-block, it should be noted that most of the houses on both sides of Haywood Avenue were built between 1920 and 1929. The house standing on the site 2540 Haywood Avenue was built before 1919. This was the home of George Lloyd, who worked at the railway right-of-ways and bridge construction in both West Vancouver and elsewhere. He worked as the maintenance man at the shingle mill located on the site around where the last relic is the cottage of 2694 Marine Drive. In the early 1930s Mr. Lloyd established a garden nursery, which was taken over by his son. The present owner is Mr. Albert Duynstee. This nursery is known today as "The Maple Leaf Garden Spot".

Just past the nursery, it will be noted that Kings Avenue diagonally intersects with Haywood Avenue from the east. Reverse direction eastwards down Kings Avenue. Three of the central homes are all dated prior to 1919. The house on 2557 Kings Avenue was known to have been built in 1913. They all have a tale to tell of Dundarave's early history.

Continue down the 2500-block of Kings Avenue to where it leads onto a pathway and footbridge over Marr Creek. Kings Avenue continues on the east side of this stream. The house on the property 2503 Kings Avenue was built in 1911.

Crossing over 25th Street, continue walking eastwards along Kings Avenue until reaching 22nd Street, then turn right (south) to connect with the principal Route A at Jefferson Avenue, Stn. A17.

At the Recreation Centre, Stn. A18, if you wish to limit your walk to the Dundarave Route D, you should continue down 22nd Street to Marine Drive. Before crossing Marine Drive, have a look at Kiwanis Park on your left, which is south of the Recreation Centre and Seniors' Centre.

After crossing over Marine Drive, continue down 22nd Street and over Bellevue Avenue into a small green park between high-rise apartments. Follow the footpath and steps down to the waterfront and Centennial Sea-Walk at Stn. A13. Turn right (west) and continue the walk back to Dundarave pier as per Route A.

A stroll along the Centennial Seawalk. (WVMA)

Marking the City of Vancouver's centennial year, the guinness family, who built the bridge, presented a sparkling night-time attraction with a display of lights. (MW)

Chapter Fourteen

CONSILIO ET ANIMIS

By Robert D. Watt
First Vice-President, Heraldry Society of Canada
and Director of the Vancouver Museum

As West Vancouver prepares to celebrate its Diamond Jubilee it is about to join a select but fast-growing company of Canadian municipalities that have been honoured by the Crown with the grant of a coat-of-arms. This ancient and beautiful form of symbolism, which has its roots in medieval Europe, flourishes today in virtually every corner of the globe but especially in parts of the world where European inheritance is strong. In the Commonwealth, these symbols have a special meaning because a grant of arms is considered, in law, to be an honor received from the Sovereign involving an exercise of the Royal Prerogative.

The heralds, the professional officers who serve the monarch by devising granting new arms in the Queen's name and regulating the use of existing arms, are present day descendants of officials who served English and Scots sovereigns as early as the 13th century. In Britain, these heralds are grouped into two bodies, the College of Arms in London, governing English heraldry and the Court of the Lord Lyon in Edinburgh, supervising Scots heraldry. The College is the younger of the two offices having been founded by a Royal Charter received from King Richard III in 1484. It has had a number of homes but since the late 17th century has occupied a beautiful brick building in the heart of the City of London just south of St. Paul's Cathedral. With the dramatic post World War II upsurge of Canadian interest in heraldry, the Government of Canada is now studying the concept of setting up a Canadian Heraldic Authority which would perform the same functions as the British authorities but exercising the Royal Prerogative of the Queen as the Queen of Canada. In the meantime, Canadian individuals and corporations are continuing to approach the College or Lyon Court with their petitions, as West Vancouver has done.

Coats-of-arms, which symbolize the authority, dignity and unique personality of the possessor, are carefully devised so that once granted they are never granted again in the same form. This ensures continuation of the medieval first principle, that is the immediate identification of the bearer. Simplicity of design elements and choice of colour from a striking and very limited palette to produce maximum dramatic effect are important considerations.

In mid-March, 1987 dignitaries and citizens will gather to witness one of the Diamond Jubilee year's most historic moments. Dr. Conrad Swan, York Herald of Arms and Registrar of the College of Arms, a native of Duncan B.C. and member of the Royal Household, will read the Letters Patent granting arms to West Vancouver in a public ceremony. After proclaiming the full text of the grant, York Herald will present the illuminated parchment to His Honour, Lieutenant Governor Robert G. Rogers (himself recently granted arms) representing Her Majesty Queen Elizabeth II. The Lieutenant Governor will then, in the Queen's name, present the Patent to His Worship, the Mayor, who will accept it on behalf of Council and the citizens of West Vancouver.

This impressive piece of pageantry will be the culmination of a story that stretches back fifty years to the spring of 1936, when the City of Vancouver was beginning the celebration of its Golden Jubilee. In March, T.P.O. Menzies, Curator of the Vancouver City Museum, had circularized the clerks of all the municipalities in the Lower Mainland asking for a copy of their coat-of-arms. He explained that these would be held in the Museum's historical archives and also exhibited during the Jubilee Celebrations. At the time Menzies' letter reached the West Vancouver Clerk of that era, William Herrin, the District used no identifying device of any kind, and Mr. Herrin referred the enquiry to Reeve Leyland for reply. The letter seems to have spurred Mr. Leyland to very quick action. Within the month the Duncan Lawson Chapter of the Imperial Order of Daughters of the Empire held a community-wide contest to design a coat-of-arms and twelve entries were received. A committee headed by Vancouver Art

Gallery founder H.A. Stone, judged the submissions and selected the one received from Albert E. Bibbs. Shortly afterwards, Mr. Bibbs' design was selected by Council as West Vancouver's coat-of-arms. Albert Bibbs must have known something about heraldry because his idea was sound aesthetically and in terms of all the basic rules of the form. The symbolism of the various elements he chose, as was outlined in a contemporary newspaper account, was drawn directly from West Vancouver's geography and economy. The heraldic sparrows, or martlets, in the upper part of the shield, represented the varied bird-life of the community. The ship, shown in the form of a heraldic galley or lymphad, referred to coastline and shipping. The chevron in the centre is one of heraldry's principal dividing elements or 'honourable or-dinaries'. The crest, which is the element shown above the shield of arms, was composed of a maple leaf flanked by two dogwood flowers. Finally, the motto, "Wisdom and Courage", was meant as a compliment to the Municipal Council.

Regrettably, the full aesthetic force of Bibbs' design was not realized, and no consideration was given to seeking lawful arms based on his concept until the 1980s. Nevertheless, the Bibbs device was widely used, appearing on municipal stationery, notices, property and vehicles such as the Blue Buses. It has been the principal visual shorthand for "West Vancouver" for fifty years.

Now, happily, the essential quality of Albert Bibbs' work is to be enshrined forever as the core element of West Vancouver's new complete armorial bearings. Council, headed by Mayor Derrick Humphreys, has been anxious that the new arms be based as fully as possible on the old device. The English Kings of Arms are granting the Bibbs' design in all its essentials together with some very beautiful and meaningful additions.

The new arms grew out of a decision taken by Council on October 17th, 1983 to petition the College of Arms for a grant of arms, in anticipation of the Diamond Jubilee on March 15th, 1987. The decision followed a meeting between Dr. Swan and Mayor Humphreys in May, 1982 when the Mayor learned of the process involved for a municipality wishing to acquire proper heraldry. Council's October, 1983 motion set up a Committee to oversee the project consisting of the Mayor, Douglas Allan, the Municipal Clerk, and Robert D. Watt, Director of the Van-couver Museum and First Vice-President of the Heraldry Society of Canada. [Mr. Watt grew up in West Vancouver and is a grandson of pioneer businessman, John T. Watt, a municipal Councillor in the 1920s.]

In June, 1986, after considerable discussion of additions to the shield and crest and some excellent suggestions from the Mayor, Aldermen and senior officials, Council approved the final design proposal from the Kings of Arms. The new arms are centred around Bibbs' shield, strengthening and extending the original colour scheme of blue and white (heraldic silver). The overall design honours the riches of West Vancouver's location and natural environment. For the first time ever in English heraldry, the ship is edged or "garnished" in gold, a symbol of the community's good fortune. The supporters flanking either side of the shield are silver mountain lions, or cougars, symbolic of the rich and varied native fauna of the District, and of power. Each bears a collar of blue fir boughs laden with golden cones. The helmet, which is granted to all arms-bearing corporations, carries the crest which has two parts. Firstly, the Bibbs' maple leaf and dogwoods are transformed into a "crown" of alternating maple leaves and dogwoods, symbolizing national and provincial ties. It is interesting to note that Bibbs' design was the direct inspiration for three similar circlets previously granted by the College' Richmond (1978), Shawnigan Lake School (1981) and the City of North Vancouver (1982). The second portion of the crest rises above the circlet in a double allusion to history and geography, the flaming holly leaves recalling the origin of the name of the mountain and the pioneer John Lawson. The Compartment, on which the shield rests and the cougars stand, represents West Vancouver's granite shoreline, marked by glacial striations, with streams flowing down to meet the ocean. The motto, "Consilio et Animis" remains the same.

Taken altogether, the arms form a beautiful, historic and highly distinctive symbol of West Vancouver's identity. Beginning in 1987, the shield of arms will fly in flag form as the municipal banner with the banner itself being painted on the armorial Letters Patent, another heraldic first, according to the experts at the College. The new arms will be used widely in 1987 as the central visual mark of the Diamond Jubilee celebrations. In the future, as they continue to identify the District's property, services and activities, they will also serve as a splendid memorial of a milestone year in the life of West Vancouver.

Albert Bibbs, creator of the Coat-of-Arms of West Vancouver came from a long line of artists and engravers, and for some years worked for a carriage firm designing automobile bodies. He later became a banker and retired to West Vancouver. (HB)

Albert Bibbs' winning entry in a Coat-of-Arms contest sponsored by the Duncan Lawson chapter of the Imperial Order of the Daughters of the Empire. (VCA)

The heraldic arms of West Vancouver as approved for the municipality's 75th anniversary in 1987.

Dr. Conrad Swan, York Herald, who was born at Duncan, British Columbia, gave formal approval to the municipal emblem.

INDEX

349

350

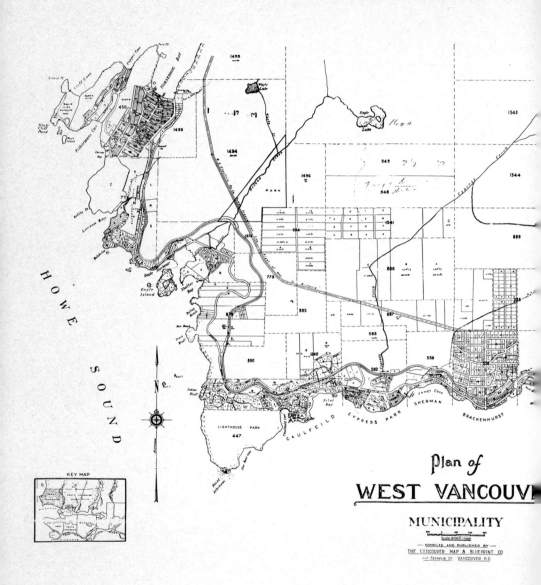

Plan of
WEST VANCOUV[ER]

MUNICIPALITY

Scale 2000 ft - 1 inch

— COMPILED AND PUBLISHED BY —
THE VANCOUVER MAP & BLUEPRINT CO
441 SEYMOUR ST   VANCOUVER B.C

KEY MAP